BEER LOVER'S
CHICAGO

D1125273

KARL
KLOCKARS

Globe
Pequot
Guilford, Connecticut

"For Nora. Thanks for those first few Oberons. "

Globe Pequot

An imprint of Rowman & Littlefield
Distributed by NATIONAL BOOK NETWORK

Copyright © 2018 by Karl Klockars

Maps by Melissa Baker © Rowman & Littlefield

British Library Cataloguing in Publication Information Available
Library of Congress Cataloging-in-Publication Data Available

ISBN 978-1-4930-1270-1 (paperback)
ISBN 978-1-4930-2511-4 (e-book)

∞™ The paper used in this publication meets the minimum requirements of American National Standard for Information Sciences—Permanence of Paper for Printed Library Materials, ANSI/NISO Z39.48-1992.

Printed in the United States

INDEPENDENT BREWPUBS 114

CONTRACT AND ALTERNATING PROPRIETORSHIP BREWERS 137

CHAIN-STYLE BREWPUBS 142

INTRODUCTION

There has never been a better time to be a beer drinker in Chicago than right now. That may sound a bit hyperbolic, or like some mild alcohol-induced exaggeration, but it's true. Chicago is awash with fresh, locally made beer from breweries in all sizes and styles—from the tiniest basement nanobrewery to the massive million-barrel super-brewery. Brewers in Chicagoland have never been more prolific, more creative, or more inspired than right now.

I've spent a good part of the last few years traveling in search of beer experiences and have been lucky enough to stumble into many great ones—from beer bars in New York City and Washington, D.C., to brewpubs and production facilities in Los Angeles and San Francisco; from amber ales at a tiny Upper Peninsula brewpub near the shores of Lake Superior to the tart, tropical weissbiers made in Miami. Each time I come home to Chicago, I'm reminded that we're exceptionally lucky to be a part of the beer culture that we have waiting to be discovered right here.

The beer revolution has been bubbling around since breweries like Goose Island, Three Floyds, and Two Brothers kicked off decades ago. In the late 2000s, drinkers saw six-packs of Half Acre lager enter the scene, followed by beers from Metropolitan, Haymarket, and Revolution, and the floodgates opened. Seven years after that, there are about 200 different breweries in Illinois, with the vast majority of them within an hour's drive from downtown Chicago. For those of us who grew up thinking that "Chicago beer" basically started and ended with Old Style, the change is seismic.

The following couple hundred pages represent an attempt to pull into one place the stories of many of these breweries, brewpubs, taprooms, bars, and beer-friendly restaurants that make up the landscape of the Chicagoland beer enthusiast. From the most traditional lager to the wildest barrel-aged stout and all the wild yeasts and adjunct ingredients in between, you don't have to look too far to find something made close to home that fits your palate.

Wanna go get a beer? C'mon, I know a good place. It's right down the road.

HOW TO USE THIS GUIDE

This book was created to deliver an overview of the many places in Chicagoland where beer is brewed, poured, and appreciated. It's one part guidebook, one part brewery mini-biography, and one part story of the growth of the city's craft beer community (and maybe even a bit of history, too).

It's also the first real full listing of the area's many beer destinations since the words craft beer entered the drinker's lexicon in the mid-2000s—and, as you can imagine, there's been a lot of changes since then.

Since the state of Illinois licenses places as either breweries or brewpubs, that's what we've done here as well. Breweries are broken out by location—North Side, South Side, and 'Burbs—whereas brewpubs receive their own catch-all category, same as beer bars/restaurants and bottle shops. Slightly illogical? Sure, but so is alcohol legislation most of the time. (Why other states allow bars and restaurants to fill growlers but Illinoisans can not, I don't know, but be glad you can buy beer on Sunday in this state.)

Hopefully this helps you find someplace new to appreciate the creations of the many brewing minds around town, allows you discover a new beloved bar or restaurant, or even helps you learn something new about an old favorite.

The actual drinking of the beer you can probably handle yourself.

GLOSSARY OF TERMS

Beer is its own world that comes with its own language. We tried to be as conversational and plain-spoken as possible in this book, but sometimes you've gotta talk the talk. From contract brews to alt-props to bbl to grain bills, here are the basics you'll need to know if you want to understand the next hundred pages or so.

ABV: Alcohol by volume—the percent age of alcohol in a beer. Most beers average around 5 percent ABV, but many stronger beers can get up to 12 percent.

Ale: Beer brewed with top-fermenting yeast. Ales take less time to ferment than lagers, which is why, in general, most craft beers are ales. Popular styles of ales include pale ales, amber ales, stouts, and porters.

Alternating Proprietorship: Often shortened to "alt-prop." An arrangement where one brewery will temporarily use another brewery's equipment to make beer. Alt-prop breweries regularly have their own fermentation tanks in their host brewery's space and often multiple brewing companies can exist in the same space.

Barrels: Breweries measure the amount of beer they produce in barrels. Barrels are 31 gallons, and a standard keg size is a half-barrel, or 15.5 gallons. A brewery that produces 1,000 bbl per year makes about 248,000 pints of beer.

BBL: Barrels

Beer: An alcoholic beverage brewed with malt, water, hops, and yeast. If you're reading this and you didn't know that, find the nearest brewery and schedule a tour—they'll almost certainly start with this information.

Body: The way a beer feels on the palate in terms of consistency and heft. Light-bodied beers are easy to drink; very full-bodied beers pour like motor oil.

Bomber: The 22-ounce bottles used to package many craft beers.

Brewhouse: The system on which breweries make their beer. Chicago area breweries work on brewhouses as small as a single barrel at a time all the way up to 250 bbl monsters.

Brewpub: Typically a restaurant, but sometimes just a bar, that brews its own beers on-site almost entirely for on-premise consumption. In Illinois, brewpubs can make 5,000 bbls per year, per location.

Clone brew: A homebrew recipe based on a commercial beer.

Collaboration: A beer brewed in combination with two different breweries. Collaborations are a way for breweries from different areas share recipe ideas, or just work together as friends.

Contract brewery: A company that pays someone else to brew and bottle its beer. Some breweries use contracting as a stepping-stone to their own facility, and others remain contracted for their entire existence.

Craft beer: The term generally used to refer to high-quality, flavorful beer made by independent craft brewers (see next definition). As craft beer grows larger and is increasingly being purchased by larger corporations, this definition is slowly becoming obsolete...but no one has a better idea about what to call it, so we're kind of stuck with it.

Craft brewer: According to the Brewers Association, a craft brewer is small (annual production of 6 million barrels of beer or less), independent (less than 25 percent of the craft brewery is owned or controlled [or equivalent economic interest] by an alcoholic beverage industry member that is not itself a craft brewer), and traditional (a majority of its total beverage alcohol volume is beers whose flavor derives from traditional or innovative brewing ingredients and their fermentation). As you can imagine, these definitions get pretty fuzzy as mergers, investments, acquisitions, buyouts, and takeovers occur.

Distribution: How the beer you drink gets to market. Most beer is delivered by a distributor, a company that takes the beer from the brewery and gets it to the retail market. Distributors are the middle-tier in the three-tier system and play a key role in selling beer as well as getting it into stores. It also keeps the breweries from directly connecting with retailers, as required after Prohibition to keep larger breweries from forcing out smaller ones. See also: self-distribution.

Double: Most often refers to a higher-alcohol version of a beer, and is often interchangeable with the word imperial. This is separate from Belgian dubbel style beers, which is a specific kind of beer as opposed to an augmentation of a smaller one.

Dry hopping: A practice of adding hops very late in the brewing process when the beer is in the fermenters in order to add hop aromas to a beer.

Grain bill: The types and amounts of malt and grain that go into a beer recipe.

Growler: A 64-ounce jug of beer, usually sold to take home. While most brewery taprooms and brewpubs sell growlers of their beers to go, Illinois bars and restaurants are prohibited from doing so (for now).

Hops: A flowering plant that grows on a bine; the hop cones are used in beers to produce aroma, bitterness, and flavor. Nearly every beer in the world has hops, which come in a near-endless and ever growing amount of varieties. German hops are often herbal; English hops are earthy and vegetal; while American hops are fruity, piney, and can be really damn bitter.

IBU: International bittering units is a measurement used to show how bitter a beer is. A beer that's 20 IBU will have a barely noticable bitterness, whereas a 100+ IBU hop bomb can be massively, palate-wreckingly bitter.

Lager: Beer brewed with bottom-fermenting yeast at colder temperatures than ales. Lagers take longer to ferment and most styles reveal flaws more readily than ales. Popular styles of lagers include pilsners, Vienna lagers, bocks, and schwarzbiers.

Malt: Typically refers to specifically malted barley, but often used as shorthand for the other grains that go into a beer. Malt provides the fermentable sugar in beers, as well as its color. The more fermentable sugar, the higher the ABV in a beer. Without malt, a beer would be too bitter from the hops.

Mash: Brewer's term for the steeping of the hot water and grains that activates the malt enzymes and converts the starches from the grains into fermentable sugars.

Microbrewery: A brewery that brews fewer than 15,000 barrels of beer a year.

Nanobrewery: A brewery that brews 4 barrels of beer per batch or less.

Tallboys: 16-ounce cans

Reinheitsgebot: The German beer purity law that states beer can only contain water, barley, yeast, and hops.

Self-distribution: Quite simply, the ability to sell your own beer to bars, restaurants, and stores. In Illinois, only breweries that produce under a certain amount of beer per year can legally self-distribute their beer. Above a certain size, the brewery is required to go through a distributor to sell its beer.

Session beer: A catch-all category for low-alcohol beer (under 5 percent) popularized in 2015. Pale ales and IPAs are the most popular session beers, and are characterized by lots of flavor without lots of kick. It's a beer you can have several of in one long drinking "session."

Taproom: A place in a brewery where the public can sample the beers produced on-site. Different municipalities have different rules for tasting beers in a taproom, but it's always the best place to go for the freshest beer, and often the only place to find certain experimental styles.

Wort: The sweet liquid that is extracted from the mixing of hot water and malt (mash). Wort contains all the sugars that will be fermented by the yeast to produce alcohol. Many brewers say they don't make beer, they make wort. Yeast makes beer.

Yeast: The living organism in beer that causes the sugars to ferment and become alcohol. When yeast eats the sugars in the wort, it produces two things—CO_2 and alcohol. While grains and hops are generally assumed to provide much of the flavor of beer, yeast strains can also contribute heavily to the final flavor and feel of a beer.

BEER STYLES

There are hundreds of different beer styles in the world, all with their own specific characteristics, flavor profiles, ABV ranges, colors, and aromas. For more details on every beer style that you could imagine, the Beer Judge Certification Program style guidelines are the go-to resource for any info you could want, and it's easy to find on their website or in their downloadable app. The styles you'll likely find at your neighborhood brewery are below.

Amber/Red Ale: A medium-bodied, caramel-malty beer with some mild hop bitterness.

American Light Lager/American Adjunct Lager: What everyone used to think American beer was. If you hear someone say to the bartender at your local brewpub, "What's the closest thing you have to Bud Light?", they're looking for a light lager. Adjunct lagers are often made with corn or rice to lighten the body (and cheapen the grain bill) but retain the fermentable sugars to create alcohol.

Barleywine: Not a wine at all, but a high-ABV ale that originated in England. English versions tend to have a sweeter, maltier balance while American versions often have large amounts of hops.

Berliner Weiss: A German-style sour wheat beer that's easy drinking, lightly tart, and low in alcohol. It is often augmented with fruit or fruit-flavored syrups.

Blonde Ale: A yellow, lightly flavored, easy drinking, generally pretty middle-of-the-road style of beer often flavored with honey.

Brown Ale: Darker than an amber, not quite a porter or stout, brown ales are generally English-style beers, notable for their nutty, malty, sweet flavor but usually easy-drinking body.

Dubbel: A Belgian-style brown ale, fairly strong in alcohol content and generally sweet, fruity, and malty.

IPA: Craft beer's favorite style and one that came into its own when American brewers began amping up the bitterness. Most believe this strongly hopped ale was created in the UK when beer was being shipped to India. The high hop content added a level of preservative to the beer to make it stay drinkable on the long trip. Nowadays most IPAs don't travel much farther than a few miles, but drinkers seem to require the high hop levels regardless.

ESB: Extra-special bitter. A traditional malt-heavy English pub ale with low bitterness, usually served on cask.

Gose: Pronounced goes-uh, this wheat beer has a tart flavor that originated in Germany and usually has a grain bill made up of at least 50 percent malted wheat as well as coriander and salt. This beer was all but forgotten until recent years, but a recent resurgence in interest in sour beers has brought the style back to the forefront.

Kölsch: A light, refreshing German-style ale originated in Cologne, Germany.

Pale Ale or American Pale Ale: Quite similar in structure to an IPA, but a little bit less intense and more easy-drinking. Generally not as strong or as hoppy, but can still be very strongly flavored.

Pilsner: A style of German or Czech lager, usually light in color. Most macro beers are by definition pilsners and so craft brewers basically ignored them for years, until recently when hoppy pilsners and the similarly styled imperial pale lagers began becoming popular again.

Porter: A dark and hearty ale, very similar to a stout, sometimes imperceptibly so. Dark, roasty, hearty, and made for cooler autumn nights.

Quad: A strong, Belgian-style ale, typically sweet and high in alcohol.

Russian imperial stout: A Russian imperial stout is a higher-alcohol, thicker-bodied version of a regular stout. Often times it features adjuncts like coffee or chocolate, or is aged in bourbon barrels for extra-complex flavors.

Saison: Also known as a Belgian or French farmhouse ale, it used to be brewed in cooler weather to be drank in the warmer season (aka saison). It is fruity, spicy, peppery, dry, and usually highly carbonated.

Seasonal: A beer that is brewed at a certain time of year to coincide with the seasons. Pumpkin beers, Christmas beers, and Maibocks are all seasonal types of beers. The seasonal beer category is one of the largest selling, thanks in part to the varying tastes of craft beer drinkers.

Sour: Less a specific style than a characteristic of many different styles, sour beers of all types have been growing steadily in popularity. Sours can be abrasively acidic or just lightly tart; some even have characteristics of vinegar.

Stout: A strong, dark beer brewed with roasted malts. Various stout styles include dry Irish stouts, oatmeal stouts, and milk stouts made with lactose sugar.

Tripel: A Belgian-style ale, lighter in color than a dubbel but higher in ABV. It usually doesn't taste strongly alcoholic, so be aware that these can get you into trouble fast.

Wheat beer: Beers, such as hefeweizens and witbiers, brewed using wheat along with barley malt and often characterized by a creamy body and a fruity or citrusy flavor. If you see a beer with a lemon or an orange slice on the rim, you're probably looking at a wheat beer.

Chicago, North

For years, Chicago beer meant one thing: Goose Island (and Old Style, but I think you get what I mean). Then, with breweries such as Metropolitan, Half Acre, and Revolution beginning to open their doors around 2009 and 2010, it ushered in a renaissance in Chicago beer production not seen since Prohibition. Nowadays most North Side residents are no farther than a walk or a quick cab ride from their closest brewery taproom or brewpub, and the city's finest bottle shops and beer bars almost all have a home north of Madison Avenue.

ALARMIST BREWING

4055 W. Peterson Ave., Chicago, IL 60646; No Phone;
Alarmistbrewing.com; @Alarmistbrewing
Founded: 2015 **Founder:** Gary Gulley **Brewer:** Gary Gulley
Flagship beer: Entrenched IPA **Year-round beers:** Entrenched IPA,
Phobophobia Patersbier **Seasonals/Special Releases:** Impulsion
Oatmeal Stout **Tours:** No **Taproom:** In Planning

The story of Alarmist Brewing is really one of perseverance, DIY dedication, commitment to quality and what happens when you straight-up say "screw it, I'm gonna chase that dream." Alarmist founder Gary Gulley spent years in the trenches of corporate America, all while homebrewing and thinking of someday maybe opening a brewery of his own.

It was a diagnosis of cancer (Gary's wife's) paired with a corporation's heartlessness that was the real kickstart to Alarmist. When his former employers found out that his wife was ill, the late-forty-ish Gulley found himself out of a job. So at that point, why not start a brewery? At the outset it was called Panic, and beer fans with an obsessive eye could follow the process from paperwork to business plan (ask Gary about it!) to the first pour on his blog. (Gary's wife turned out okay and his gamble paid off, too.)

Gulley went to brewers' school, took an internship with the Metropolitan Brewery team (as so many do), attended brewers' conferences, and throughout it all kept a phenomenal sense of humor about the whole thing. After finding a space for the brewery on Peterson in the far-northwestern neighborhood of Sauganash (on a former site of the Siebel Brewing Institute, crazily enough), he finally released his first beer in March 2015, the **Pantsless** pale ale.

But it wasn't enough to just release the first beer. Gulley dumped the full first batch of pale ale and posted the video to Facebook, explaining that the beer just wasn't up to his standards. The move surely hurt in the financial short–run, but it earned him a lot of fans who appreciate that kind of dedication to quality. A Belgian single, **Phobophobia** followed, as did **Entrenched**, an IPA. Then came beers in bottles and cans, and eventually a taproom.

Hopefully by now, with the brewery open and underway, the alarm has turned down a notch. Perhaps the panic is over. (Okay, probably not. But it's nice to think so.)

ALL RISE BREWING COMPANY

235 N. Ashland Ave., Chicago, IL 60607; (312) 226-6300; allrisebrewing.com; @Allrisebrewing
Founded: 2014 **Founders:** Tommy Nicely and Sean McKeough
Brewer: Tommy Nicely **Flagship beer:** Wonder Beer Pale Ale **Year-round beers:** Three Orange Wit, Reverend Bob's Uber IPA **Tours:** No
Taproom Hours: Mon through Fri, 11 a.m. to 2 a.m.; Sat, 5 p.m. to 3 a.m.; closed Sunday.

Brewer Tommy Nicely took the long way to opening this brewery with the help of the team at Cobra Lounge. Nicely started out brewing with his dad in high school and got his professional start in the 1990s at Goose's Fulton & Wood facility just a few blocks away. From there, Nicely spread his wings and headed to Harpoon in Massachusetts, then Lagunitas in California and eventually came home to help the Half Acre brewery get off the ground on Lincoln Avenue. That's where he created the **Daisy Cutter,** a legendary pale ale.

Once Half Acre was established, Nicely moved to the Ashland Avenue space to set up the brewery then known as Greyskull Brewing. The rollout was slow but determined, and in fact Nicely wasn't planning to be leading the All Rise charge. His best friend "Reverend Bobby" Kittrell was going to be the original brewer, with experience bouncing around Baltimore breweries, as well as time spent at Stone and Goose Island. When Kittrell passed away in 2012, Nicely stepped in as a way to both honor his friend and take the opportunity to build something of his own.

Nicely brews on a 10 bbl brewhouse, which is a decent size for a brand new brewery but tiny in comparison to the 50 bbl at Goose and 200 bbl he worked with at Lagunitas. It is good, though, as the smaller setup gives the All Rise team an opportunity to be creative and flexible with the twleve lines available at the bar. The lineup focuses on traditional English- and German-style beers with an eye on the aggressively–flavored American beer sensibility as well. Their first beer, the **Wonder Beer** pale ale, was poured at the 2014 Riot Fest, a concert event co-organized by All Rise and Cobra Lounge owner Sean McKeough.

Other beers include the **Temporary Solution** robust porter, an IPA, and an ESB called **Exploding Sky**, a style not often explored by most brewers. The beer that strikes to the heart of the Chicagoan experience (at least for those who are Blues Brothers fans to the core) is the **Three Orange Wit**, a nod to the order John Candy places in the seminal Belushi/Ayckroyd film before chasing the brothers Blues across Cook County. It's a highly seasoned and spiced wheat beer chock full of bright citrus.

BEGYLE BREWING COMPANY

1800 W. Cuyler Ave., Chicago, IL 60625; (773) 661-6963; begylebrewing.com; @BegyleBrewing
Founded: 2012 **Founders:** Kevin Cary and Brendan Blume **Brewer:** Matt Ritchie **Flagship beers:** Crash Landed Pale Ale, Begyle Blonde **Seasonal beers:** Don't Bring Me Down, Zeus DIPA, Imperial Flannel Pajamas Coffee Stout, Maybe Next Summer APA **Tours:** Yes **Taproom Hours:** Mon through Thurs, 12 to 9 p.m.; Fri, 12 to 10 p.m.; Sat 11 a.m. to 10 p.m.; Sun, 12 to 8 p.m.

Begyle's story started with a pedicab and a dream.

The founders of Begyle, Kevin Cary and Brendan Blume, were working for their pedicab business, shuttling people around Wrigleyville one pedalstroke after another. At the end of a shift, they'd sit on the back of their rigs and shoot the shit, as people will do. One day one of them said, "We should open a brewery." And really, that was that.

Friend and homebrewer Matt Ritchie was brought on board—Cary and Ritchie used to brew together in a turkey fryer after college—and the three of them set out to launch Argyle Brewery. (We'll get to that in a second.) Space was acquired on Cuyler Avenue at Ravenswood, a small brewhouse was purchased, fermenters acquired, and everything was set to go until an Oregon winery intervened and said they had dibs on the Argyle name.

After some brief consideration, they landed on Begyle, a bit of a cross between *beguile* and *partigyle*, the process of making two beers with one mash. Also, as Cary would say, "If you can't Argyle, Begyle." They debuted their beers in August 2012 at the Oak Park Microbrew Review, coming out the gate with their **American Blonde** and **Crash Landed** hoppy wheat.

Begyle's main focus was being a neighborhood brewery, super-serving the bars, restaurants, and other local establishments around North Center and Lincoln Square. Their first account was at Lincoln Square's Grafton restaurant (whose beer buyer would go on to open Only Child Brewing) and they delivered the beers by pedicab. Begyle guests can still view that pedicab on the weekly brewery tours, if you want to see where it all began.

Part of being dedicated to their immediate surroundings was opening a Community Supported Brewery (CSB). Begyle would go on to be the first brewery in Chicago to offer "subscriptions." Patrons would sign up for a monthly charge and receive anything from growler fills to sixtel kegs at a slight discount for being regular customers, the idea being that folks in the surrounding blocks would sign up and regularly bring home a few beers from their local brewery.

Their efforts were low-key and fairly humble as breweries go, but it was enough to get people to take notice. *Chicago Magazine* named them the city's best new brewery in 2013. Ongoing construction, expanded brewing capacity, and a barrel-aging program soon followed, as well as collaborations with Fountainhead's Cleetus Friedman, chef Kevin Hickey of Allium and Bottlefork, and the DryHop brewpub on a beer named for a song called "Johnny Quest Thinks We're Sellouts," which eventually became a "collaboration" with the writers of that jam, the ska band, Less Than Jake.

In 2015 a taproom finally opened, so folks could sit and have a beer in a space that once held artist studios and be surrounded by the four walls that became a quintessential neighborhood brewery. It took three years, but Begyle finally came full circle—the neighborhood they began serving from the back of a bike could now be served beer face-to-face.

EMPIRICAL BREWERY

**1801 W. Foster Ave., Chicago, IL 60640; (773) 349-2739;
empiricalbrewery.com; @empiricalbrew
Founded:** 2014 **Founder:** Bill Hurley **Brewer:** Nevin McCown
Flagship beer: Infinity IPA **Year-round beers:** Infinity IPA Main
Seasonal beers: Phase Transition Porter, 1st Law Belgian Table Beer,
Double Helix IPA, Heliotropic Hoppy Pale Ale, 3rd Law Belgian Tripel,
Chromatic Imperial Red Ale **Tours:** Yes **Taproom hours (when
available):** Sun and Tues through Thurs, 12 to 10 p.m.; Fri through Sat,
12 p.m. to 12 a.m.

Some breweries name themselves after places. After attitudes. After their last names. After socks. (Begyle's original name of Argyle was partially based on one of the owner's preference for plaid-patterned foot coverings.) Empirical Brewery's name comes from their process—they aim to create data-driven beers for the best possible flavor combinations. Considering the wide palates of Chicago drinkers, it's an ambitious endeavor.

Empirical works out of the corner of Ravenswood and Foster Avenue on the border of Lincoln Square and Andersonville. Plans for the brewery started in 2011 when owners and homebrewers Bill Hurley and Sumit Mehta put their brains together with a love of beer and science, though Empirical wouldn't start sending kegs to market until the second half of 2014.

They started big, while most breweries kick off with anything from a nano-sized 1.5 bbl system up to a reasonable 7 bbl system, Empirical planned for the long haul by purchasing a 30 bbl setup and a couple of 60 bbl fermenters at the get-go so they could hit the ground running. The industrial space along the Metra tracks has plenty of room to grow and, with neighbors like Metropolitan and Aquanaut literally just a few minutes walk away, they need not be lonely for brewer conversation.

They also started with a pro at the helm. Empirical recruited Art Steinhoff, whose experience dates back three decades and includes time at a Kenosha brewpub and at Flatlanders in Lincolnshire, to be their brewmaster. One of their first beers was an eye-opening single IPA called **IBU Overload**, clocking in at a massive 105 IBUS, aka massively bitter.

Their taproom opened in late 2015, pouring their already-established lineup of **Gamma Ray Ginger Wheat, Infinity IPA,** and **Phase Transition Porter** made with Mexican brown sugar for some latent sweetness and a touch of rum. Enterprising beer geeks could get themselves a flight of experimental beers, however, brewed on Empirical's test batch system.

Empirical's motto is "Exploring the Science of Beer," which informs their logo, crafted to embody the original cuneiform word for beer found on a

7,000-year-old piece of hieroglyphics. It really lives and breathes in their flight program, which serves a regular beer (the "control" of the experiment) and variations on that beer, with differences in hops, malts, or yeasts. Data collected from the drinkers will help inform future releases of the brew.

Beer purists may scoff at the idea of literally crowdsourcing a beer— shouldn't all beers come from the heart and soul of a skilled brewmaster, whose recipes come from a pure core of belief and drinking experience? But really, most brewers riff on beers and vary their recipes all the time, they just don't tell you about it. Many things in the craft beer are still basically an experiment. The only thing that makes Empirical so different is that they're up front about it . . . and they want your data. It's the easiest science fair project you'll ever work on.

FINCH'S BEER COMPANY

4565 N. Elston Ave., Chicago, IL 60630; (773) 283-4839; finchbeer.com; @finchbeer
Founded: 2011 Founder: Ben Finch Brewers of the Round Table: Mike Jacobs, Gordon Scott, Nick Webster, and Grant Thompson Flagship beer: Hardcore Chimera Imperial IPA Main Seasonal beers: Brewers Reserve Series Tours: Soon Taproom: Opening Summer 2016 (Albany Park)

Finch's has been a brewery in transition almost since the day they opened. Originally created by graphic designer Ben Finch with his brother Mike and father Ben, they started sending beer out the door in June 2011. Their original lines included **Golden Wing, Cutthroat,** and a **Threadless IPA** made in conjunction with the Chicago clothing brand. Cans came out in 2012, and to this date, Finch's beer is primarily in cans with distribution to more than twenty states.

Finch's started in the early rush of Chicago brewing but quickly established itself as a regional player, sending beer fairly far and wide. They expanded from their core lines to add more extreme beers like their **Secret Stache** vanilla milk stout and the **Hardcore Chimera** double IPA. They eventually stopped brewing their original beers altogether in favor of new flagships like a pale ale and a new IPA called **Chimera,** the "baby brother" of the original older hardcore version.

They also started off with one head brewer, but have transitioned to a form of brew-by-committee, with a team of four brewers who collaborate to come up with new products. Working from a 15 bbl brewhouse into a field of 30 bbl fermenters, the team cranked out about 10,000 barrels in 2015 on the city's northwest side. Though an expansion is underway, it didn't shape up the way they thought it would.

Plans for a brewery along the Chicago River were released in December 2014, but were officially taken off the table six months later. At the end of 2015, though, the ever-transitioning brewery found space in Long Grove and started serving as a warehouse in November. A package store, a taproom, and new brewing facility were originally planned to operate from that location, but in May 2015, news broke that Finch's would pivot their plans once again to take over the Breakroom brewpub in Albany Park, rebrand it as the Finch Kitchen. Brewery investors removed founder Ben Finch from the top of the company, changed the name simply to Finch Beer and also took on the Hopothesis contract brand of beers.

Things moved along for about six months when things changed *again*—Finch announced that they were walking away from the brewpub, closing their Elston Street brewery and moving to an all-contract setup. Many breweries move from contract to their own place, but very few ever make the reverse trip. Like the Chicago weather, if you think you know what Finch Beer is up to, wait five minutes and it'll change again.

ILLUMINATED BREW WORKS

415 N. Sangamon Rd., Chicago, IL 60642; no phone; ibw-chicago.com; @IBW666
Founded: 2012 **Founders:** Matt Shirley and Brian Buckman **Brewers:** Brian Buckman and Jason Monk **Flagship beer:** Orange Sunshine **Year-round beers:** Fnord, Ed's Legs, Kallisti Main **Seasonal beers:** Orange Sunshine, Brown Reason to Live **Tours:** Yes **Taproom:** Not yet

As breweries become increasingly media savvy and brewers get more and more recognizable, it's not often you get to describe one as "mysterious," but the small-batch creations from Illuminated Brew Works fit the bill. Brewing on a 7 bbl system in a small well-hidden West Loop space on gear cobbled together with the help of co-founder Jason Monk's years of welding experience, he and fellow founder Brian Buckman, along with Matt Shirley, create beers fueled with Belgian yeasts.

Plans for the brewery go back to the late 2000s and really got underway when Buckman made efforts to open a brewpub in Oak Park but was stymied by investor financing. After that experience, the team collaborated with Andersonville Brewing and DryHop, brewed for a few months at Une Année, and got their first kegs into the world in February 2014.

They opened their shop later that year and have since expanded their reach to bars around the West Loop as well as being reliably on draft at Avondale's nationally praised Parachute restaurant. Beers include the **Kallisti Belgian** strong ale, the **Orange Sunshine** saison, and the **Black Maw,** a Belgian strong dark. Plans for 750 ml bottles are in the works, but if you find an IBW beer on draft, snag some before it disappears into the inky black depths of their hidden brewing lair.

GOOSE ISLAND BREWERY (FULTON & WOOD PRODUCTION FACILITY)

1800 W. Fulton Ave., Chicago, IL 60612; (800) 466-7363; gooseisland.com; @gooseisland
Founded: 1995 **Founder:** John Hall **Brewers:** Jared Jankowski (brewmaster) and Mike Siegel (head of brewing innovation) **Flagship beer:** Goose IPA **Year-round beers:** 312 Urban Wheat Ale, Goose IPA, Honkers Ale, Sofie, Matilda, Four Star Pils, Green Line Main **Seasonal beers:** Bourbon County Stout, Summer Ale, Winter Ale, Goose Island Oktoberfest, Festivity Ale, Lolita, Halia, Gillian, Madame Rose, Juliet **Tours:** Yes **Taproom hours (if available):** Thurs through Fri, 2 to 8 p.m.; Sat and Sun, 12 to 6 p.m.

You'll find the bulk of the Goose Island origin story over in the brewpubs section (see page 127), as the Clybourn place is where a lot of the original legend was built. This production facility, located at Fulton & Wood on the city's industrial West Side amongst coffee roasters, metal manufacturers, and auto shops, is where that legend was cemented.

Opened in 1995, the brewery cranked out the original lineup of flagship beers like **Honkers, IPA, Nut Brown,** and the **Oatmeal Stout.** In 2003, they introduced their now-famous **312** wheat beer, which went on to win four GABF medals in the English-Style Summer Ale category. The massive popularity of the easy-drinking beer would basically turn the facility into a 312 machine until 2011, when . . . it happened.

The ire and rage of the nation's beer geeks descended on the Fulton & Wood facility on March 28, 2011. It was that morning that owner John Hall announced that he was selling his brewery to Anheuser-Busch for $38 million dollars. The brewpubs remained independent and owned by Hall (for the moment, at least), but Fulton & Wood, the brands, and the brews all belonged to the King of Beers.

This announcement, in a world not yet numbed to massive billion-dollar craft beer buyouts, was nothing short of jaw-dropping. For decades Goose Island had been one of the long-time shining beacons of craft beer nationwide, along with breweries like Deschutes and Great Lakes that also opened in 1988. Now it was owned by the same company that had accomplished the feat of making one out of every five beers sold in America a Bud Light. Craft became a commodity that day. And yet, all was not lost.

Lines like **Honkers, 312,** and **Goose IPA** were soon outsourced to Bud breweries in Colorado and New York (and no, the irony of **312** being made in a different area code was not lost on many). This allowed the team of brewers at Fulton & Wood to stretch their legs into new and interesting territories, like creating as much **Bourbon County Brand Stout,** their heralded barrel-aged brew, as they could to go into national release. Bud helped take one of the craziest, biggest, brashest beers to all points of the country.

There were casualties. Beers such as **Summertime, Nut Brown, Mild Winter,** and **Pepe Nero** were sidelined. Other brews such as **Sofie, Matilda,** and **Green Line** grew and grew. The brewers were freed to experiment with flavors like pomegranate, chai tea, and cucumber on a much larger scale. Bourbon County added variants like **Bramble Rye** and **Proprietors and Rare.** Over a few years, most level-headed beer fans came to realize that even though A-B/InBev signed the checks, the beer hadn't suffered a bit. (In fact, I like **Goose IPA** even better now than I did when it was made at Fulton.)

The facility came full circle in early 2015 when Goose opened the facility for tours, along with an eighty-seat taproom. Finally the brew-happy public could come in and see what all the fuss was over—a relatively small brewery packed wall to wall with fermenters, a state of the art brewhouse, a special facility for their sour beers, and a small garage holding some of the barrels aging a variety of beers. (A much larger facility farther west holds the bulk of the beer waiting out its time in the barrel.) The taproom featured special one-off beers brewed on a small pilot system, taking the Goose team from brewpub to massive ever-growing brewery back to messing around on a 2 bbl test-batch setup. Kinda poetic.

HALF ACRE BEER COMPANY

(Taproom and brewery) 4257 N. Lincoln Ave., Chicago, IL 60618, (Production facility) 2050 W. Balmoral Ave., Chicago, IL 60625, (773) 248-4038; halfacrebeer.com; @HalfAcreBeer Founded: 2006 Founders: Gabriel Magliaro, Matt Gallagher, Maurizio Fiori, and Brian Black Brewers: Matt Gallagher (head brewer), Matt Young (lead brewer), Ryan O'Doherty, Stephan Mance, Justin Emmons, Lee McComb Flagship beer: Daisy Cutter Pale Ale Year-round beers: Daisy Cutter Pale Ale, Pony Pilsner Main Seasonal beers: GoneAway IPA, Lead Feather Black Ale, Akari Shogun American Wheat Ale, Vallejo IPA Tours: Sat, 11:00 a.m., $10 (cash only), 4257 N. Lincoln Ave. Taproom Hours: Closed Mon. Tues through Wed, 11 a.m. to 11 p.m.; Thurs, 11 to 12 a.m.; Fri through Sat, 11 to 1 a.m.; Sun, 11 a.m. to 11 p.m.

O f all the breweries in Chicago, very few of them have proceeded through three very distinct phases in their lifespans, but Half Acre has. Starting as a contract brewer producing a middle–of–the–road lager in Wisconsin, they proceeded to open a small neighborhood brewery in Lincoln Square and produce some astonishingly good beers, the popularity of which forced them to grow into a massive facility a short distance north. From having your beers made by someone else to becoming a Chicago powerhouse, Half Acre's progress shows what the power of a great pale ale can accomplish.

Founder Gabriel Magliaro started out blowing glass in Colorado after graduating from the School of the Art Institute. Originally from New Jersey and Pennsylvania (the brewery's name comes from the town of Devil's Half Acre near where he grew up), Magliaro found himself falling in love with the culture of beer, specifically Avery Brewing Company. He returned to Chicago and started working on the brewery in 2006, with six-packs of lager hitting the shelves in August 2007.

In March of 2009, Half Acre took a big step toward becoming the company that it is today, with the opening of their brewery on Lincoln Avenue. They opened their storefront a few months

later, and finally folks could go to the source and take home bombers of an ever-growing variety of beers. The Lincoln brewery, using a 15 bbl system purchased from Ska Brewing in Colorado, became the first place where Chicago craft beer was ever canned, the lineup of **Daisy Cutter, Gossamer,** and **Over Ale** soon became a must-have for all discerning Chicago beer drinkers.

A taproom followed in 2012, pouring Half Acre favorites as well as allowing the brewers the chance to experiment with new pale ales, IPAs, brown ales, porters, barleywines, and even the occasional lager. Beers like **Akari Shogun,** a wheat beer, and **Pony Pilsner** became new favorites on draft and in cans. The team developed some annual offerings as well, including **Big Hugs,** the imperial stout released in winter, the **Chub Step** porter, their **Sticky Fat** harvest beer and the **Lager Town Oktoberfest.**

Half Acre's ascendency was confirmed in 2014 at the Great American Beer Fest. Their **Heyoka IPA** was named the second best in the nation at a time when American-style IPAs were more competitive than any other part of the craft beer world (the category received 279 entries, the most of any category). Since then, Heyoka has changed names out of sensitivity to a Native American tribe who requested the term not be used, then changed again after the new name (Senita) was too close for comfort for another unnamed brewery. Now, if you see **GoneAway** in cans, grab it.

Half Acre opened a huge new brewing facility a couple miles north in Bowmanville in 2015, taking the pressure off the Lincoln location, which at that time was brewing a massive amount of **Daisy Cutter** to try and keep up with demand for the brewery's cans. Moving production of **Daisy Cutter** and other year-round beers gave the original brewery the breathing room to start experimenting again, including with sours, something untouched until now. Finally, the company added a restaurant to their original taproom in January 2016, bringing the world what it never knew it needed: a menu focused on upscale stoner burritos served alongside some of the city's best beer.

In a world where brewers are becoming as recognizable as celebrity chefs, Half Acre remains thankfully enigmatic—the label artwork is the most distinctive "personality" the brewery has, with beautiful and cartoonishly subversive designs by Phineas X. Jones. The beer speaks enough for everyone, and their beer is awesome. On the Mount Rushmore of Chicago beer, you'll find a can of Daisy Cutter. It's a classic.

HOPEWELL BREWING COMPANY

2760 N. Milwaukee Ave., Chicago, IL 60647; (773) 698-6178; hopewellbrewing.com; @HopewellBrewing
Founded: 2016 **Founders:** Samantha Lee, Stephen Bossu, and Jonathan Fritz **Brewer:** Stephen Bossu **Flagship beer:** First Lager
Year-round beers: First Lager, Endgrain Lager, Swift IPA, 24:37 Red IPA, Farm and Family Saison **Tours:** Yes **Taproom Hours:** Tues through Thurs, 4 to 11 p.m.; Fri, 4 p.m. to 12 a.m.; Sat, 12 p.m. to 12 a.m.; Sun 12 to 9 p.m.

Hopewell came to Logan Square in February 2016 by way of New York, by way of Portland, by way of California (with a quick trip to Scotland), by way of Champaign-Urbana. It's a long path, but it leads to a succession of good, crisp, clean beers in Chicago, so stick with us.

Like many breweries, this one started during backyard homebrew days at the University of Illinois, which brought lead brewer Stephen Bossu to the Brewing Science department at the University of California-Davis. While studying there, Bossu won the 2010 "Crisp Malting" award from the

Institute of Brewing & Distilling in Scotland, and from there took his learnings to Widmer Brothers in Portland. A three-year stint at Brooklyn Brewery followed, but Chicago still beckoned.

Along the way, Bossu wed fellow beer lover/maker and University of Illinois alumna, Samantha Lee, while their friend and partner Jonathan remained in Chicago. The original plans for Hopewell go back a few years, back when the brewery landscape wasn't so jam-packed in Chicago. But much like the hundreds of vintners that dot the landscape around UC-Davis, there's still plenty of room for variety in the city's beer world.

Located in an awesome-looking, terra cotta–clad building that housed a Goldblatt's Department Store in a former life, the Hopewell team brews on a 20 bbl system into a few 40 bbl fermenters for the core brands as well as a 20 bbl for the fun and wild one-off stuff. Hopewell's focus leans toward lager beers, but ale styles like IPAs and saisons find a home as well.

Their real focus is making beers that are "something that speaks to who we are—approachable and friendly," says Lee. Their west coast–style **Swift IPA** is heavy on pine and tangerine by design, because "that's what's interesting to us, when you can have those really clear notes. The common thread to our beers is dry and clean flavors. We don't have anything that's super sweet or leaves too much of a funk in your mouth."

"Approachable and friendly" basically defines the look of their taproom: a bright, airy space that's almost Nordic in its refinement. The team aims to produce about 1500 to 2000 barrels annually for the taproom and draft accounts throughout Logan Square and Chicago.

LAKE EFFECT BREWING COMPANY

4727 W. Montrose Ave., Chicago, IL 60641; (312) 919-4473; lakeeffectbrewing.com; @LakeEffect_LLC
Founded: 2012 **Founder:** Clint Bautz **Brewers:** Clint Bautz, Eric Ullrich **Flagship beers:** Falcon Dive IPA, Lake Effect Snow, Bitchin' Blonde **Year-round beers:** Falcon Dive, Bitchin' Blonde **Seasonal beers:** Espresso Gone Stout, Brett Frambois, Pateque Watermelon Saison, Superdawg Varieties, Morton Arboretum Beer **Tours:** Yes **Taproom:** In planning along with a bottle shop

When the economy imploded in 2008, then-architect Clint Bautz recognized an opportunity to see what else might be out there for him. "It was an awakening," he said. "The time was now to do something for myself." As a homebrewer for six years, he saw a chance to open his own small brewery on the city's northwest side. It was partially a way to get some square footage back in his home. "Basically all I wanted to do was take what I was doing at home and find a new location to get it out of the house . . . in a lot of ways I've just moved my man cave over to this location," he said. Bautz set up shop for Lake Effect off an alley on West Montrose near the Blue Line and the Metra in April 2012 and was delivering beer by September. The intention was to keep Lake Effect small to start, since it was a part-time effort for him as he transitioned out of his day job.

Eventually the brewery demanded his full-time efforts, thanks in part to a late delivery. His 2 bbl tanks showed up six months after they were expected. "In the meantime, I was already licensed to brew, and Jerry [Nelson] from Une Année pointed me to [Sawyer, Michigan's] Greenbush," Bautz explains. "They were expanding, and we picked up four of their 7 bbl tanks. That immediately changed the whole dynamic."

Lake Effect's offerings, brewed on a 4 bbl Psychobrew system, exist on a few different tiers. Their flagship line of beers, the **Falcon Dive** IPA and the **Lake Effect Snow** witbier, are the main sellers. Previously only available on draft and in bombers, those beers recently moved into six-packs of 12-ounce bottles.

The second tier is their wild/sour collection aged in things like wine barrels, which includes their **Cerise, Framboise,** and **Pamplemousse** beers.

The third tier is focused on collaborations—few breweries work with as many different people and organizations as Bautz does. A beer made in partnership with then-Fountainhead chef Cleetus Friedman named **27 Blocks** refers to the straight-line distance between the two places on Montrose. There's also a beer made for the Morton Arboretum, for the Medinah Country Club, and finally a series of beers made for the iconic Superdawg restaurant just a few miles up the road from the brewery. The **Superbier** is a kolsch with a bit of smoke and a touch of spice, brewed to pair with the restaurant's namesake Superdawg. The **Whoopskibier**, a German-style amber, offers a pairing for the restaurant's Polish sausage while the final collaboration is made to embody a rich, malty chocolate shake.

A taproom is part of Lake Effect's future plans; in the meantime, a bottle shop for package goods and growlers opened at the very end of 2016.

MAPLEWOOD BREWERY & DISTILLERY

2717 N. Maplewood Ave., Chicago, IL 60647; (773) 270-1061; maplewoodbrew.com; @maplewoodbeer
Founded: 2014 **Founders:** Adam Cieslak, Ari Megalis, and Paul Megalis **Brewers:** Adam Cieslak and Adam Smith **Distiller:** Ari Megalis **Flagship beer:** The Charlatan American Pale Ale **Year-round beers:** The Charlatan American Pale Ale, Fat Pug Oatmeal Milk Stout, Azacca Morris IPA, Creepy Ginger Belgian Golden Strong with Organic Ginger, Brownie Points Northern English Brown Ale, Juice Pants IPA **Seasonal beers:** Lemondrop American Wheat Ale, Crushinator Session IPA, Mind Fk Russian Imperial Stout, Mikhail Gorbachev Russian Imperial Stout **Tours:** Yes **Taproom:** Yes (opening soon)

The team at Maplewood Brewery & Distillery operates a little differently than just about every other brewery on earth. Maybe you noticed it in the name, but Maplewood is one of the rare combos able to both produce beer and spirits for mass consumption, putting them in the rarified air of similar dual-purpose places like Ballast Point, New Holland, and Rogue. All of them, however, gradually worked their way from brewing into spirits—Maplewood jumped into both as fast as they could, and the creativity this allows them will be pretty fascinating to observe.

Brewer Adam Cieslak, along with fellow founders and brothers Ari and Paul Megalis, started homebrewing in 2006. They got into craft beer after sampling their way around the craft beer section of Sam's Wine & Spirits (in their pre-Binny's days) and a copy of Charlie Papazian's *The Homebrewer's Companion*. At the same time, Cieslak (who has a background in engineering) "may or may not" have been trying his hand at distilling on a test still as well. "We all really enjoyed beer and different spirits and whiskeys," he says. "So it seemed natural to us to marry the two, since the processes are very similar."

Doing the two in the same place has never been done in Illinois. At the brewery, they've got distinctly separate spaces (including lines spray painted on the floor) to designate the separate sections of both; beers come from a 10 bbl brewhouse, while the spirits are distilled in a 250L column still from Kothe, the same manufacturer who built the system with which the nearby Koval Distillery works.

Maplewood's main beers—**The Charlatan American Pale Ale** and the **Fat Pug** stout—were first released in October 2014 under the brewery's original name, Mercenary. Unfortunately that name was too close for comfort to the Myrcenary Double IPA made by Colorado's Odell. Rather than burn a bunch of time, and effort, and lawyer fees on fighting for the name, they rebranded as Maplewood, named for a section of Chicago that survived the Great Fire (as well as the street on which the brewery space sits).

Beers have been out since late 2014, but the spirits side has taken longer to get underway. The final distiller's license finally cleared midway through 2015 and Maplewood is underway with both sides of the business. After that, a taproom will round out Maplewood's efforts so guests can try beers and spirits side by side—sometimes of the same base brew. For example, a stout could be brewed with a selection of grains, and those same grains can also be distilled into a more pure alcohol. Distillations of straightforward beer can be done as well.

In addition to whiskeys, ryes, and gins hitting streets in early 2016, Maplewood expects to get creative in other ways. Thanks to their two licenses, they're able to make a true eisbock beer. Making that kind of beer involves freezing the beer to raise the ABV, which is technically a distillation process, and is otherwise illegal for brewers to pursue.

METROPOLITAN BREWING

3057 N. Rockwell St., Chicago, IL 60618; no phone; metrobrewing.com; @MetroBrewing
Founded: 2009 **Founders:** Doug Hurst and Tracy Hurst (no relation)
Brewers: Doug Hurst and Ryan Murphy **Flagship beer:** Krankshaft Kolsch **Year-round beers:** Flywheel Bright Lager, Dynamo Copper Lager, Krankshaft Kolsch, Magnetron Schwarzbier **Seasonal beers:** Generator Doppelbock, Iron Works Alt-style, Arc Welder Dunkel Rye, Heliostat Zwickelbier, Afterburner Oktoberfest **Tours:** Not yet
Taproom: Yes

If you are looking for a patron saint of Chicago craft beer, you can find it in Metropolitan. Call them the guiding star, or the pioneers with the arrows in the back to prove it, but you should definitely call Metro (as it's often shortened to) 100 percent devoted to the art of brewing beer. If there were a Ten Commandments of brewing, one of the first would be co-owner Tracy Hurst's saying "lagers tell on you." She should know. She and brewer Doug Hurst have simultaneously carved a path for Chicago craft beer and taken it their own way all at once.

Somehow, Metropolitan, remains pretty much the same as when they started out. They remain committed to making unimpeachable German lagers, from their bright **Flywheel** to their dark **Magnetron Schwarzbier.** They're unabashedly nerdy, with fermenters named for *Star Trek* references, and they are still sorta outsiders in the scene they helped create.

Despite being the vanguard for craft brewing in Chicago, they don't count themselves among the ranks of the Illinois Craft Brewers Guild. Some people just aren't "joiners."

They opened shop in 2009 and had to forge their way through a tangled bureaucratic process. Metro was the first brewery to open within city limits in the decade since Goose Wrigley took over an existing brewpub in 1999. They set a precedent by opening in an old autobody shop in Ravenswood, and many other brewers would follow in their wake, some just blocks away. Their small space remained basically the same through the late 2000s to the mid 2010s, save for many more tanks crammed into open spaces where staff used to roam free. Their main constant is, appropriately enough, their consistency. Their flagship beers, **Dynamo, Flywheel** and **Krankshaft,** all evoke a Germanic mechanic-cism that matches the fine-tuned craftsmanship of the long-fermenting lager. Their love of robots, which appear on their labels and pour their beers at events, also drives that home.

While almost all other Chicago breweries only dabble in lager beers like pilsners and the occasional marzen, nearly everyone else is overwhelmingly ale-centric. Lagers take more time. Ales are quicker, thus are more profitable. Metro takes the long view, and has taken the harder road from day one. (Okay, so a kolsch is an ale yeast fermented at lager temperature, but let's not split hairs here.)

All of these are reasons to hold Metro aloft in the Chicago brewing firmament; to make them the Abe Lincoln of the city's brewing Mt. Rushmore. Beyond that, they've fostered brewers who've gone on to create their own operations. Off Color and Alarmist might not exist without Metropolitan—John Laffler and Gary Gulley both worked at Metro before launching their own efforts. The number of brewers that have Tracy and Doug on speed dial for a hose, a clamp, a piece of advice, or a recommendation on how to deal with the city, can't be counted. The truism that Chicago craft brewing is a collegial community full of helpful people can draw a straight line back to Doug and Tracy's open doors and phone lines.

Plus, did I mention they make damn good beer?

In 2015 Metro finally expanded their reach into perhaps the one state that would appreciate their lagers as much as Chicago—Wisconsin. A state built on lager beer earned Metro's first outside-Illinois accounts, as well as making for a homecoming of sorts. Doug hails from Madison and found his brewing muse in the guise of a project at the University of Wisconsin-Madison, and Tracy is a former Greenville resident (north of Appleton), so it makes sense that their first interstate beers would make their way north of the Cheddar Curtain.

In November 2015 they announced plans to pick up stakes and move west of the river to a new space at Belmont and Rockwell, which would allow them to double capacity and add a taproom. Not a single person in Chicago would begrudge them a newer, bigger space or a chance for a bigger piece of the beer pie . . . but once those Spock-clad fermenters move out of Ravenswood and Winona, it'll be a piece of the city's brewing history moving on. Metro's new brewery and taproom opened in October 2017. More Metro lager is nothing but a good thing.

MIDDLE BROW.

No physical address, no phone; middlebrowbeer.com; @MiddleBrowBeer
Founded: 2011 Founders: Nick Burica, Pete Ternes, Bryan Grohnke
Brewer: Varies Flagship beer: Robyn Farmhouse Blonde Year-round beers: Robyn, White Light, White Heat, Ad Astra Seasonal beers: Milk Eyed Mender Tours: No Taproom: No

If breweries of the 2010s are the spiritual equivalent of the alt-rock and indie bands of the 1980s and '90s, middle brow. is kinda like Fugazi. Their stuff is a little weird and out there, they're very socially conscious, and those who get it, *get it.* If middle brow. decided to pair a beer with a self-produced album on vinyl of remixed recordings of their wort boiling as part of a release, I don't think anyone would be too surprised.

They started in 2011, with the mission of making beer that did good for others as opposed to just doing well for themselves. From the beginning, the brewery set out to provide a portion of the proceeds from all their beers to benefit a variety of charities. Those earnings have gone to places as varied as Ceasefire and the Interrupters on the south and west sides of the city, to Lurie Children's Hospital, to immigration services providers, and more.

Middle brow. is a contract-brewed beer, produced at places like Ten Ninety's former facility in Zion and Church Street's brewery in Itasca, but head brow-ers Nick Burica, Pete Ternes, and Bryan Grohnke are all hands-on in the process. From zesting limes to popping popcorn to stripping vanilla beans, the unique but subtle styles of their beers all require their attention, which it receives. (See page 137 for more on Chicago's other contract breweries.)

The brewery also was one of the first in Chicago to crowdsource some of their recipes. In addition to donating to charity, with their semi-regular brewing contests are also helping homebrewers get a leg up. Some of those contests have led to beers such as their first one, a dark saison with vanilla and cinnamon called **The Life Pursuit.**

Other beers reflect a musical influence. Their most well-known brew, **Robyn,** is named for the Swedish singer, and they made a Belgian pale ale called **Summer in Pain** for the release of a local artist's debut record. Similarly, the inspiration for the witbiers **White Light,** made with apricot and cardamom, and **White Heat,** made with ancho chili and sweet orange peel (which you buy in a four-pack stocked with two of each beer for blending or drinking separately) come from the Velvet Underground.

Other beers simply reflect the city we live in—the **Keep It Copacetic** cream ale, brewed with lime zest, ancho chile, and 240 pounds of popped popcorn was made to evoke the idea of elotes, the street food available in so many parks around Chicago.

OFF COLOR BREWING

3925 W. Dickens Ave., Chicago, IL 60647; no phone; offcolorbrewing.com; @OffcolorBrewing
Founded: 2013 **Founders:** John Laffler and Dave Bleitner **Brewers:** John Laffler and Dave Bleitner **Flagship beers:** Troublesome, Scurry **Year-round beers:** Troublesome, Scurry, Apex Predator, **Seasonal beers:** Le Woof Biere de Garde, Le Predateur, DinoS'mores **Tours:** No **Taproom:** No **Bottle shop Hours:** Wed through Thu, 3 to 7 p.m.; Fri, 2 to 8 p.m.; Sat, 12 to 6 p.m.

The genesis of Off Color Brewing goes as far back as 2008, when principal players John Laffler and Dave Bleitner attended Siebel and interned at Metropolitan together just as the city's craft beer scene was getting started. They started spitballing the idea of opening their own facility in 2009, but those plans got kicked into a higher gear when Goose Island was sold to A-B/InBev in March 2011. Laffler, then an "innovation brewer" doing R&D work for Goose, was responsible for managing Bourbon County Brand Stout (BCBS) and eventually decided that the emerging corporate structure from the A-B sale made it a good time to step out on one's own.

It's a decision that was made again and again by other Goose employees in the years that followed—Greg Hall started Virtue Cider, Claudia Jendron started Temperance, Tom Korder started Penrose, John. J. Hall helped build 5 Rabbit, and Jared Rouben left the brewpub to start Moody Tongue. Laffler's higher profile from working on the vaunted BCBS program, however, gave Off Color an immediate kick into the "most anticipated brewery" category.

Bleitner was working at Two Brothers as a brewer and started scouting spaces before Laffler's departure. Together the two formed a sort of Super Twins of avant-garde Chicago brewing as their plans to revive forgotten styles like gose, kottbusser, gotlandsdricka, and sahti emerged. (Bleitner explained their inspiration to the *Tribune* more bluntly: To make "very bizarre beer no one has heard of or knows about.") A space on the near West Side by Logan Square was acquired, a brewery went in, and some of the most interesting beers in Chicago began pouring out in June 2013.

The first main beers were two Germanic styles. Their **Troublesome** gose was a blend of two different beers, one funky and acidic and one that was a more staid wheat beer. At the time they came out, the gose style was so unknown they simply marketed it as a "tart wheat ale" to get past the immediate questions of why they were trying to sell a salted coriander sour beer. The other beer, a kottbusser called **Scurry** made with honey, oats, and molasses was darker, richer, and a little more accessible, even if not immediately pronounceable.

These two beers pretty much encapsulate the Off Color ethos—underappreciated or near-extinct styles plucked from old brewing texts, revived and delicately crafted for adventurous drinkers and curious palates. (They also introduced us to the city's cutest brewery mascot featured on all their labels. It's a little line-drawn grain mouse, chosen per their FAQ because "it's the only mammal that's at the brewery more than us.")

They've also released the juniper-infused **Bare Bear** sahti, an excellent saison called **Apex Predator,** the lusted-after **Dino'Smores** imperial stout with vanilla and graham cracker, and one of the city's best Berliner

Weiss beers, **Fierce.** Their dedication to the obscure and interesting can be seen in their collaborations with other like-minded, small-batch breweries such as St. Louis's award-winning Side Project, Austin's Jester King, and Denmark's Amager.

An up-close look at those obscure and interesting beers can be seen at the onsite bottle shop they opened at the brewery in February 2016, offering a place for fans to get their hands on large-format wild beers as well as beers like **Troublesome** fresh from the bottling line. Even better, 2017 should see the opening of an Off Color taproom and second brewery in Lincoln Park.

PIPEWORKS BREWING CO.

3921 McLean Ave., Chicago, IL 60647; (773) 698-6154; pdubs.net; @PipeworksBrewin
Founded: 2012 **Founders:** Gerrit Lewis and Beejay Oslon **Brewers:** Kate Brankin, Scott Coffman, John Dunne **Flagship beer:** Ninja Vs Unicorn Double IPA **Year-round beers:** Ninja vs Unicorn DIPA, Lizard King Pale Ale, Glaucus Belgian Pale, Blood of the Unicorn hoppy red, Close Encounter hoppy stout, Lil Citra session IPA Main **Seasonal beers:** "Epic Battle" Double IPA, "Abduction" Series of Russian Imperial Stouts, Rotating Honey DIPAs **Tours:** No **Taproom:** No

Think of the craziest beer you've ever had. I bet if you look through the listings of beers that Pipeworks has made, you can find something similar if not more insane. And for Pipeworks, that's just another day brewing some of the most creative, explosive, varied, sought-after beers in Chicago. There's only one shop in Chicago that's been named "Best New Brewery in the World" (Ratebeer, 2013) after all, and Pipeworks didn't earn that designation by being timid.

Owners Gerrit Lewis and Beejay Oslon met behind the counter of noted bottle shop West Lakeview Liquors (see page 198) in 2008 and quickly bonded over their love of beer—if you bought a beer at West Lakeview Liquors around that time, you probably remember talking about your purchases with either one of them. Their appreciation for beer is both memorable and contagious. The plans to move from retail employee to brewery owners happened in line at Dark Lord Day shorly thereafter.

Both Lewis and Oslon started as homebrewers. Additionally, Oslon headed to Belgium for a few months to apprentice at De Struise Brouwers, one of the world's top breweries. Stateside, the plans for Pipeworks were revealed in one of the country's first Kickstarter efforts to create a brewery. It simultaneously resulted in an influx of capital and a lot of pre-opening press. When bombers of their first beers, the **Ninja Vs. Unicorn DIPA** and **End of Days** imperial stout, started flowing in March 2012, they were snatched up immediately. Those two beers remain an excellent example of the Pipeworks ethos: Big, big, big. Big bottles, big flavors, big ideas, even big bright colors on the labels, mostly designed by Oslon.

Pipeworks hit the ground running and didn't let up—they produced a variety of beers in the first couple of years that many breweries don't make in a decade. Rarely replicating a brew, they tweaked, updated, reworked, or revamped beer after beer. The Ninja series showcased varietals of different hops, their **Abduction** stout did the same thing for adjunct flavors like orange, raspberry, mint, or pistachio. The combination of hugely varied beers did a couple of things for the brewery—it kept beer fans guessing, and it kept them coming back for more, reviewing and writing online about the newest version of this or that. All that conversation led Ratebeer to award Pipeworks the aforementioned Best New Brewery less than a year later.

Lewis and Olson let inspiration for beers come from movies, like the **Hey Careful, Man, There's a Beverage Here** milk stout, inspired by the White Russians preferred by The Dude from *Big Lebowski*. They riffed on beers made to resemble mixed drinks like the **Brown & Stirred** for the Michelin-starred Longman & Eagle, inspired by a Manhattan and brewed with rye, cherry puree, lemon peel, and bittering roots. They even partnered with the world-renowned Aviary bar, using their rotary evaporator to extract the heat and spice from fresno peppers to make a big passionfruit infused chile DIPA. (Like I said: crazy stuff.)

After working for three years in their facility on Western Avenue, Pipeworks picked up shop and moved it a little west to a new production facility, which allowed them to greatly expand capacity and move into 16-ounce cans for the first time. They also became neighbors with Off Color, making a little production-brewery hub in west Logan Square. The canning line prompted Pipeworks to produce their first year-round brews, as opposed to the unpredictable parade of releases they were known for. Not that these beers are now identifiable as "flagships" in the traditional sense of the word; they're more of a natural expansion of their mindset—big hoppy ales, some dark, some light, all in-your-face.

REVOLUTION BREWING (PRODUCTION FACILITY)

3340 N. Kedzie Ave., Chicago, IL 60618; (773) 588-2267; revbrew.com; @RevBrewChicago
Founded: 2012 Founder: Josh Deth Brewers: Jim Cibak (head brewer), Glenn Allen (brewing manager), Marty Scott (brewery quality & innovation lead), Matty Kemp (brewer), Miguel Miguitama (brewer), Matt Voelker (brewer) Evan Isaac (brewer), Tim Mason (brewer) Flagship beers: Anti-Hero IPA, Eugene Porter, Bottom Up Wit, Fist City APA Seasonal beers: Oktoberfest, Rosa, A Little Crazy, Fistmas Tours: Yes Taproom Hours: Wed through Thu, 2 to 10 p.m.; Fri, 2 to 11 p.m.; Sat, 12 to 11 p.m.; Sun 12 to 8 p.m.

Maybe it's the amount of space they have there, but there's something peaceful about drinking a beer at the Revolution production facility on Kedzie. Maybe it's the roof being dozens of feet above your head. Maybe it's the view spanning through the glass walls hundreds of feet past the canning line, fermentation tanks, and brewhouse. Maybe it's just having room to stretch your legs instead of being shoulder-to-shoulder with someone at any other overhyped bar in town. Revolution Brewing is one of the biggest places you'll find in the city for a beer, and most certainly the largest independent one.

The production space opened in May 2012, a couple of years after the Revolution brewpub proved to be a massive hit in Logan Square. The

RevBrew team quickly realized they needed way more space to pump out the **Antihero IPA, Eugene Porter, Bottom Up Wit, Rosa,** and **A Little Crazy** that the city desired. As Chicago breweries go, it's one of the more unassuming—you wouldn't know it was there unless you were hunting for it, lumped as it is alongside other industrial spaces on an otherwise residential stretch of Kedzie north of the Kennedy. Parking sucks, but hey, that's what keeps the tours from getting overcrowded.

Speaking of tours, if you want to take a quick (and free) tour in one of the biggest breweries in Illinois, take this one over the Lagunitas tour. Sure, Lag is bigger and you get to look down on all their shiny stainless steel toys, but Revolution takes you into the guts of their operation, through the cold room, the grain mill, the brewhouse, the fermenter farm, and the canning line (a 1970s-era beast they picked up from the RC Cola company). It's fun, it doesn't take up your entire afternoon, and they give you a beer. What's not to like?

You can also sit yourself down at the bar in one of the rare places where legitimate famous people have been documented drinking craft beer—the 2012 film *Drinking Buddies* by local director Joe Swanberg was filmed in part at the Rev Kedzie space, so pull up a stool where actors such as Olivia Wilde and Jake Johnson pounded pints.

SPITEFUL BREWING

1815 W. Berteau Ave., Chicago, IL 60613; no phone; spitefulbrewing.com; @SpitefulBrewing
Founded: 2010 **Founders:** Jason Klein and Brad Shaffer **Brewers:** Jason Klein and Brad Shaffer **Flagship beers:** Spiteful IPA, Alley Time Pale Ale, Goddamn Pigeon Porter **Seasonal/rotating beers:** Jackass O'Lantern Pumpkin Ale, Jingle Balls Winter Ale, GFY Stout, Malevolence Russian Imperial Stout, Belligerent Bob Barleywine **Tours:** No **Taproom:** No

If you want to see what a Chicago brewery looks like as filtered through the punk-rock view of a collective of bike messengers, artists, and musicians, Spiteful is your place. A more irreverent, smartassed, DGAF group of brewers you'll not find in Chicagoland—not even Pipeworks rises to the middle-fingers-extended attitude of Spiteful. But also, they're nice dudes who make good beer.

When they opened in 2010, Spiteful's story at the get-go was their size. In a 2.5 bbl system crammed into a tiny basement in North Center, they blasted out bombers of buzzsaw stouts like **GFY Stout** (with a label featuring a cartoon bear flipping folks the bird), zippy pale ales like **Alley Time,** and crazy porters that riff on a variety of flavors like peanut butter, raspberry, chocolate fudge, and banana.

They use labels to make fun of their friends (the **People Against Colin series** of beers), office drones (**Working For the Weekend DIPA, I Hate My Boss Coffee Stout**) and really, anything worth skewering (see also the **Selfies Are For Wieners** DIPA). Call it comical, but the folks at Spiteful are being true to themselves.

Spiteful is also one of the smallest Illinois breweries offering cans on a reliable basis. Whereas most breweries get their cans printed by the (literal) truckload, Spiteful labels their cans by hand, allowing them to get their beer into a bike-friendly, light format while still having the flexibility to offer many different versions of their beer in aluminum. Those cans rarely make it too far out of the neighborhood, but Lincoln Square and North Center patrons are plenty happy to have them around.

As the operation got a little more sophisticated, they edged into things like barrel–aging in ways that other breweries wouldn't touch. An absinthe-barrel program saw new versions of their stout, while Belgian-style single and saison all got an anise-flavored edge. The crazy ones are decidedly fun experiments, but two of their more mainstream cellared beers earned hardware at the 2015 Festival of Wood and Barrel-Aged Beers (FoBAB)—their **Chocolate Caliente Malevolence Russian Imperial Stout** and the **Belligerent Bob Barleywine.**

In January 2016, the Spiteful team announced they'd be leaving the underground lifestyle behind (speaking literally, not figuratively) for a bigger brewing facility in Bowmanville next door to the Half Acre production facility, with enough space for lots more beer and a taproom. Spiteful has grown from being just the tiny brewery to being the brewery with a bunch of awesome crazy beers. I don't think anyone will be too surprised or saddened by their expansion.

UNE ANNÉE BREWERY

9082 W. Golf Rd., Niles, IL 60714; no phone; uneannee.com; @UneAnnee
Founded: 2012 **Founder:** Jerry Nelson **Brewer:** Jerry Nelson
Flagship beers: Maya Belgian IPA, Esquisse American Wild Ale **Year-round beers:** Maya, Esquisse, and Le Seul series of American Wild Ales with fruit **Seasonal beers:** Airing of Grievances Belgian Imperial Stout
Tours: No **Taproom:** In planning

Downtime on a military base isn't where you expect most breweries to have their roots, but Une Année's Jerry Nelson isn't most brewers. He picked up the hobby while serving in the marines in the mid-90s, and continued the hobby until enrolling in school for architecture. Sadly, there wasn't a big homebrew scene at the Illinois universities where Nelson studied, and brewing was left by the wayside.

It was a friend's homebrew kit that got him back into it in 2010. Nelson was invited over to pitch in on said friend's first batch and that reignited the need to brew. After running the numbers, getting some Siebel education and building his brewhouse, he got underway with Une Année in early 2012. He brought a new and much-needed Belgian and French focus (Une Année means "one year" en francais) and a seasonal mindset to his beers, which immediately distinguished the company from the parade of new and emerging breweries at the time.

Originally working on a homemade 7 bbl brewing system and building it up to an 18 bbl setup, Une Année produces about 400 to 500 barrels per year, split equally by draft and package. Rather than go to market with a parade of bombers, Une Année again distinguishes itself by serving most of its beers in 750 ml bottles, using a few smaller 375 ml bottles from time to time.

Though Russian Imperial Stouts and IPAs have made their way out of the brewery, the change didn't sit right with Nelson. "In the last couple years, I realized doing American styles under the name Une Année doesn't work very well. I realized I should probably split [those] off and make a side label really focused on that."

Based on that inspiration, beers from a new label called Hubbard's Cave emerged in late 2015. Meanwhile, Une Année has doubled down on the Belgian–style and increased focus on saisons and sours as well. This mirrors the way a few other breweries operate—18th Street opened a second project called Sour Note, and Michigan's funk-focused Jolly Pumpkin has a second brand for their more mainstream American-style beers called North Peak.

In late 2016-early 2017, Une Année moved to a new facility elsewhere in the area in order to open a taproom. The zoning at the original Une Année space made it near impossible to acquire a liquor license, so the town of nearby Niles became the beneficiary of Une Année's move out of town.

THE LOOP BAR CRAWL

For years Chicago's downtown Loop area was a great place to be between 8 a.m. and 6 p.m., then everyone cleared out and headed home. Over the past decade or so, shops have stayed open longer, people are out later, and restaurants and bars have reemerged to provide some options after the workday is done.

Sky Ride Tap, 105 W. Van Buren, Chicago IL 60605; 312-939-3340; no website (like any true dive)

Just outside the literal edge of the loop is this shot-and-beer bar for day traders, blue-collar workers, and commuters ready to head home after a day at the office. Decor-wise, it's pleasantly stuck in the 1980s, with wood-paneled walls, drop ceilings, news on the TV, and the ghost of thousands of cigarettes smoked before the indoor ban kicked in. It's a great place for a beer, even if the selection is slim; great experiences can be had with the smallest of beer lists. **High Life and a Beam** is a good order here.

Walk west on Van Buren and north on Wacker to…

South Branch, 100 S. Wacker Dr., Chicago IL 60606; 312-546-6177; southbranchchicago.com.

Just a few blocks northwest, South Branch gives you a more upscale option right along the Chicago River. The long, dramatically lit bar runs along the restaurant with huge windows offering expansive views of the skyscrapers across the river. In summer months, the large outdoor patio is a huge draw, with next to no chance of grabbing a table between 5 and 7 p.m. South Branch is from the same restaurant group behind Howells & Hood (see page 162) and Old Town Pour House (see page 173), so you know at least a few good beers will be onhand.

Keep heading up Wacker, then east on Washington and a little further north on Wells to…

Stocks and Blondes, 40 N. Wells St., Chicago IL 60606; 312-372-3725; stocksandblondesbar.com.

In the same vein as Sky Ride, Stocks and Blondes sits right beneath the Washington & Wells El stop and pours for a commuter crowd and after-office happy hour clientele. (Don't count on getting a drink here on the weekend; S&B is closed. Some Loop places are still happy to work hard and fast only during the weekdays for their daily bread.) They do have a reliably good selection of beers in a small space—it can get loud, raucous, and crowded though. It's a solid Chicago bar in a part of town that doesn't have many true tavern options.

Head north on Wells to Lake and then head a little west on Lake Street to...

Monk's Pub, 205 W Lake St., Chicago IL 60606; 312-357-6665; monkspubchicago.com.

Head up to the northwest corner of the Loop for this stop. Monk's sits right by the intersection of the Green Line and the Orange/Purple/Brown lines, but you'll find that the crowd more than drowns out the rattle of public transit. If you're looking for a downtown beer release party or a rare craft to try, Monk's is one of your best Loop bets. (See page 172.)

Head east on Lake Street and turn south on State Street for a nice hike down to Adams where you head east and then north on Wabash to...

Miller's Pub, 132 S. Wabash Ave., Chicago IL 60603; 312-263-4988; millerspub.com.

Another historic Chicago restaurant and bar. (So many of these choices exist directly underneath the El, for some reason. Miller's is no different.) While Miller's doesn't have any incredible local history, it's just a very good bar that has stood the test of time. Open since 1935, Miller's was, for a time, a favored spot for celebrities in the mid-twentieth century. The pub could have easily rested on the laurels of the autographed pictures that line their walls. Instead, they keep serving good food and they keep buying really good beer. One-off brews from locals like Half Acre and Off Color find room on the lines as do fresh beers from new breweries from all over Chicago that many beer bars haven't even gotten their hands on yet. Of course, if it's winter and you don't get a Miller's hot toddy, well, that's on you.

Head east over to Michigan Avenue and north one block to...

The Gage, 24 S. Michigan Ave. ,Chicago IL 60603; 312-372-4243;
thegagechicago.com

When the Gage opened in 2007, it was a bit of a signal that the
Loop was coming back as an after-hours option. This bistro-style
spot with highly elevated pub/comfort food matched cocktails, wine,
and, notably, a wide variety of quality beers just steps from the new
Millennium Park. (Don't miss the scotch egg.) The bar evokes a certain
nineteenth-century vibe, one where you expect the bartender to have
garters on his sleeves and his hair parted down the center, slicked with
oil. The view onto the Avenue is great, the patio dining in summer is
equally excellent.

*This one's easy – exit The Gage, face north, and walk about a hundred
feet north. You'll find yourself at...*

The Game Room, Chicago Athletic Association (CAA) Hotel, 12 S. Michigan
Ave., Chicago IL 60603; 844-312-2221; gameroomchicago.com.

When the CAA opened in May 2015 after years of renovation,
it immediately became one of the hottest spots in town. It was
transformed from a private club for the city's elite (folks like William
Wrigley and Marshall Field were once members) into a boutique hotel
with five different drinking and dining options. The whole building
looks like it was preserved from its 1890-era opening day, as though
capitalists and robber-barons were just next door in a meeting room,
smoking cigars and planning their next railroad purchase.

The Game Room gives you the feeling that you could be one of them,
with an indoor bocce court, shuffleboard, foosball, and table games such
as chess and checkers. High ceilings, rich, dark-wood-paneled walls,
and tile floors are lit by era-appropriate Edison bulbs; the room echoes
with conversation and energy. The bar pours local beers alongside
Schlitz. Once you walk into The Game Room, it won't matter what you're
drinking, you'll really be drinking in the look of the room itself.

Chicago, South

The City's South Side brewing scene may not be as densely packed as it is in points north, but there's still everything from the tiny storefront brewpub to one of the largest craft breweries in the world.

Chicago, South

Chicago

Lower West Side

Cicero

Little Village

McKinley Park

Archer Heights

Back of the Yards

Hyde Park

Bedford Park

South Side

Burbank

Auburn Gresham

South Shore

South Chicago

Oak Lawn

Washington Heights

East Side

Pullman

West Pullman

Whiting

Alsip

Crestwood

Little Calumet River

Dolton

LAKE MICHIGAN

Calumet River

ILLINOIS
INDIANA

Chicago

N

0   2   4 miles

BREWERIES

ARGUS BREWERY

11314 S. Front Ave, Chicago, IL 60628; (773) 941-4050;
argusbrewery.com; @ArgusBrewery
Founded: 2009 **Founders:** Bob and Patrick Jensen **Brewer:** Mary
Pellettiere **Flagship beers:** Pegasus IPA, Jarret Payton's All American
Wheat Ale, Holsteiner Lager, Ironhorse Chicago Common, EZ Rider Pale
Ale **Tours:** Yes **Taproom:** No

Perhaps the oldest Chicago brewery that the fewest people might recognize, Argus's brewing career goes all the way back to 2009, when the father and son team of Bob and Patrick Jensen opened shop. Located in the far South Side neighborhood of Pullman, the brewery operates out of a building formerly used as distributions stables for the Schlitz brewery in the early twentieth century when horses delivered beer to thirsty Chicagoans.

Argus began as a company brewing house brands for restaurants and bars around the city—if you had a beer at the Ballydoyle Irish Pub in Downers Grove or the Country House restaurants in Clarendon Hills, Geneva, or Lisle, you may have had an Argus and not known it. They've branched out since then into their own line of beers, including the **Holsteiner Lager** and **Pegasus IPA** (you can see the horse theme developing from the stables location) as well as a special wheat beer for Jarrett Payton, scion to Chicago sports royalty Walter Payton.

Argus was one of the first and only breweries in the state to self-distribute their beer, and that right came into question during the legislative argument in Springfield over Anheuser-Busch, craft breweries, and who could sell their beer where. Argus and Big Muddy in downstate Murphysboro were the only breweries in the state who could, and did, self-distribute their beer in 2011. The legislative agreement known as SB754 would solidify their right to bring their beer to bars and restaurants themselves. That bill would go on to be the starting point, legally speaking anyway, for many craft breweries to follow. (See sidebar on page 50.)

Argus is also one of the few Chicago breweries to distribute beer abroad. (This, they don't self-distribute.) Goose Island has been in the UK for years, and Revolution occasionally sends kegs out to Japan, while Argus distributes their beer to England and Germany. They also help with new contract beers for growing Chicago breweries from time to time—their lager knowledge came in handy when the Baderbrau line launched out of Argus well before their South Loop brewery came online.

There are not many Chicago breweries that can claim their beer has been enjoyed by a President, but Argus can wear that particular feather in their cap. When news broke that President Obama would be naming the Pullman Historic District as a national monument, they brewed a special **Monumental Lager** for the occasion. When the President came to Pullman in February 2015 to make it official, Argus provided the lager for a celebration at the Pullman Visitors Center.

A special request came through from the Secret Service, and four cases found their way to Air Force One. Considering President Obama helped bring homebrew to the White House for the first time, it's probably safe to say he sampled some Argus beer on the way back to D.C.

BADERBRAU

2515 S. Wabash Ave., Chicago, IL 60616; (815) 263-1309; baderbrau.com; @baderbrau
(Re)-Founded: 2012 Founder (Reviver): Rob Sama Brewer: Nathan Tertell Flagship beers: Baderbrau Chicago Pilsner, South Side Pride Helles, High Noon Hefe Seasonal beers: Red Velvet, Lawnmower Lager, Naked Selfie, Oktoberfest, Velociradler Tours: Yes Taproom Hours: TBD

The story of the revival of the Baderbrau pilsner reminds me of Tim "Ripper" Owens, who was at one time the singer for Judas Priest. (I assure you, this will make sense.) Owens was the guy who famously fronted a Priest tribute band only to end up actually singing for the band when original vocalist Rob Halford went solo. I'm not saying Baderbrau owner Rob Sama is the "Ripper" to the original brand's brewer, but . . . well, he went from superfan to running the place as well, so that's close enough for me.

The original Baderbrau was almost completely forgotten when Sama revived it. The beer was brewed in the 1980s and '90s by the Pavichevich brewery in Elmhurst, and when they went under Goose Island took over making the brand for a few years and even won a medal at GABF with it before leaving it by the wayside. It was a beer once famously proclaimed by Everyone's Favorite Beer Writer, the late Michael Jackson, to be "the best [he'd] ever tasted in America." *(I've thought about this quote a lot and considering the relatively unimpressive state of American brewing in 1989*

when Jackson made that comment at the Conference on Gastronomy (held in Chicago, by the way), I really have to wonder if Jackson kindly meant "best pilsner in America" at the time like one would say "best Soviet-era automobile" to describe the Yugo. Either way, it's a cool story.) And quickly, Baderbrau was basically forgotten about. Except by Sama.

Really, you can thank a URL search for the revival of the brand. Sama was a fan of the beer from the days when he drank it as a college student at the University of Chicago, and when he looked it up online, there was no website for it. Sama grabbed the domain name, started a fan website, and started looking into who owned the brand. As it turned out, Goose Island had let the trademark lapse (after purchasing it in 1997 for a reported $100,000), so Sama acquired that as well. After that, the original brewmaster was hunted down (also via the wonders of the Internet), the original yeast strain acquired from a Canadian university, and contract brewing began in 2012.

After re-introducing the original pilsner, Sama added more German-style beers including the hopped-up bock **Red Velvet**, a roasty black lager called **Naked Selfie,** a traditional Oktoberfest and the John Deere color-pallette-appropriating **Lawnmower Lager IPL.** Beers were originally brewed at Argus on the south side, and then moved to the Stevens Point brewery in Wisconsin. Finally, those beers returned home.

A space in the South Loop was acquired and converted to a full brewery, taproom, and store for their lager-focused efforts. Sama wanted a South Side space to honor the University of Chicago days where he learned to love locally crafted pilsner beer. He found such a space in a former plumbing supply space on Wabash. From there he brought in Nathan Tertell from Lagunitas as brewmaster. Baderbrau is a big notch in the belt of the South Loop brewing renaissance, kicked off by Motor Row and Vice District just a few blocks away. Its opening in June 2016 brought the brand's brewing story full circle—from being the city's first packaged beer in decades, to a decline into almost total obscurity, and back to a brewing home of its own near the heart of Chicago.

LAGUNITAS BREWING COMPANY

2607 W. 17th St., Chicago, IL 60608; (773) 522-2097; lagunitas.com; @lagunitasbeer
Founded: 1993 **Founder:** Tony Magee **Brewer:** Mary Bauer
Flagship beer: Lagunitas IPA **Year-round beers:** Lagunitas Sucks, Daytime, New Dogtown Pale Ale, A Little Sumpin' Sumpin', Lagunitas Pils, Maxiumus, Hopstoopid **Seasonal/occasional beers:** Equinox Pale Oat Ale, Brown Shugga, Cappucino Stout, Undercover Investigation Shut-Down Ale **Tours:** Yes **Taproom Hours:** Wed through Sun, 12 to 9 p.m.

I t's the only Chicago brewery that could also be considered an import. Lagunitas started in California in 1993 when Rogers Park native Tony Magee fired up his stove and boiled up a kit of homebrew. Now it's one of the biggest breweries in America. That's the shorthand version. The longer version takes some more time.

Lagunitas was already well on its way to being a craft beer powerhouse when they announced their plans to build a massive brewery on the city's South Side in April 2012. Even in a city growing numb to beer news, the announcement (made via Magee's Twitter account, of course) was jawdropping—hundreds of thousands of square feet; a 250 bbl brewhouse on order from overseas; the capacity for about a million barrels of craft beer every year. The scope of it was damn near inconceivable for a city used to the word "big" being applied to a few 50-barrel batches from Goose Island.

Chicagoans watched every move of the buildout via Magee's social media outreach. It started with photos from the empty space, inviting viewers to imagine the potential for the city's scale of craft beer. After that came updates on huge tanks arriving from Europe. We watched a hole get opened in a wall to accomodate the massive lauter tun. News sites posted video of huge pieces of stainless that shut down city streets due to their massive size, all while Magee narrated from the middle of the road with a bottle of **Daytime** in his hands.

Finally, no less than Governor Pat Quinn showed up to cut a ribbon (metaphorically speaking, that is, as the opening was actually a chain cut by bolt cutters) and get the place down to business. The governor wore a suit and a purple tie. Magee wore black jeans and an untucked, open collar green shirt; circus performers stood in the background; and a marching band led the way into the brewery after the ceremony.

Brewing actually started in April, with hundreds of barrels of IPA coming out of the brewery at a time. The taproom overlooking the brewery with catwalks extending out over the brewing and packaging lines became some of the best views a beer manufacturer could offer. The scale of the brewery continues to be really unfathomable—it's best to just have a pint of the freshest beer you can ask for and try to absorb it all. It helps to let the rhythm and rattle of the packaging line numb you into a sort of meditative Zen state. It's awesome in the literal sense of the word, heavy on "awe."

It's still hard to imagine that this was just one of many chapters Lagunitas planned on writing, and not a defining one. Within eighteen months, another 250 bbl brewhouse was on its way to complement its partner. More and more fermenters were added to the farm of tanks. A third brewery in southern California was announced, expected to be of equal scale and made to impact the burgeoning craft beer movement in Central America. The most notable moment came in September 2015, when Heineken announced that they'd bought a 50 percent stake in the company, with the intent to bring American craft beer overseas and essentially take Lagunitas global.

Magee made an announcement on his Tumblr page at the same time the official press release made it to the world. The financial pages paid attention to what Heineken officials had to say; beer geeks around the globe only wanted to know what it meant from the man who had decried purchase attempts from A-B and shunned sales of craft breweries like 10Barrel and Elysian. He quoted Heraclitas, he name-checked Nietzche. It was classic Tony. It came down, very simply, to finding what he called "a mutual respect society, a meeting of equals, a partnership of peers."

If the end result of Lagunitas's growth into Chicago is the eventual world domination of their IPA, Pils, **Little Sumpin' Sumpin'** and other high-hopped west coast–style craft brews, well, it was fun to watch it sorta start here. Remember the events of 2014 when you're sipping a Lagunitas IPA in Costa Rica, Madagascar, or Mongolia.

MARZ COMMUNITY BREWING

3315 S. Halsted Ave., Chicago, IL 60608 (new facility forthcoming); (331) 223-3226; marzbrewing.com; @marzbrewing
Founded: 2014 Founder: Ed Marzewski Brewer collective: Tim Lange, Eric Olsen, Alex Robertson, Pete Alvorado, Kazys Ozelis, Eli Espinoza Flagship beers: Jungle Boogie Pale Wheat Ale, Bubble Creek Berliner Weiss, The Machine APA Seasonal/occasional beers: Ruby's Tears Gose, Citra! Citra! Citra! DIPA Tours: No Taproom: No

This band of freaks, misfits, lumpens, and other ne'er-do-wells is led by Ed Marzewski, longtime artist, writer, organizer, agitator, gallery owner, former bar owner, and the greatest ambassador for the Bridgeport neighborhood (non-Daley division). After many late-night discussions with a variety of folks in the brewing scene at his family's drinking establishment, Maria's Packaged Goods & Community Bar (see page 171), he decided to open a brewery with a rotating collection of brewers.

Marz Community Brewing could have found a home next to the bar or in any number of different places around the neighborhood, none of which panned out. When a small storefront on Halsted opened up just a few blocks from Maria's, as Marzewski puts it, "we said screw it. Let's open this thing." And so, a brewery was born.

Working from a 5 bbl Psychobrew system, the community brewery makes beers with the help and recipes of a variety of homebrewers including many from the HOPS and CHAOS homebrew groups. Co-lead brewers Tim Lange and Eric Olson help coordinate the brewing of beers like the **Bubbly Creek** berlinerweiss, the **Ruby's Tears** gose with coriander and lime sea salt, the **Machine APA,** and the **Citra! Citra! Citra!** double IPA.

While working at the Halsted space, Marzewski continued looking for new spaces, checking out dozens of properties around the neighborhood. When a spot near 37th and Iron Street opened up, Marzewski went to check it out and, "it was like it was destined to happen," he explains. His mother suggested he go check out the factories south of the bar and, as he pulled up to a building next to a friend's space, he noticed a sign for an available building.

As he was set to call the number, a car pulled up next to him. It was his friend, Tim, who also happened to be a real estate agent and who had taken over the building that day. You can imagine the pull of fate at that moment. A 15 bbl brewhouse was placed on order and Marz expects to be up and running there in 2017 or 2018 . . . sometime. To tide them over, the brewery released a series of highly experimental beers called **Zewski's Brewskis,** like the **Earl Olaf** wheat wine aged in imperial stout bourbon barrels and the **Nasal Cavity** golden milk stout with wasabi. Yes, wasabi. These dudes made a pho-inspired beer as well as a mushroom beer aged it soy sauce barrels. Things get weird sometimes. But that's what keeps things fun.

MOTOR ROW BREWING

2337 S. Michigan Ave., Chicago, IL 60616; (312) 624-8149; motorrowbrewing.com; @MotorRowBrewing
Founded: 2015 **Founders:** Bob and Frank Lassandrello **Brewers:** Frank Lassandrello and Justin Lincoln **Flagship beer:** Reclamation Lager **Year-round beers:** New Phenix, Out of the Loop IPL **Seasonal beers:** Amber Sunrise, Bipolar Bear Pale Ale, Fleetwood Black Schwarzbier **Tours:** Yes **Taproom Hours:** Tues through Thurs, 4 to 10 p.m.; Fri and Sat, 12 to 11 p.m.; Sun, 12 to 8 p.m.

Pouring beers, scrubbing floors, leading tours. That's where Frank Lassandrello started at the Goose Island Clybourn pub after finishing school in 2004, while also homebrewing and angling for a gig at the brewery. When a job working in the cellar opened up at Fulton Street, he grabbed it and immediately started . . . feeding cardboard into a packaging machine.

"I was taken aback. I thought I'd start training in the brewery right away. Thankfully, they gave me experience in all places—packaging, shipping, and receiving," he said. "I learned how to be a really good forklift driver, which is very underrated in the industry."

Like so many, starting at the bottom gave Lassandrello a chance to earn some stripes in every part of the brewery, as well as to discover what he really loved there.

"Learning to do filtration, taking samples, working in the lab to count yeast—that's where my passion is, in the lab," he says. "I love working with finished beer. Knowing that I'm the last line of defense before the beer goes into that package . . . I enjoy that pressure."

That education led to Lassandrello taking over at Milwaukee's Lakefront Brewery as director of Quality Control in 2008, where he also learned to make lager beers instead of the Belgian and English styles that Goose was really focused on. Along the way, he started thinking of opening his own place, too.

A big step in kicking Lassandrello in that direction was being asked to judge at GABF alongside "the best of the best," as he puts it. "When I came back I felt very strongly about my skills and what I'd developed . . . I came back and I said, 'I think I can do this.'"

They landed on a space in the South Loop way down on Michigan Avenue near McCormick Place, a landmark building that housed one of the many early automobile sales and manufacturing places in the early 1900s. A complete refurbishing of the building followed, and a 10 bbl brewing system went in, custom built to Lassandrello's specifications.

Like so many best-laid plans, this one had some twists and turns—the original name of Broad Shoulders changed to Motor Row plans to open a brewpub got sidelined when the city didn't land the Olympics (the location is near where the athlete's village would have been), and, thanks to the historic nature of the building, the buildout took longer than expected. Far longer—South Loop residents waited years for Lassandrello to open his doors.

Beers finally started flowing in January 2015 out of the small storefront taproom, and a grander second-story space opened in October. With a focus on both lagers and Belgian-style beers in sessionable ABVs—4.5 to 6.5 percent is what they aim for—the brewery's flagship beer is a zwickel-style, unfiltered lager with rye called **New Phenix,** named for the auto manufacturer that operated out of the same building between the two world wars. Originally available on draft only, Motor Row moved into tallboy cans in December 2015.

MOODY TONGUE BREWING COMPANY

2136 S. Peoria Ave., Chicago, IL 60808; (312) 600-5111; moodytongue.com; @MoodyTongue
Founded: 2013 **Founders:** Jared Rouben and Jeremy Cohn **Brewer:** Jared Rouben **Flagship beers:** Steeped Emperor's Lemon Saison
Year-round beers: Steeped Emperor's Lemon Saison, Sliced Nectarine IPA, Caramelized Chocolate Churro Baltic Porter, Applewood Gold
Seasonal beers: Bourbon Barrel Aged Chocolate Barleywine **Tours:** Not yet **Taproom:** Yes

As more and more fine-dining chefs get into the brewery game, you can basically thank Moody Tongue's Jared Rouben for the spark of inspiration that got them going. While he served as the brewmaster for the Goose Island Clybourn brewpub, he worked with over fifty chefs, including the likes of Rick Bayless, Stephanie Izard, Paul Kahan, and other top Chicago chefs. They responded well to his style of "culinary brewing" as well as his background as a graduate of the Culinary Institute of America and his time spent working in Michelin-starred restaurants.

After crafting beers with food-friendly ingredients at Goose, Rouben split off in August 2013 to announce his own culinary brewery, Moody Tongue, a name directly inspired by the discerning palates he was looking to reach. Rouben moved a 20 bbl brewhouse Into a Pilsen in a former glass factory. The fermenters are specifically designed for his style of brewing, made to help extract the flavors from ingredients like farm-fresh paw paw fruit, toasted cacao beans, brandied blackberries, and dehydrated tangerines.

Beers emerged on draft in June 2014 and in bottles in April 2015. Brews included **Steeped Emperor's Lemon Saison** infused with citrusy tea (named to *Draft Magazine*'s list of Best Beers of 2015), the **Caramelized Chocolate Churro** baltic porter that tastes like a light-bodied rich chocolate cake in a glass, and the **Sliced Nectarine IPA,** with the sharpness of the fruit balancing out the bitterness of the hops. Other experiments included a dehyrdrated tangerine peel wheat, a padron pepper Belgian IPA, a green coriander witbier, and a surprisingly true-to-style Czech pilsner made just for the team at the nearby Thalia Hall.

Moody Tongue's biggest blast of attention came when Rouben introduced a beer made with one of his wildest ingredient experiments yet—the $120-a-bottle **Black Truffle Pilsner.** Perhaps the most expensive bottle of pilsner ever made, this beer featured hand-shaved truffles that usually run upward of $3,000 a pound. The price tag was high, but really it was basically a break-even beer for the young brewery that bought a whole world's worth of press.

The delicately flavored beer was deliciously complex with the earthy truffles contributing a rich bouquet of nutty, savory, almost briny flavors. It was also a way for Rouben to come back home to the food world that created him—it was served at Per Se, the New York restaurant helmed by Rouben's former boss, Thomas Keller. For any other brewery on earth, a $120 beer with a weird ingredient would have seemed like just another PR-grabbing stunt beer, but for Rouben, it was a natural extension of what he's been doing all along—great ingredients put into a bottle instead of on a plate. One more additional extension of that culinary focus came into being in November 2016, when the Moody Tongue taproom opened. You'd think that the home base for a noted chef/brewer would have an awesomely ambitious restaurant as part of it, but you'd be wrong – Rouben pairs his taproom beers with just two items: oysters and chocolate cake.

VICE DISTRICT BREWING COMPANY

1454 S. Michigan Ave., Chicago, IL 60605; (312) 291-9022; vicedistrictbrewing.com; @Vice_District
Founded: 2014 **Founders:** Curtis Tarver and Quintin Cole **Brewer:** Charlie Davis **Flagship beers:** Everleigh ESB, Habitual Dark Cascadian Ale **Seasonal/occasional beers:** Cluster, Damn Near Killed Her DIPA, Metrosexual Chocolate Stout, The Usual Suspects Steam Beer **Tours:** No **Taproom Hours:** Tues through Thurs, 4 to 11 p.m.; Fri, 4 p.m. to 1 a.m.; Sat, 2 p.m. to 1 a.m.; Sun, 2 to 9 p.m.

Vice District isn't the biggest brewery in town. Hell, it's not even the biggest brewery on the street. But if every neighborhood had a taproom this friendly, pouring a variety of local beers and bringing together a community to kick back and enjoy themselves, with owners that welcome guests like friends, the city might be in better shape. (Yes, a better city through beer. Don't look at me like I'm crazy.)

The brewery has its roots in a snowstorm, which may be the most Chicago-y origin story until a brewery conceived over Italian beefs opens its doors. (I give it three years.) The Snowmageddon of February 2011 that dropped 2 feet of snow on the area and shut down Lake Shore Drive also found Curtis Tarver II helping dig out his new neighbor, Quintin Cole. The two bonded over good beer, then homebrewing, and then, after a number of late-night tasting panels and equipment trades made by running across the street, the two found themselves faced with a bit of an ultimatum from their wives—you guys need to just go ahead and get out of the basement(s) and open your own place. So they did.

Vice District is a small, sparse, no-frills space with communal tables and a tall bar; if you like concrete and wood, the District is your place. They pour up to ten different in-house beers brewed on a 7 bbl system viewable from the taproom. They have a few flagships but mostly rotate through whatever they see fit to brew. It's friendly as hell, with folks playing board games, families eating takeout dinner over pints of beer, and folks just watching Michigan Avenue go by from the big floor-to-ceiling windows.

Cole and Tarver brought on Charlie Davis, formerly of North High Brewing in Ohio and Finch's Brewery on the north side to handle the production. Main brews include the **Everleigh ESB,** named for the sisters who ran an infamous brothel back when this part of the city was a literal district of vice; their **Habitual Black IPA** is a nice, roasty brew that doesn't suffer from over-the-top pineyness.

It's a much-needed but entirely casual neighborhood spot in a place that most people don't consider much of a neighborhood—achieving any sense of community in this high-rise happy corner of town is a true accomplishment. Vice District announced in late 2015 that they'd be adding another member of the family to the community with plans to open a larger production facility in Homewood, as well as another taproom.

LINCOLN SQUARE/ NORTH CENTER BAR CRAWL

This part of the city has a very high density of breweries; one could drink at a handful of different places and never have a beer that was made farther than 20 feet from where you're sipping it. That said, in addition to the breweries, there are a lot of great bars around as well. Draw a straight line up Lincoln Avenue and you hit plenty of great options; it's the best drinking street in the city if you're looking for quality, not quantity.

Big Bricks, 3892 N. Lincoln Ave., Chicago IL 60613; 773-525-5022; bigbrickschicago.com.

A sibling to the Lincoln Park pizza place, Big Bricks adds house-smoked barbecue to the mix, and a small but great selection of draft beer choices from locals and from across the country. Christmas time finds them breaking out a vertical selection of Sierra Nevada Celebrations from throughout the years; it's a rarity to find that many draft lines devoted to multiple ages of one kind of beer. The smoked wings are excellent, the pizzas are very good (try the Ditka).

From Big Bricks, walk northwest up Lincoln Avenue and take a right on Irving Park to find...

The Globe Pub, 1934 W. Irving Park Rd., Chicago IL 60613; 773-871-3757; theglobepub.com.

While most new bars and restaurants are laying their fealty at the feet of American craft beer, the Globe is happy to focus on brews from all over, including European selections from Estrella Damm and Bellhaven. They are a football/soccer bar, opening their doors bright and early on weekends for footy fans looking for some communal drinking and sport (and a classic fry-up breakfast). The Lounge next door was an expansion that added another couple dozen draft lines to an already populous list; their beer selection comes in a thick, many-paged pamphlet that can be intimidating to those who don't know their ales from their lagers.

Head back west on Irving to Lincoln Avenue and keep heading northwest about 5 blocks to...

Half Acre Beer Company Tap Room, 4257 N. Lincoln Ave., Chicago IL 60618, 773-248-4038; halfacrebeer.com.

It's a rare evening when every stool isn't filled at this bar and every table doesn't have folks packed into each seat, sipping beers and eating takeout from nearby restaurants. The Half Acre taproom is one of my favorites in the city. You can sit and order pints and hypnotize yourself studying the intricately curved and carved wooden walls. Gaze up at the large bear's head emerging from above the taps, sit and enjoy the sun pouring through the skylight (you are day drinking, right?), and listen to the raucous crowd's high-volume conversations rattle around the room's hard walls. Now that this brewery is open for their experimental beers, you can find some ridiculously fun stuff on draft. **Daisy Cutter** is easily found everywhere else; order the fun stuff, especially on Firkin Friday, when they pack a small barrel of beer with weird/unique/fun ingredients for a specialty beer that disappears quick.

Doesn't get any easier than this – Half Acre is just a couple doors south of...

Wild Goose Bar & Grill, 4265 N. Lincoln Ave., Chicago IL 60618; 773-281-7112; wildgoosebar.com.

The neighborhood is lucky to have a straight-up sports bar that serves good wings, a damn fine quesadilla, and a wide selection of craft beers where other sports-minded establishments would start and end with no more than the bucket of domestics of your choice. Naturally there's always Half Acre available, along with the likes of Lagunitas and Three Floyds reliably on hand. Large-format bottles can get interesting, especially paired with their award-winning, freshly fried chipotle barbecue wings.

Another easy one: walk out of the Wild Goose and cross Berteau and then Lincoln – the bar is kitty-corner from...

Bad Apple, 4300 N. Lincoln Ave., Chicago IL 60618; 773-360-8406; badapplebar.com

Although Bad Apple is also covered in the restaurants section (see page 149), it's worth pointing out again how amazing a beer list this hamburger restaurant has. Don't skip the cheese curds.

Stay on the same side of Lincoln and head northwest three very long blocks to...

Fork, 4600 N. Lincoln Ave., Chicago IL 60625; 773-751-1500; forkchicago.net.

Smack dab in that Goldilocks zone of Square restaurants—a just-right menu of comforting cuisine with a just-right beer list featuring a mix of locals and imports. Despite calling itself a wine bar, Fork offers a reliably good selection of local beers on tap. The food offers a good selection of cheese, charcuterie, and small and large plates; brunch is solid as well. Hard to Google, though.

Keep heading up Lincoln. Yep, there's a lot of great places to drink beer on Lincoln. Once you get north of Leland, look for the little wooden shack which indicates the presence of...

Huettenbar, 4721 N. Lincoln Ave., Chicago IL 60625; 773-561-2507, huettenbar.com.

One of my favorite bars in the city, Huettenbar opened in the mid-80s when the neighborhood was populated with a large number of German immigrants. A bierstube that wouldn't feel out of place in the Black Forest, this place offers two bars pouring the likes of Stiegl, BBK, Weihenstephan, Spaten, and Kostritzer. It's a European lager lover's dream. They've branched out and added an occasional handle of local craft like Revolution and at Christmas time, Anchor, but you want a draft pour of a sparkling, crisp lager and a seat at one of the tables by the windows up front. When those are thrown open wide for the first time each year, it's a symbol that spring has truly arrived.

Walk outside. Cross the street. Turn right. Walk about a hundred feet. Congrats! You're at...

Gene's Sausage Shop, 4750 N. Lincoln Ave., Chicago IL 60625; 773-728-7243; genessausage.com.

Gene's is a polish specialty grocer whose original location is on far-west Belmont, but when they opened in the space of the former Meyer Delicatessen, they brought many Germanic touches to the market. Pierogis sell alongside sauerkraut, and hunter's sausage, herring, and potato pancakes fill the deli cases. The seasonal rooftop is the real draw in summer, though—pitchers of beer, sausages, potato salad, and more beer at a picnic table on a sunny afternoon is nirvana.

You already walked past the Brauhaus to get to Genes, so head back outside and walk a couple doors south because we wanted to end this crawl at...

The Chicago Brauhaus, 4732 N. Lincoln Ave., Chicago IL 60625; 773-784-4444; chicagobrauhaus.com.

As true a German bierhall as you can get in the city, The Chicago Brauhaus is large, loud, and boisterous; the food is hefty, the beer is strong, and yes, you can order it in a glass boot. After walking out the front door at the close of your crawl, take a brief moment to offer your condolences to the Lincoln Square Lanes that once stood a few blocks northwest. They were destroyed in a massive fire in late 2015 that razed the bar and bowling complex. The bowling alley stood for decades and had completed a renovation in recent years that completely re-energized the place (and added a dozen draft lines of good beer), and it disappeared overnight.

BEER AND POLITICS

Politics and beer have gone hand in hand in Chicago since the city's inception. The Lager Beer Riots of 1855 occurred after legislation aimed at German and Irish immigrants closed taverns on Sundays—the only day of the week most people weren't working—and raised the cost of a liquor license six times over. Thankfully, alcohol legislation is a lot more wonky these days and a lot less violent, but recent changes have helped remake the brewery scene in Illinois more than most realize.

The explosion of craft breweries in Illinois was getting underway in 2011, with breweries like Metropolitan, Revolution, and Half Acre just getting up and running. In the eyes of state law, there was no differentiation between someone like Metropolitan, operating out of a tiny industrial space along Ravenswood Avenue in Chicago, and someone like Miller or Budweiser. A brewer was a brewer.

Thanks to the three-tier system of alcohol distribution in the US, a system in effect since Prohibition to make sure breweries couldn't monopolize how people get their beer, a brewer could also not operate as a distributor, which was something Anheuser-Busch (A-B) had a problem with.

A lawsuit in 2010 ruled that A-B could not, under the current law, purchase more of a stake in a distributor called City Beverage, because out-of-state breweries could not legally self-distribute their beer. A-B cried foul because two small in-state breweries, Argus and Big Muddy, could and did distribute their beers. A-B called that discriminatory, and sued the Illinois Liquor Control Commission. A judge agreed, and said no one could self-distribute, unless the Illinois legislature could untangle the mess of liquor laws that needed defining.

Over the months that followed, the legislature, the Associated Beer Distributors of Illinois, and a whole bunch of lawyers hashed out what would become SB754, or the reason we have so many new craft breweries today. Basically, it did a few things: It created a new license for craft breweries. It made it legal for craft breweries to self-distribute their beer as long as they make less than 15,000 barrels and distribute 7,500 barrels of it or less. It also stated that breweries could not hold a distributor's license, ensuring that A-B could not take over City Beverage, or any other distributor. This prompted the Ebel brothers, owners of Two Brothers Brewing and Windy City Distribution, to divest themselves from that company.

It certainly wasn't a perfect bill—owners of brewpubs like Revolution's Josh Deth weren't happy that the new rules treated brewpubs and production breweries differently. Revolution would have to build a separate production facility to distribute their beer outside the brewpub. There were also limits in place that didn't line up with the rapidly expanding world of Illinois beer. The fact is that while 15,000 barrels is a lot of beer, there were a lot of thirsty people in Illinois in 2011, and a few breweries rapidly blasted past that number, Revolution being one of them. In 2011 the bulk of the dues-paying members of the Illinois Craft Brewers Guild (ICBG) were brewpubs, and because of those restrictions, the ICBG was actually opposed to the bill. Many considered it mostly a win for the big-money distributors.

Time has shown that SB754 was a really good start, though. During the debate over the legislation, licensing of breweries slowed to a near halt. After the craft brewer's license was created, things took off like a shot. Dozens of breweries opened in 2012 and 2013, and many of them took advantage of the opportunity to deliver their beer themselves to bars and stores throughout the area. One great example of that exists in Begyle Brewing.

Begyle set up shop in North Center, almost a straight shot south down Ravenswood from Metropolitan. From the get go, their focus was simple and straightforward—to be a Community Supported Brewery (CSB), which was a new angle on the community-supported agricultural programs that brought products from farmers directly to consumers. Begyle's CSB plan based itself on bringing its beer directly to members through "subscriptions" to pick up a growler or two a week, as well as walking their beer right out their front door and into the bars and restaurants up and down Lincoln Avenue (see also the Lincoln Square/North Center Beer Crawl on page 147).

Breweries starting with tiny amounts of capacity oftentimes can't afford the cost of adding a distributor to sell, store, and ship their beer. Self-distribution allows a small brewery the luxury of controlling where their beer goes and how it gets there, while receiving that revenue directly. It keeps the beer fresh, with delivery time measured in hours and days instead of weeks, and it allows the brewery to build their reputation how and where they want it.

It seems a little counterintuitive as to why the collective beer distributors of Illinois were on board with giving away this right to smaller brewers. Wouldn't the distributors want everyone forced to go through their service? You'd think so, but the ABDI took the long view. Keeping the big beer guys out protected the family companies who were distributing their beer for them, and small breweries often grow up to be bigger breweries who then need their beer distributed for them. SB754 gave them a whole new customer base. After a while, when a brewery gets big enough, it makes sense for them to spend their time making great beer instead of putting it in a van to drive it places.

An additional piece of legislation was passed in 2015 that served as a "fix" to the wrinkles of SB754. It created a new class of craft brewer license, making the original license a Class 1 license and adding the new Class 2 license. Class 1 breweries could still brew up to 30,000 barrels and distribute up to 7,500; the new law clarified that they could not hold a brewpub license, though. Class 2 brewers could brew up to 120,000 barrels and own three different brewpubs, but they could not self-distribute their beer. These changes were negotiated between the ICBG and the ABDI. With both on board, the legislation sailed through both houses and was signed by Governor Rauner.

It's a lot of legal language to wade through, but the result of it is a better state in which to brew and sell beer, which benefits all of us who love fresh, creative, local beer. In addition to creating a fair system for breweries to start up in—it's also brought us breweries originally planned for other states.

The 'Burbs: North, South, West, Northwest Indiana

If the beating heart of Chicago's beer scene is in the city, the surrounding suburbs are the arteries and veins that keep the brewing community's creativity and passion flowing for miles beyond municipal boundaries. From the Wisconsin border to the fox river valley and into Indiana, there's far more local beer than you might expect, and some of these breweries aren't very micro at all.

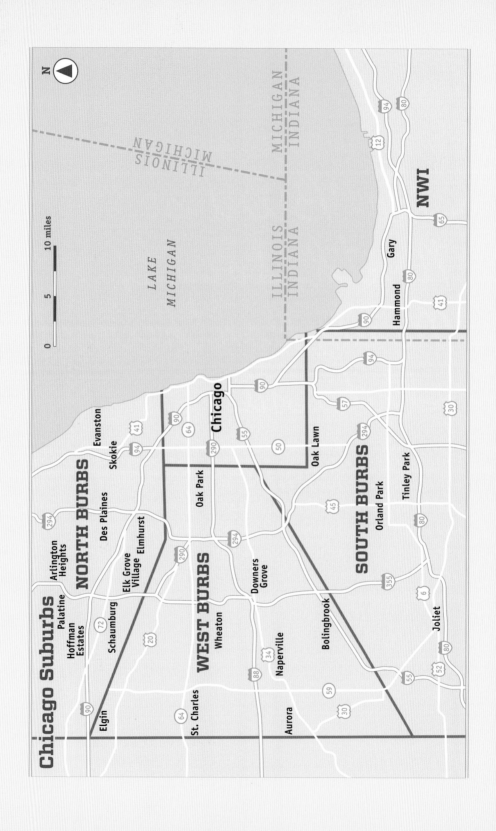

ALTER BREWING COMPANY

2300 Wisconsin Ave #213, Downers Grove, IL 60515; (630) 541-9558; alterbrewing.com; @AlterBeer
Founded: 2015 **Founders:** David Yob, Mark Hedrick, Pete Kosanovich
Brewer: Mark Hedrick **Tours:** Yes **Taproom Hours:** Tues through
Thurs, 3 to 10 p.m.; Fri, 3 to 11 p.m.; Sat, 12 to 11 p.m.; Sun, 12 to 6 p.m.

Picture three guys working in the pit at the Chicago Mercantile Exchange, yelling out orders and waving frantically at screens displaying prices of corn and cattle futures. Now picture those same three guys, overseeing a taproom and brewery in suburban Downers Grove. A brewery taproom can seem like a raucous place from time to time, but compared to a day at the Board of Trade, it's gotta be downright relaxing.

Owners David Yob, Mark Hedrick, and Pete Kosanovich met at the CME in the 1990s, trading options and futures. Hedrick brewed beer in his off hours and attended Siebel, and Yob was previously involved in a brewery startup in Denver called Living the Dream. A shared love of beer and a desire to build a business closer to their homes in the west suburbs brought them together and soon plans emerged for a brewery briefly called Mad Ape (coming from the first couple letters in each of their names).

As plans progressed, the word "alter" kept coming up in describing the brewery plans to family and friends. "We're altering our lives [and] it kinda fit with what we wanted to do in not pigeonholing ourselves. We wanted to brew anything," Yob says. Thus Alter Brewing was born. Working on a 20 bbl system, the brewery aims to produce 1000 barrels in its first year all in self-distributed draft products. Plans to move into bottles and cans will come, but primarily the beers pour from their 1500-square-foot tasting room in a small industrial corner of Downers Grove a short walk from the Metra line.

Not tying themselves to any one style ("completely unfocused" is how Yob jokingly refers to them), Alter's beers focus on classic ale styles using mostly traditional ingredients, with the **ALTERior Motive IPA** emerging as a quick fan favorite. Guests may notice some particularly advanced artwork on the chalkboards denoting the names and types of the beers on tap—in addition to being the head brewer, Hedrick was also an artist and art major in college, so now his work goes in your glass and also tells you what you're drinking.

BLUE NOSE BREWING COMPANY

6119 East Ave., Hodgkins, IL 60525; (708) 905-5198; bluenosebrewery.com; @BlueNoseBrewery
Founded: 2012 **Founders:** David Kelley, Jordan Isenberg, Nathan Garcia **Brewers:** David Kelley (brewmaster), Jordan Isenberg, Robert Kelley, Nathan Garcia **Flagship beers:** True Justice Pale Ale, The Nothing brown ale **Year-round beers:** Pipa American Lager, XXX Honey Belgian Tripel, Archer Ave Pale Ale, Past Due Stout **Seasonal beers:** Peppermint Maggie, Blind Doggery chipotle stout, Saison Sarandon, Garden Party Lager, Fall Harvest, Bear Trap. **Tours:** Wed, 5 and 7 p.m.; Fri and Sat, 5 p.m. **Taproom Hours:** Mon through Thurs, 3 p.m. to midnight; Fri and Sat, 12 p.m. to 2 a.m.; Sun, 12 to 8 p.m. winter, 10 p.m. summer

B rewer and Blue Nose co-founder David Kelley actually didn't want to start a brewery when he met his fellow cofounders Jordan Isenberg and Nate Garcia. He was teaching a series of homebrew classes, and usually when students talked to him after class and told him they wanted to open a brewery, he'd nudge them off the idea.

"I'd be like, 'You don't want to open a brewery. It's an insane amount of work and the last thing you'll be doing is brewing beer.' If it was just brewing and drinking your beer, everyone would be doing it," he explained. Kelley would know—after starting as a bartender and assistant brewer at Emmett's in West Dundee, he moved on to a job with Northern Brewer, the homebrew supply giant in Wisconsin. He eventually became their main recipe formulator (if you used to brew with a NB kit, you might have kinda already drank Kelley's beers) and began working on recipes for a few other breweries as well.

During that period, he got to work on all manner of systems, from a 10 bbl kit all the way up to a 60 bbl machine, from direct fire to steam, with all permutations of equipment in between. Eventually he came back home to the suburbs to lead the aforementioned homebrew classes; instead of the usual "I want to open a brewery" talk, Isenberg and Garcia got Kelley to have a few drinks at a bar, where they laid out their experience (bartenders), their passion (craft beer) and their business plan—all it needed was a brewer.

"So basically, I said, 'f— it. let's do it,'" Kelley laughs,

They originally set up shop in June 2012 in a converted garage space in Justice, practically in the shadow of Midway Airport. Working on a 15 bbl system, they sold their beer one tiny batch at a time and worked day jobs to build up the capital to expand into a bigger facility with a taproom. They found their current space in a then-unfinished building in Hodgkins just a few miles west; after slaving in a tiny, cobbled together space they were able to basically build up from scratch—trench drains, gas mains, sinks everywhere, and a bar from which they could sell their beer.

The new space opened in July 2015 with ten draft lines for Blue Nose beer; core options range from their balanced **True Justice** pale ale to the **XXX Honey Belgian** tripel that clocks in at 10 percent ABV to the **Pipa** lager, made in what Kelley calls the "World War American style" of beer—made with corn because the bulk of the grains were being dedicated to the war effort. If you want a beer to go, you can take it in a 32-ounce canned crowler (no growlers, though) and their beers make it into the city at a few discerning beer-friendly accounts if you can't make your way to Hodgkins. (You should though.)

BLUE ISLAND BEER COMPANY

13357 Olde Western Ave., Blue Island, IL 60406; (708) 954-8085; blueislandbeerco.com; @BlueIslandBC
Founded: 2015 **Founders:** Bryan Shimkos and Alan Cromwell
Brewer: Bryan Shimkos **Flagship beers:** Massive Political Corruption,
Tours: Yes **Taproom Hours:** Wed through Thurs, 2 to 9 p.m.; Fri, 2 to 10 p.m.; Sat, 12 to 10 p.m.; Sun, 12 to 6 p.m.

Blue Island was once home to a handful of breweries in the late 1800s that tunneled into the local landscape to keep their beers cool. Over a century later, a new business opened providing locally crafted beer to the community, but advances in refrigeration technology keep the Blue Island Beer Company team above ground.

Plans for the brewery began in 2011 when events promoter Alan Cromwell met brewer Bryan Shimkos, then working at Flossmoor Brewing Company, at a brewery event. Both had an interest in opening their own place on the south side, with both of them having family in the area, but

Shimkos went to help open Rosemont's Hofbrauhaus and then served as head brewer for the now-closed Ale Syndicate for a short time before heading back south to open Blue Island (BIBC).

Beers started flowing from the 10 bbl system in May 2015 with a focus on true-to-style recipes as well as some more avant-garde creations. Located in the historic district near other craft beer destinations like Rock Island Public House and Maple Tree Inn, BIBC pours beers like their pre-Prohibition style ale called **Massive Political Corruption,** a **Hard Luck IPA,** and a black session beer called **Early & Often.** They also self-distribute draft products throughout the Blue Island area. Guests to their taproom can play foosball or take swings on the putting green.

BUCKLEDOWN BREWING

8700 W. 47th St., Lyons, IL 60534; (708) 777-1842; buckledownbrewing.com; @BuckleDownBeer Founded: 2013 **Founders:** Ike Orcutt and Sean Mahoney **Brewer:** Ike Orcutt **Flagship beers:** Fiddlesticks Belgian-style IPA, Belt & Suspenders American IPA, Painted Turtle Extra Pale Ale, Shady Aftermath Robust Porter **Tours:** No **Taproom Hours:** Wed, 4 to 10 p.m.; Thurs, 12 to 10 p.m.; Fri and Sat, 12 to 11 p.m.; Sun, 11 a.m. to 5 p.m.

While most breweries try to differentiate themselves by creating the craziest, adjunct-filled stouts or the hoppiest IPAs, BuckleDown is betting on their dedication to consistency to win out. Owners Ike Orcutt and Sean Mahoney originally met while they were working in marketing in the West Loop. They were both also homebrewers, and decided to dive headfirst into the brewing world in 2013, with the taproom and brewery releasing their first beers in early December.

The pair got a hand up from Pete Crowley at Haymarket Brewing, who allowed them to brew their first few batches of collaborative beer on the Haymarket system. Crowley is "our mentor, our guardian angel, you name it," Orcutt says. Their 15 bbl brewing system is even from the same manufacturer, with some slight modifications for BuckleDown's brews.

Working out of near-west suburban Lyons, the brewery operated in draft only for the beginning of the brewery's run and added two beers in cans in July 2015—the **Painted Turtle** session pale ale and the **Belt & Suspenders American IPA.** A DIPA and a lager were canned in 2016, but there's no rush to get a few dozen BuckleDown beers in the market. "The most important thing is quality . . . If you have a foundation of quality, of consistency, you can have fun," Mahoney explains. "Everything we're going to put out is something we're proud of. Not because we're chasing after a trend."

The BuckleDown name comes from the idea that the brewing business involves a lot of hard work, and Orcutt and Mahoney embrace that—doing things by hand, working long hours, and putting in sweat equity. It's paying off, with an annual output of about 3000 bbl and growing.

CHURCH STREET BREWING COMPANY

1480 Industrial Dr., Itasca, IL 60143; (630) 438-5725; churchstreetbrew.com; @ChurchStBrew
Founded: 2012 **Founders:** Lisa and Joe Gregor **Brewer:** Joe Gregor
Flagship beer: Heavenly Helles **Year-round beers:** Heavenly Helles, Brimstone IPA, Tale of the Shony Scottish Ale, Lubelskie Polish Pilsner, and Devil's Advocate Golden Strong **Seasonal beers:** Crimson Clover Irish Red, Magisterium Maibock, Hauch von Himmel Hefeweizen, Itascafest Marzen, Bob's Your Dunkel, Pontificator Doppelbock **Tours:** Yes **Taproom Hours:** Wed through Thurs, 4 to 8 p.m.; Fri, 4 to 10 p.m.; Sat, 1 to 9 p.m.; Sun, 1 to 6 p.m.

Lisa and Joe Gregor's son, Steven, came home one day and remarked that maybe dad needed a hobby, and maybe it should be making beer. Things moved pretty quickly after that. "We went to Brew & Grow, and on Christmas Day in 2007 they were brewing on the stove in our house," Lisa

says. "By March it was all-grain and by summertime there was a lagering fridge in the garage." When the homebrewing hobby hits, it can hit hard.

The natural next step in the process was a brewery their own, of course, and Joe jumped in with both feet. They incorporated in 2011, found a space in early 2012, and were brewing in September of that year in a full-on 30 bbl system. This would be a huge jump upward for most homebrewers, but Joe, a chemical engineer by trade, had the skills and technical wherewithall to scale up quickly. The brewery also does the same thing for small contract brewers in the area looking to take a step into the game—take a recipe, dial it up, brew it, and see how it does.

Church Street (named for the intended original location for the brewery; the lease didn't materialize but the name stuck) serves up a lager-focused lineup but one that is not strictly limited to bottom-fermented beers. They have a scotch ale and an IPA but their flagship is the **Heavenly Helles Lager.** It's made utilizing a special technique called a decoction mash, which involves taking some of the wort from the kettle, heating it to a higher temperature, then returning it to the rest of the boil. It adds a richness of flavor and a higher clarity to the beer—German and Czech breweries used it for ages, though it's rarely done any more, as it's time- and effort-intensive.

The Helles, along with their other beers like the **Brimstone IPA** and the **Continental Lager,** are served up to a few dozen people at a time from their taproom, and on draft or in bottles at accounts in all points north of Peoria. If you're at a festival and they've got the Helles pouring, make it a point to stop by, you'll probably find a few brewers nearby sipping it as well.

CRYSTAL LAKE BREWING COMPANY

150 N. Main St., Crystal Lake, IL 60014; (779) 220-9288; crystallakebrew.com; @CrystalLakeBrew
Founded: 1994, opened August 2014 **Founders:** John O'Fallon and Chuck Ross **Brewer:** Ryan Clooney **Flagship beers:** Slalom King Rye IPA and Beach Blonde Golden Lager **Year-round beers:** Slalom King Rye IPA, Beach Blonde Golden Lager, Wake Maker Session IPA and Lakesider American Märzen **Seasonal beers:** Spring Fever Raspberry Hibiscus Ale and Overboard Oatmeal Stout **Tours:** Yes **Taproom Hours:** Mon through Thurs, 4 to 10 p.m.; Fri, 3 p.m. to 12 a.m.; Sat 12 p.m. to 12 a.m.; Sun, 12 to 9 p.m.

Located in downtown Crystal Lake in a former car dealership, Crystal Lake Brewing Company is a production facility that brews and cans a handful of true-to-style beers. Founders Chuck Ross and John O'Fallon opened the brewery in August 2014 after working with the city council to create a brand new liquor license classification in order to get the operation up and running.

Brewmaster Ryan Clooney joined Crystal Lake after thirteen years at the Emmett's family of brewpubs, where he won a number of GABF and World Beer Cup medals, including a Silver in 2011 for his **Helles Lager.** Clooney added to that award case with a World Beer Cup Bronze Medal for Crystal Lake's **Beach Blonde** in May 2016, also a helles-style lager. The brewery quickly expanded in June 2015 to add a canning line and more fermenters to help with lager production in August 2015.

Flagship beers include the **Slalom King** rye IPA, the **Beach Blonde** golden lager, **Wakemaker** session IPA and the **Lakesider** marzen. The brewery expanded to add a line of **Boathouse Reserve** barrel-aged beers in 22-ounce bombers in December 2015. Growlers and howlers can be taken to go from the taproom, and food trucks regularly stop in to provide sustenance.

DRY CITY BREW WORKS

120B N. Main St., Wheaton, IL 60187; (630) 456-4787; drycitybrewworks.com; @DryCityBrews
Founded: 2014 **Founders:** Ben and Jessica Sampson and David and Lori Carr **Brewer:** Ben Sampson **Flagship beer:** Providence Coffee Milk Stout **Reliable beers:** Ryejacked Rye IPA, Baby's Toupee Copper Ale, I Saved the King Scotch Ale **Seasonal beers:** Stout-Man Imperial Stout, Pumpkin Pyro Porter with Smoked Pumpkin **Tours:** No (But you can see the whole brewhouse from the bar) **Taproom Hours:** Wed through Thurs, 4 to 9 p.m.; Fri, 3 to 10 p.m.; Sat 2 to 10 p.m.; Sun, 2 to 6 p.m.

I t's continuously impressive that this tiny little taproom, hidden in a parking lot off Wheaton's main drag, even exists at all. The western suburb mostly known for being home to churches, heavily evangelical Wheaton College, churches, John Belushi, and churches, was notably dry for decades. You had to get out of town to a bowling alley or VFW hall to find a beer nearby. Now there's a team making it up fresh in the heart of downtown. Amazing.

Still, you have to work to find it—the brewery's location itself implies a certain sense of the city wanting to hide them away. You have to walk through an alley off Main Street or thread your way through some back parking lots to find the place, stowed into a tiny concrete-clad space just big enough for their 5 bbl brewing system and a handful of fermenters.

State tasting room rules keep Dry City from getting too wet—they can only serve three pints or flights per person per day, then they can send you on your way with a growler. Beers rotate frequently, but if they have the **Providence Coffee Milk Stout**, grab it. Also, as a nod to the generally non-alcoholic nature of Wheaton, they always have a house-made soda available to sample.

18TH STREET BREWERY

5725 Miller Ave., Gary, IN 46403 and 5417 Oakley Ave. Hammond, IN 46320; (219) 939-8802; 18thstreetbrewery.com; @18thStreetBrew
Founded: 2010 **Founder:** Drew Fox **Brewers:** Drew Fox, Richard Mendoza, Bucky Sisson, Kyle Reed **Flagship beer:** Sinister DIPA **Year-round beers:** A selection of ever-rotating beers **Main Seasonal beers:** Hunter Double Milk Stout and variants **Tours:** No **Taproom hours:** Sun, 12 to 8 p.m.; Mon through Thurs, 12 to 10 p.m.; Fri and Sat, 12 p.m. to 12 a.m.

Northwest Indiana is still Chicagoland in my mind, even though some people seem to think that line of the city's influence should stop at the state line. Not so, and NWI is growing into a craft beer culture all its own (as in: more than just Three Floyds) along with the rest of the city and other suburbs. Of the many new area breweries, the one that has the highest profile is Drew Fox's 18th Street Brewery.

Fox was working in the city's restaurant industry managing a spot at a downtown hotel when, after a trip to Belgium in the early 2000s, he came back invigorated by the beers he'd drank. He moved a lot of craft beer after taking over the buying for the bar at the hotel, and from there made the leap to homebrewing, going so far as to try and get the brewery he built behind his house licensed. When the Powers That Be gave the thumbs down, Fox spent time working at other breweries, notably Pipeworks, who eventually trusted Fox's skills enough to make him a full-time brewer.

From there the leap to a place of his own was next. After getting things started with some contract brewing with Pipeworks and Spiteful, Fox created a successful Kickstarter that raised more than double its initial goal of $12,000. Fox moved 18th Street into a former dry cleaners in the Miller Beach neighborhood of Gary, just a few steps from the South Shore line station that so many Chicagoans would alight from in search of Fox's hefty brews. (No, it's not actually on 18th Street—the name comes from the main drag of Fox's beloved Pilsen neighborhood, where the dream for the brewery began.)

They opened at the very tail end of 2013, and began cranking out beers like their **Sinister DIPA, Deal With the Devil** pale ale, and most notably their **Hunter Double Milk Stout,** which went on to include variants like vanilla, coconut, orange, and cherry—the barrel-aged version release days have lines out the door. Response to 18th Street was so strong that those initial few days in 2013 were enough to earn 18th Street the honor of being named Ratebeer's Best New Brewery in Indiana.

Collaborations with brewers like Prairie, Against the Grain, Mikkeller, and (of course) Pipeworks quickly followed, and a second line of sour beers brewed under a new name—Sour Note—emerged in March of 2015. In February 2016, Fox and the 18th Street team took an even larger step, opening a new production facility and brewpub in nearby Hammond.

EXIT STRATEGY
BREWING CO.

7700 W. Madison St., Forest Park, IL 60130; (708) 689-8771; exitstrategybrewing.com; @ESBrewingCo
Founded: 2015 **Founders:** Chris and Katherine Valleau **Brewers:** Chris Valleau and Jacob Kell **Flagship beer:** Exit Strategy APA **Year-round beers:** Knoblocked Out Blonde Ale, Persephone Pomegranate Wheat, Apologize Witbier, Rue Dauphine Saison, Exit Strategy APA, Posthumulus American IPA, Judgmental Dick Double IPA, Nobody Reads the Copy ESB, Dougan's Brown English Brown Ale, Scotsquatch Scottish Ale, Rufus Porter, Valleaudated Milk Stout **Seasonal beers:** Whaddachooch Belgian Dubbel, Mittens with Grip Vanilla Porter **Tours:** No **Taproom Hours:** Tues through Thurs, 3 to 10 p.m.; Fri, 3 p.m. to 12 a.m.; Sat, 11 a.m. to 12 p.m.; Sun, 11 a.m. to 4 p.m.

There are a lot of breweries in Chicagoland that have served as an escape from the corporate world, but only one has been so up front about making beer their specific Exit Strategy. Owners Chris and Katherine Valleau were working in the fields of law and education, respectively, and had been homebrewing for a couple years when they entered a Battle of the Brews in Oak Park and swept the damn thing! The couple won for dark and light beers with their milk stout and pomegranate wheat.

Located in what is essentially a brewery desert between the city's Near West Side and Elmhurst, Exit Strategy threw open the doors on Forest Park's main drag in April 2015, adding a much-needed option for fresh beer in the area. They pour beers made on their 5 bbl system that are mostly available only in their taproom, though you can find them reliably at the nearby Beer Shop and Kinderhook Tap.

In addition to the **Persephone** pomegranate wheat and the **Valleaudated** milk stout, you can also find the **Knoblocked Out** blonde, **Rufus** porter and the awesomely named **Judgmental Dick** double IPA. Beyond just the beer, the dining menu is creatively fun as well, with Thai-style nachos, a pork belly BLT, bourbon-bacon grilled cheese, and housemade sodas.

5 RABBIT CERVECERIA

6398 74th St., Bedford Park, IL 60638; (312) 895-9591; 5rabbitbrewery.com; @5RabbitBrewery
Founders: Andres Araya and Isaac Showaki **Brewer:** John J. Hall **Flagship beers:** 5 Rabbit, 5 Lizard, 5 Grass, 5 Vulture **Seasonal beers:** Huitzi, Chocofrut, Yodo Con Leche, the Gringolandia & Paleta series **Tours:** Yes **Taproom Hours:** Wed through Fri, 4 to 10 p.m.; Sat, 2 to 8 p.m.

Pairing south-of-the-border marketing and business skills with Chicago-area brewing masterminds, the team behind 5 Rabbit prides itself on being the first Latin American–themed brewery in the states. Their beers, however, go well beyond your average Bohemian lager with a lime wedge jammed into it. Using the flavors of Latin America as inspiration, 5 Rabbit features recipes that range all the way from light, fruity, summer crushers to big, spicy, winter comfort beers.

The brewery started when Andres Araya and Isaac Showaki (who are from Costa Rica and Mexico respectively) began working together for a marketing company assisting breweries like Heineken, Florida Bebidas, and Cervecería Cuauhtémoc-Moctezuma. The brewery bug bit them both, and after looking into markets with a heavy Hispanic-American base like Austin, Los Angeles, and Miami, they decided to set down roots in Chicago.

The two began working with Chicago beer author, brewery consultant, recipe formulator, and general mastermind Randy Mosher on the beers themselves, working with traditional styles amped up by Latin ingredients like passionfruit and ancho chiles. Beers brewed on a contract basis at Argus rolled out in June of 2011 and a GABF Gold quickly followed in the Fruit Wheat Category for their **5 Lizard.** Brewing operations moved to a couple other contract places from there, and soon the team moved to a brewery in Bedford Park just outside the city's southwest border.

With former Goose Islander John J. Hall at the helm as brewmaster, the brewery's new 30 bbl brewing system allowed them to both brew their own beers but also contract for other new outfits as well. Their core line of beers, called "The Fives", like the bright, tart **5 Lizard,** lightly spicy **5 Vulture,** and the hoppy **5 Grass** were brought in-house. (Why the constant 5 references? It goes back to Aztec mythology and a collection of deities, one of whom, 5 Rabbit, symbolized over-indulgence.)

Just a few months after the opening of the new brewery, things between the two owners went south. Lawsuits were filed by both Araya and a brewery intern over accusations of theft and infidelity made by Showaki. Showaki agreed to a buyout and parted ways with the company. He went on to open Octopi Brewing in Wisconsin in 2015. Since then, the 5 Rabbit team has been happy to let the beers do the talking for them. They won another GABF medal in 2014, this time a silver, for their **5 Rabbit Golden Ale,** and they continue to produce new, innovative, and interesting varieties of beer seemingly nonstop.

Their release of the low-alcohol **Paleta** series, inspired by the popsicle vendors that roam the city streets in warmer months and featuring rotating flavors like guyaba, watermelon, and tamarind, is becoming an annual summer highlight. The flip side of that light summer fruit beer is their **ChocoFrut** line of stout beers, with flavors like mandarin or blackberry, released in winter 2015.

Other beers include the **Yodo Con Leche,** made with Costa Rican coffee, and **Ki'Chun,** made with chantarelle mushrooms. If that's not weird enough, they released an experimental gose at the 2015 Beer Under Glass made with beetles and grasshoppers (the dried insects are also used in Mexican cuisine).

FLESK BREWING

200 Applebee St., Suite E., Barrington, IL 60148; (630) 233-4997; fleskbrewing.com; @FleskBrew
Founded: 2011 **Founders:** William and James O'Brien **Brewer:** James O'Brien **Year-round beers:** Haus Helles, Moped Traveler Pale Ale, Ghost Relic IPA, Running Man Milk Stout **Seasonal beer:** Big Pointy Teeth DIPA **Tours:** No **Taproom:** Yes

It started with a Mr. Beer in 2008. Yes, the plastic barrel of beer with the screw-on lid, available at better hardware stores everywhere. The beer-in-a-box kit that made so many homebrewer's first couple gallons of brew, usually awful in retrospect. That's how Lombard's Flesk got its start.

After that initial Mr. Beer experience, the O'Brien brothers, Will and James, continued their homebrewing efforts but were also inspired by the 2009 movie *Beer Wars,* the documentary showcasing the efforts of outsider brewers like Dogfish Head and Stone up against beer behemoths Miller and Budweiser. "It kinda galvanized us," Will says. James enrolled in Siebel, and went to Germany to continue his beer studies. When he came home he worked for Lunar Brewing for a couple years, moving from washing kegs up to brewing on their small tavern system.

In the meantime, the brothers were batting around plans for their own brewery. The name Flesk originated from a castle in Ireland, the subject of stories in their childhood of their dad's travels around the auld sod on a moped in the 1970s. In love with the idea of telling stories through beer like Dogfish did, along with the tradition of spinning yarns with a beer in hand, they named their brewery Flesk because "it encapsulated the idea of storytelling for us. It's about sharing, it's about hanging out and having beers and telling stories."

Flesk tells those stories via 22-ounce bombers, 16-ounce cans, and a few draft accounts at a time. They originally work off of a 3.5 bbl system in an industrial section of Lombard, making balanced beers that are at turns hoppy, dark, or German-styled as influenced by James's experiences working near Munich. They are the house brewer for the Radler, a haute bierstube in Logan Square that uses their helles

lager to make the restaurant's namesake citrus radler. They also make dunkels, maibocks, and hefeweizens.

One of the smaller breweries in town by output, they recently were brewing around 300 barrels per year, but in June 2017 moved from Lombard to Barrington and added a taproom.

FLOSSMOOR STATION RESTAURANT & BREWERY

1035 Sterling Ave., Flossmoor, IL 60422; (708) 957-2739; flossmoorstation.com @FlossmoorBrewCo
Founded: 1996 **Founders:** Dean and Carolyn Armstrong **Flagship beer:** Pullman Brown **Year-round beers:** Zephyr Golden Lager, Gandy Dancer Lager, Station Master Wheat, Fruit Beer (Raspberry, Blueberry or Cherry), Panama Red Ale, Pullman Brown Ale, Shadow of the Moon Stout and Rail Hopper IPA **Seasonal beers:** Hefeweizen, Blonde Sided and Flossy IPL **Tours:** available upon request **Full bar and restaurant hours:** Sun through Thurs, 11:30 a.m. to 11 p.m.; Fri and Sat, 11:30 a.m. to 12 a.m.

Located along the Metra Electric District line in a century-old converted train station, Floosmoor Station has been one of the area's premiere breweries since their opening in July 1996. Flossmoor natives Dean and Carolyn Armstrong set out to open the brewpub after discovering the joys of microbrewed beer on a vacation through Michigan.

Flossmoor's beers immediately began earning praise, with their flagship **Pullman Brown Ale** earning a bronze at the GABF in 1997 and a silver in 1998, the same year their **Imperial Eclipse Stout** took gold. The hardware isn't limited to the brewery's early years—their **Shadow of the Moon** stout earned a GABF silver in 2014. If there's a top to this plateau, it's 2006, when they were named Best Small Brewpub. Not bad for a little spot a fifty-minute train trip outside the city.

Flossmoor's more mainstream beers include the **Station Master** American wheat, the **Gandy Dancer** honey lager, the **Rail Hopper IPA,** and the **Panama Red Ale.** They introduced bombers of their beer to store shelves in 2008. Railroad fans will love feeling the trains pulling past the building while they dine on menu items appropriately subdivided into sections like Whistle Stop Salads, Roundhouse Wraps, and Boxcar Deli sandwiches.

Many notable brewers have spent time brewing for Flossmoor over the years—Todd Ashman brewed here for years before departing for FiftyFifty

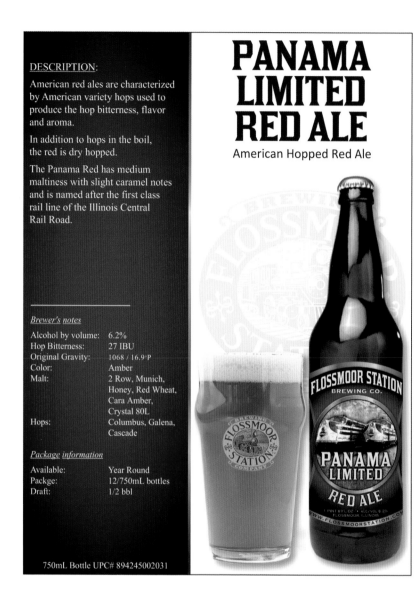

DESCRIPTION:

American red ales are characterized by American variety hops used to produce the hop bitterness, flavor and aroma.

In addition to hops in the boil, the red is dry hopped.

The Panama Red has medium maltiness with slight caramel notes and is named after the first class rail line of the Illinois Central Rail Road.

Brewer's notes

Alcohol by volume:	6.2%
Hop Bitterness:	27 IBU
Original Gravity:	1068 / 16.9°P
Color:	Amber
Malt:	2 Row, Munich, Honey, Red Wheat, Cara Amber, Crystal 80L
Hops:	Columbus, Galena, Cascade

Package information

Available:	Year Round
Packge:	12/750mL bottles
Draft:	1/2 bbl

750mL Bottle UPC# 894245002031

PANAMA LIMITED RED ALE
American Hopped Red Ale

FLOSSMOOR STATION BREWING CO.

PANAMA LIMITED RED ALE

1 PINT 9 FL.OZ. • ALC/VOL 6.2%
FLOSSMOOR, ILLINOIS
WWW.FLOSSMOORSTATION.COM

brewing. Matt Van Wyk, brewer for the 2006 GABF Best Small Brewpub win, now helms Oakshire Brewing in Oregon. Bryan Shimkos brewed for Flossmoor before starting his Blue Island Brewing Company. And Nick Barron brewed for Flossmoor before taking over the Goose Island Clybourn brewpub operations after the departure of Jared Rouben.

Plans to expand and add a production facility have been discussed and nearly came to fruition with a Hammond, Indiana, location but sadly didn't come to be. In a world of super-new upstart breweries opening left and right, the world could use some more beer with heritage to it, and a few thousand more barrels of the deliciously nutty **Pullman Brown** would be a great way to start.

HAILSTORM BREWING COMPANY

8060 186th St., Tinley Park, IL 60487; (630) 631-7173; hailstormbrewing.com; @HailstormBrew
Founded: 2014 **Founders:** Brandon Banbury, Chris Schiller, Gene Wabisczewicz **Brewer:** Brandon Banbury **Flagship beers:** Vlad Russian Imperial Stout, Dominatrix DIPA, Prairie Madness Pale Ale **Seasonal beers:** South Side Irish Red, Crash Test Dummy Tripel, Jesus Toast Belgian-style IPA, Fruitcake & Shame Cranberry Dark Ale **Tours:** No **Taproom hours:** Tues through Thurs, 12 to 8 p.m.; Fri and Sat, 12 to 10 p.m.; Sun, 12 to 8 p.m.

Owner and co-brewer Chris Schiller got into the brewing industry in a way that's a little different from most other homebrewers. Instead of deciding to jump in after the hobby got out of hand, he started brewing with the intent of opening a brewery from the very start. Hailstorm opened in Tinley Park in April 2014 after building the space entirely on their own, from digging trench drains to plumbing to glycol lines.

Schiller started homebrewing in 2008 and joined the Brewers of South Suburbia homebrew group, where he met Brandon Banbury. As Schiller explains it, "We had been homebrewing for about the same amount of time on the calendar, but he'd brewed two or three times as many batches as I'd done. He's a younger guy with a better back and a stronger liver. I'll be the back office, finance guy." If only all workplace tasks delegations were so simple.

Banbury and Schiller work on a 15 bbl brewhouse with some slight updates like a larger mashtun, which helps them brew beers with enough grain to get them some massive ABVs. They turn out about 1,000 barrels a year, and although they don't assign themselves to any particular style, they find themselves brewing bigger beers than most. "Word of mouth seems to be that we're known for fairly big beers," Schiller says. "We didn't intentionally do that—it's just the beers we like to drink."

Hailstorm pours most of these at their taproom, though they also bottle a number of their beers in bombers and cans. They've produced an 11 percent triple IPA, a variety of Russian imperial stouts named **Vlad,** and once created a small batch of a 20 percent ABV barley wine. Initially it was brewed and regularly fermented to 12 percent, then fed corn sugar twice a day to keep the alcohol building, then pitched with Champagne yeast to tolerate the higher alcohol levels that killed off the regular ale yeast.

Barrel-aging is a big focus of Hailstorm's as well, with wine barrels for sours, along with whiskey, tequila, and rum barrels for other varied experiments. Their experiments seem to be working—Hailstorm hauled in a GABF silver for their maibock in 2015. Taproom guests visiting for a taste of their award-winning beers may find themselves right in the midst of the action—the tables and chairs sit right in the middle of the warehouse floor.

IMPERIAL OAK BREWING

501 Willow Blvd., Willow Springs, IL 60480; (708) 330-5096; imperialoakbrewing.com; @ImperialOak
Founded: 2013 Founders: Grant Hamilton, Chris DiBraccio, Brett Semenske, Brewers: Brett Semenske, Grant Hamilton, Matt Glazier, Dan Kupres, David Dayhoff Flagship beers: Udderly Black Milk Stout, Prediction?...Pan! Imperial IPA, Farmer's Daughter Saison Year-round beers: Crank It Hop IPA, Prediction?...Pan! Imperial IPA, Udderly Black Milk Stout Main Seasonal beers: Quiet Giant Imperial Stout, Das Boot Oktoberfest, Crank It Fresh Wet Hop IPA, Sugar Shack Maple Brown, Billy Dee's Coconut Pecan Porter Taproom Hours: Sun through Wed, 12 p.m. to 11 p.m.; Thurs to Sat, 12 p.m. to 1 a.m.

When you graduate from school, they give you a diploma, shake your hand, and send you out into the real world. When you're ready to graduate from your homebrew club, sometimes you end up running a brewery with the guy whose bar you hang out in. That's the story behind Imperial Oak, an experimental small-batch brewery with a barrel-friendly focus in the southwest 'burbs.

Owner Grant Hamilton and head brewer Brett Semenske met at their homebrew club after each of them had been making beer for the better part of a decade. Hamilton was a video producer at the time while Semenske was a teacher; they both quickly realized they were serious about changing their business cards to read "Brewery Owner" instead. They partnered up with Chris DiBraccio, owner of Brixie's in Berwyn where their meetings were held, to get things started.

Hamilton and Semenske both live in close proximity to Willow Springs, and found their perfect space there after looking at eight to ten other spots.

"It faces a forest preserve, there's a Metra stop right in front; it spoke to us and said 'hi, this is a cool place to sit outside, face some trees, and have a pint,'" Hamilton explained. The taproom houses a 7 bbl brewhouse and six fermenters at the moment. They have a brewpub license, so in addition to their house beers they can also serve cider, wine, and cocktails.

True to their name, they make strong beers (Imperial) and barrel-aged offerings (as in, rested in oak). Brewing two or three times a week allows them to roll through a variety of different beers, but guests find a healthy mix available at any given time—light, dark, Belgian-y, hoppy. The benefit of a smaller system means more chance to experiment; various beers have included infusions of spices, peppers, fruits, and nuts. Some beers have even seen ingredients like cactus or saffron.

The barrel-aging program finds them also experimenting with a variety of options, not just whiskey or bourbon barrel–aging but also tequila, rum, and brandy. Some beers are brewed to fit the barrel, as a Belgian dark strong ale was for a rum barrel, or a Scottish ale for a former scotch barrel. Some of these beers find their way into bottles for a monthly release; the vast majority of Imperial Oak's beers go right into their patrons systems at the taproom.

KINSLAHGER BREWING COMPANY

6806 W Roosevelt Rd, Oak Park, IL 60304; (844) 552-4437; kinslahger.com; @kinslahger
Founded: 2016 **Founders:** Keith Huizinga, Steve Loranz, and Neal Armstrong **Brewer:** Steve Loranz **Year-round beers:** Munich Dunkel, Altbier, Prohibition Pilsner, Baltic Porter and a Chicago Common **Tours:** Yes **Taproom Hours:** Wed through Fri, 3 p.m. to 10 p.m.; Sat, 11 a.m. to 10 p.m.; Sun, 12 p.m. to 5 p.m.

It's a bit of a testament to the difficulty of producing lager beers that for nearly all of Chicagoland's recent craft beer history, only one brewery was willing to do nothing but lagers: that being Metropolitan. A new challenger appeared in March of 2016, in the form of Oak Park's Kinslahger Brewing Company, a brewery twenty-five years in the making and dedicated to the art of bottom-fermenting or cold-fermented beers.

Owners Keith Huizinga, Steve Loranz, and Neal Armstrong had all separately dreamed of opening their own brewery going back to the mid-1990s. After meeting at the Oak Park Homebrewers Club, they began making their long-held plans into reality, with head brewer Loranz attending Siebel and working with breweries like 5 Rabbit and Lake Effect. A space in long-dry Oak Park was found. With the nearby BeerShop bottle shop and tasting room and the forthcoming Oak Park Brewing Company, there was a mini beer renaissance happening.

After some trademark issues with their original name of Noble Kinsman, the three pivoted that name to a mashup of their belief in Kinship along with their lager focus to land on Kinslahger. What's with the extra "H"? That makes "LAH," which is the last initial of each of the three founders. Working on a 4 bbl system, the new brewery aims for 1,000 barrels annually, mainly on draft but moving into cans eventually.

With that lager focus comes some traditional style beers like an **Altbier,** a **Prohibition Pilsner,** a **Dunkel,** and a **Baltic Porter** (also all their individual names – no crazy beat-poetry names or metal band name logos here), but Kinslahger is also working to create a style all its own called the **Chicago Common.** Taking one of the characteristics (the hybrid yeast strain) of the well-known California Common beers popularized by San Francisco's Anchor, the **Chicago Common** has its inspiration in . . . bricks.

The Chicago Common brick was the building material of choice that rebuilt the city after the Great Chicago Fire—it was cheap and abundant, and made up the bulk of the bungalow-belt buildings . . . except for the fronts. It was when Oak Park resident Frank Lloyd Wright brought those bricks to the front of the building that you saw other architects realize the beauty available in an otherwise underappreciated product.

From that, you get the heart of the **Chicago Common** style beer. "It's got lots of red malt. It's a firm, fuller-body beer, with an earthy, piney hop character. It's a little under 7 percent [ABV]— slightly warming but a real balanced, medium/full bodied beer. And there's a little bit of rye in there for added intrigue," Huizinga explains. It all feeds into what he explains is their credo: "Lager, sustainability, and fellowship. This is a business [we] have planned on and looked toward for a long, long time. This isn't a whim; it's not some mid-career crisis." Like lager beer itself, it takes a little extra time to create, but styles—and breweries—are often best when they take a bit longer than ordinary.

LAKE BLUFF BREWING COMPANY

16 E. Scranton Ave., Lake Bluff, IL 60044; (224) 544-5179;
lbbrew.com; @lbbrewco
Founded: 2011 **Founders:** Rodd Specketer and David Burns
Brewers: Mike Dorneker, Ryan Morrill **Year-round beers:** Honey
Badger Golden Ale, Skull and Bones Double Pale Ale **Seasonal beers:**
Udderly Oatmeal Milk Stout, Undertow Belgian IPA, Velvet Hammer
Imperial Robust Vanilla Porter **Tours:** No **Taproom Hours:** Tues
through Wed, 5 p.m. to 10 p.m.; Thurs, 5 p.m. to 11 p.m.; Fri, 4 p.m. to 12
a.m.; Sat, 12 p.m. to 12 a.m.; Sun, 12 p.m. to 6 p.m.

Owners Dave Burns and Rodd Specketer started on Lake Bluff Brewing Company back at the very front edge of the craft beer explosion in 2010. Both were homebrewers and part of an area homebrew club. People had been clamoring for them to open their own place, but as there were still just a handful of super-new breweries in the world, they were a bit hesitant—until they got their beer into the Hoptacular event at the Aragon Ballroom. When they exhausted their kegs before other more well known places had kicked, that response from the crowd was what they needed to really get into the game.

They opened in March 2011 in a taproom just across the street from the Lake Bluff train station, a mile from the beaches of the North Shore and steps from the Robert McClory bike path, becoming an instant stop for thirsty folks on two-wheeled transport. Burns and Specketer, both family men with day jobs, quickly realized that they couldn't brew, bartend, and clean up the place on their own. They fell in with Michael Dorneker, another homebrewer and Siebel grad who'd cut his teeth interning at Metropolitan and headed north to become LBBCo's head brewer.

The team quickly distinguished itself, with their **Gamma Ray** pale ale named (along with Half Acre's **Akari Shogun**) the best pale ale in town in a tasting panel organized by *Chicago Magazine* in 2013 for a craft beer cover story. They received a gold medal for their barrel-aged **Kosmonaut** imperial stout at the US Beer Open Championship in the same year.

Visit today and you'll find eight to ten beers pouring at any given time, with the flaghip **Gamma Ray** pouring alongside other favorites like the **Honey Badger** golden ale and the **Skull and Bones** double pale ale. They don't have a kitchen of their own, but you can order from the Maevery Public House restaurant next door. Lake Bluff also serves up something few other breweries do—a soundtrack entirely provided by vinyl, spinning records

from a library hundreds deep. Got some fun wax to spin of your own? Stop by on Tuesday for BYOV night.

LIGHT THE LAMP BREWERY

10 N. Lake St., Grayslake, IL 60030; (847) 742-8489; lightthelampbrewery.com; @LTLBrewery
Founded: 2012 **Founders:** Bill Hermes, Jeff Sheppard, and Dave Cavanaugh **Brewer:** Daniel Ray **Flagship beer:** 1980 Miracle American Pale Ale **Year-round beers:** Bench Minor Blonde Ale, Red Line Ale, Sin Bin Stout, Center Ice Session Pale Ale, Shorthanded IPA, Powerplay IPA Main **Seasonal beers:** Drop The Puck Oktoberfest Marzen, Strawberry Blonde, Hat Trick Hefe, Pumpkin Stout, Belgian Triple **Tours:** Yes
Taproom Hours: Daily, 11 a.m. to 12 p.m.

There's something simply comforting about people who love a couple of things *a lot*. And man, do these dudes love hockey. After a trip to Europe to watch the Blackhawks play, three colleagues of beer decided to start a hockey-centric brewery and name all their beers things like the **Sin Bin Stout,** the **1980 Miracle American Ale,** the **Hat Trick Hefeweizen,** and the **Wrap Around Wheat.** Their Instagram is equal parts beer photos and headshots of Blackhawks players. It's that level of dedication that brings people to Light the Lamp, named for (what else) when a goal is scored in hockey.

Around six to seven beers from brewer Daniel Ray (a Metropolitan alum) are usually pouring from the handles at this small taproom in leafy downtown Grayslake, decked out in red walls and hockey jerseys aplenty. Opened in 2012 by a group of homebrewing fathers with a combined appreciation for center-ice faceoffs as well as the fermented arts, the brewery hosts pond hockey championships while the taproom also hosts live music, pub trivia, chili cookoffs . . . and of course, it's a pretty reliable place to find a broadcast of a 'Hawks game.

LUNAR BREWING CO.

54 E. St. Charles Rd., Villa Park, IL 60181; (630) 530-2077
Founded: 1998 **Brewer:** Ted Furman **Flagship beer:** Moondance IPA
Seasonal/occasional beers: Raspberry Cream Ale, Neil Armstrong Belgian Strong Ale, Total Eclipse Oatmeal Stout **Tours:** No

Out of all the breweries in Chicago and its surrounding suburbs, Lunar might be the one that has me the most stymied, even after all these years. Throughout the massive growth of the Chicago area beer scene, Lunar has been there the whole time, just hanging out in a bar in Villa Park, making their own beer, pouring some other good ones, just kinda doing their own thing. Hell, they *still* don't even have a website. (They do still have a MySpace page, though.)

Lunar started in 1996, and exists in pretty much the same capacity as when they opened—they're a corner tavern that happens to make their own beer. They brew on industrial-sized soup kettles, just 90 gallons at a time. Brewer Ted Furman has beer heritage that goes even further beyond the mid-1990s, working at the now-defunct Golden Prairie (where Revolution's Josh Deth originally cut his teeth as well). With over forty ever-changing recipes to brew, Lunar has more than a few moon-themed brews to cycle through, including their flagship **Moondance IPA, Jumping Cow** cream ale, the **Total Eclipse Stout, Dark Side** dubbel, or the **Neil Armstrong** Belgian tripel. The bar also hosts a variety of guest drafts, so there's really something for everyone. You

can regularly find beers from Lagunitas and Founders; Lunar has to be one of the few "breweries" in the nation that also serves Little Kings and Mickey's malt liquor. (I love them for this.)

Current proprietor and self-described "grain miller and hops weigher" for the brewery, Charlie Tierney, was a regular before he was the owner; he came to the bar after a career in restaurants and hotels and has kept it true to the original intent. Which is not to undersell the Lunar beers—they've medaled at FoBAB and can rival the guest handles also available on their lines.

Don't expect to see them anywhere other than a few festivals or on tap behind their bar, though. Lunar has made a career of keeping its head down, making its beer, and happily getting along outside the currents and tides of the city's craft beer flow. Kind of refreshing, in a world where most breweries can't expand fast enough.

METAL MONKEY BREWING

515 Anderson Dr #900, Romeoville, IL 60446; (630) 862-9595; metalmonkeybrewing.com; @MetalMonkeyBrew **Founders:** Dan Camp, Brett Smith, Brandi Nassenstein, Jason Janes, and Rachel Hampton **Founded:** 2016 **Brewers:** Jason Janes and Dan Camp **Flagship beers:** Fonkey Mucker Chocolate Peanut Butter Imperial Stout **Year-round beers:** Simian Fever Hibiscus Wheat, Tony's Car DIPA **Seasonal beers:** Monkey Knife Fight Pale Ale **Tours:** No **Taproom Hours:** Sun and Mon, 12 p.m. to 9 p.m.; Fri and Sat, 12 p.m. to 11 p.m.

You can thank a job layoff for the existence of Metal Monkey Brewing in Romeoville. Co-founder Dan Camp got a pink slip in the early 2000s and started reading about homebrewing to pass the time, which eventually led to buying brew gear, shopping at the Two Brothers "Brewer's Coop" homebrew store, making beers at his apartment, and well, you know where this is going.

After meeting Jason Janes at a gathering of the Joliet Brewers Guild, the two quickly moved onto opening a brewery of their own, with Jason as head brewer and Camp as "simian overlord" (seriously, check his business cards). The Metal Monkey name (one that's certainly more fun than many other cooler-than-thou breweries) came from the combination of Dan and Jason's other passions—Dan loved metal music and Jason . . . yeah, Jason loves collecting monkey stuff.

"Most every monkey you see at the brewery is something [Jason] brought from home," says Camp, which is something to look forward to, and I'd love to see someone smash together a cartoon with Spiteful's GFY Bear and the metal-horn-throwing cartoon chimp that makes Metal Monkey's logo.

Beers flow from a 3 bbl DIY-Psychobrew setup cobbled together with some kettles picked up "from one of the Carolinas" as well as fermentation tanks inherited from One Trick Pony. After the brewery's grand opening, the team splurged on a bigger 7 bbl tank that will allow them to churn out a total estimated 400 to 500 barrels per year.

The recipes maintain that hyper-creative, no-rules homebrew spirit, with their main flagship being a big ol' imperial stout chock full of cocoa and peanut butter called **Fonkey Mucker,** along with another six or seven on tap at any one time, including the **Tony's Car** DIPA, the **Simian Fever** hibiscus wheat, and the **Bikini Bottom Pineapple Gose.**

One of the more thoughtful nods to the realities of working in an industrial space is the attempt to batten down the volume of sound bouncing off the hard concrete walls. In many other similar taprooms, volume levels can rise to a not-so-dull roar when it's even moderately full, so the Monkey team came up with an ingenious plan to a) keep the echo down, b) add some decoration, and c) do something with the many concert t-shirts that were sitting around collecting dust. Look around and you'll see shirts from the likes of Slayer, Megadeth, Metallica, and Led Zeppelin, stretched around wooden frames and mounted artfully on the brewery walls, dampening the reverberations (at least a little).

MIKERPHONE BREWING COMPANY

107 Garlisch Dr., Elk Grove Village, IL 60007; no phone; mikerphonebrewing.com; @mikerphonebrew
Founded: First started in 2010, went pro in 2015 **Founder:** Mike Pallen **Brewer:** Mike Pallen **Flagship beer:** Smells Like Bean Spirit **Year-round beers:** Berliner Weisse-Style Ale Variants, Spin Doctor APA, Special Sauce IPA, I Want My IPA Main **Seasonal beers:** One Man Wrecking Machine sweet stout, Innocent Criminal double milk stout **Tours:** Not yet **Taproom Hours:** Fri, 3 p.m. to 10 p.m.; Sat, 11 a.m. to 10 p.m.; Sun,11 a.m. to 7 p.m.

This newly suburbanized brewery has its original home in the city's Southwest side, though the roots go back north of the Cheddar Curtain to a class at the UofW Madison. (Actually, if you consider the fact that Pallen's dad was a pipefitter for the Miller company in Milwaukee, the roots in beer go back farther than that.)

Mike Pallen started homebrewing as part of a botany class while in college back in 2002. His interest was piqued, and when he purchased a home in 2010, he outfitted the basement with all the bells and whistles of a home brewery—all the way down to the special pitched floors for easier cleaning.

Back then, as a homebrewer working in marketing, Mike knew he needed a brand. Pallen's other love was music, so Mikerphone was a natural portmanteautastic connection, and all his beer names have a musical influence or reference to them. At the same time, he was volunteering with folks like Pipeworks and 18th Street, who began to encourage him to make the jump into brewing for himself.

The original plan was to open as part of 18th Street, but when SlapShot in Little Village extended the option to come work as the head brewer of their beers while still being afforded the opportunity to get Mikerphone off the ground as well, Pallen took it. After brewing there for most of 2015, SlapShot decided to find a new southwest suburban space for a taproom and moved to contract production in the meantime. Pallen was then able to acquire their 7 bbl system solely for Mikerphone beers.

Main brews include the **One Hit Wonderful,** a Belgian-style IPA; the **Misty Mountain Hop** IPA; and the **One Man Wrecking Machine** imperial stout. In addition to the beers themselves, Mikerphone's main packaging distinguishes them—rather than go with cans or bombers, they opened up packaging their beers in the 24-ounce "BigAss" can. With a couple more ounces than a bomber and a lower price point, grabbing a Mikerphone can off the shelf makes for an easy decision.

MISKATONIC BREWING COMPANY

1000 N. Frontage Rd., Darien, IL 60561; (630) 541-9414; miskatonicbrewing.com; @miskatonicbeer
Founded: 2015 **Founders:** John Wyzkiewicz and Josh Mory **Brewer:** John Wyzkiewicz **Year-round beers:** The Eternal Series: Wise Fool IPA, Shield Maiden Pale Ale, Catchpenny Session Rye, Ingenue Belgian Farmhouse Ale **Seasonal beers:** Chapter Series of rotating IPAs, Angry Mob English Mild, Antsy Prole Coffee Porter, Grendel Old Ale, The Revenant Imperial Stout, Long Tongue Liar dry-hopped session sour, Achtoberfest Scotch Ale, The Craven dry stout with lemon, The Wicker Mann Maibock **Tours:** Yes **Taproom Hours:** Weds through Thurs, 3 to 10 p.m.; Fri, 3 to 11 p.m.; Sat, 12 to 11 p.m.; Sun, 12 to 7 p.m.

Darien's Miskatonic, a production brewery and taproom with a Lovecraftian edge, is the brainchild of two longtime Chicago-area brewers, John Wyzkiewicz and Josh Mowry. Wyzkiewicz cut his teeth at Goose Fulton before running Gordon Biersch's Bolingbrook location, while Mowry was the packaging brewer at Two Brothers in Warrenville. (He's also married to Wyzkiewicz's niece.) Both are graduates of the American Brewing Guild, so when this spot opened in July 2015, there were many years of ground-laying going into it.

Wyzkiewicz worked at Goose Island in the mid-2000s, a hugely creative time when they were just kicking off lines like Matilda and just as Bourbon County began its ascent to its annual nationwide frenzy. Before that, though, his homebrewing hobbies started in his late teens.

"In college, I had to order a kit from the back of a magazine . . . and my family had an oven in our basement that my grandma did a lot of canning on. I did it on the sly in the base at like 19 or 20 years old. I remember thinking

This is gonna be a trainwreck . . . but I was kinda surprised to find it tasted like beer," remembers Wyzkiewicz.

Thus another homebrewer entered the world. After spending some time in the world of finance, Wyzkiewicz made the leap out of the cubicle and into his education.

The Miskatonic name comes from a fictional setting in the writings of H.P. Lovecraft, and they use that inspiration as a springboard to name beers: **Shield Maiden, Wise Fool,** and **Catchpenny.**

"There's somewhat of a connection there between our view of the creative process and the way Lovecraft influenced people," Wyzkiewicz says. "Stephen King, the monsters in Ghostbusters, H.R. Giger . . . it's the 'standing on the shoulders of giants' concept. Everything we do, there's a little Goose in there. A little Two Brothers in there. We liked that connection."

You can also see it in their logo, a lady in sillouette holding a parasol while tentacles slither from beneath her gown. To paraphrase Lovecraft himself, "Searchers after horror haunt strange, dark breweries indeed."

The brewery threw open its taproom doors for draft pours in July 2015, while cans of the **Wise Fool** IPA and **Shield Maiden** pale ale began to emerge in early 2016. Cranking out brews off a 15 bbl system, Miskatonic doesn't limit their beer to any particular influence, as both ales and lagers are on the brewery's recipe sheets. While the off-premise options are focused on the canning line, there's a barrel-aging program that will see limited release in bombers, with beers like an **Old Ale** aged in Bulleit bourbon barrels or a chardonnay-barrel-aged saison.

Miskatonic took a while to find its home—between funding and finding the right location, it took five years to get up and running—but now that it's settled into its home just off the Stevenson, they're built with an eye on the future. Their facility is already created to expand as needed, fast or slow, but smart—and if you're at the taproom and you spot a tentacle slithering up from a trench drain, well, that's just part of how these guys make beer.

NOON WHISTLE BREWING

800 E. Roosevelt Rd., Lombard, IL 60148; (708) 906-3625; noonwhistlebrewing.com; @NoonWhistle
Founded: 2014 **Founders:** Mike Condon, Paul Kreiner, and Jim Cagle
Brewer: Paul Kreiner **Flagship beers:** Cozmo American Pale Ale and Bernie Milk Stout **Year-round beers:** Cozmo, Bernie, The Parker Wit & Face Smack Berliner Weiss **Seasonal beers:** Seasonal Saisons (including the Cumbersome cucumber Saison) and a Smack Series of sour beers **Tours:** No **Taproom Hours:** Weds and Thurs, 12 to 10 p.m.; Fri. and Sat, 12 to 11 p.m.; Sun, 12 to 7 p.m.; closed Mon and Tues

When three friends from grade school get together, more often than not the result is just hanging out and drinking beer, not starting a company to make it. (At least that's my experience.) But when Mike Condon, Paul Kreiner, and Jim Cagle, friends for two decades, decided to follow Kreiner's passion for craft beer, it resulted in the opening of Noon Whistle Brewing in January 2015.

The three were dabbling in the finer stuff going back a decade or so, drinking Fin du Monde and deciding they liked it better than your average American light lager. Kreiner got a job with Burke Beverage as a beer distributor and along the way started brewing, became Cicerone certified, and went to Siebel. The three always knew they'd love to do something together as a business, and one day Kreiner sat the other two down and said, "This could be our idea. And if it's not, I'm going to just run with it." Turns out it was theirs, and they set out to make a brewery.

The trio, all Lockport natives, wanted to be based in the suburbs, and originally had their eye on the beer desert of Oak Park. When that didn't materialize, a space in Lombard made itself known (next to the shockingly good beer list at Whirlyball on Roosevelt Road). The open space made sense for their 15 bbl brewhouse, along with the team's desire to have little to no separation between the brewery and the taproom. Brewers work right alongside patrons, and guests requiring a bathroom actually have to walk through the field of stainless to visit the facilities.

"We hope that when people come in, they are . . . part of our small family and friends," Condon explains.

Much like the location, the brewery's name was originally supposed to be something else. Noon Whistle was going to be a beer name, and comes from a Kreiner family tradition in northern Wisconsin, where a whistle blows daily at noon to mark the lunch hour. They'd made it a tradition that that's when the day drinking would begin, and accordingly, Noon Whistle's beers are made for the long haul.

With a specific focus on session beers, the vast majority of their recipes are under 5 percent ABV, including a "session dubbel", a cucumber saison, and a milk stout. They do have a handful of bigger beers, including a barleywine and a DIPA, but their plan is for most of their beers to allow you to have more than a few and still remain upright.

Noon Whistle also has a stronger focus on sours than most young breweries, with a wide array of Berliner weisses, goses, and other tart brews. Most sours are naturally lower in ABV and their kettle-soured offerings are no different, with their standout **Face Smack** berlinerweiss at just 4 percent. Beers are mostly draft only, though cans are on the horizon, including a pale ale and a packaged version of the **Face Smack,** which would be one of the few canned berliners on the market.

ONE TRICK PONY

17851 Chappel Ave., Lansing, IL 60438; (708) 889-6683;
ponybrewing.com
Founded: 2011 **Founder:** Mark Kocol **Brewer:** Jonathan Hickey
Flagship beer: Storm Cat, Warlander **Year-round beers:** Storm Cat,
Warlander, Spotted Saddles, Marsh Tacky **Seasonal beers:** Kentucky
Mountain, Cocoa Butter Kisses, Stallion, Georgia Grande **Tours:** No
Taproom Hours: Tues through Sat, 3 to 11 p.m.; Sun, 2 to 10 p.m.;
Mon, 6 to 11 p.m.

❝F— you, I'm not going to be some one trick pony."

That was owner and brewer Mark Kocol's response to his hophead friend (and future business partner) Dave Murphy's request to help brew with him, knowing that Dave would want to make one thing and one thing only—IPAs. A few years and about a hundred recipes after opening the One Trick Pony brewery in Lansing, this horse indeed has a few tricks.

One Trick began to emerge after a previous entrepreneurial brewing project of Kocol's failed to get off the ground. "The brewing at home started to become therapeutic at that point," he says. "Instead of just brewing beer and enjoying myself, I started to pick up those other hours that I was

spending trying to get the other project open, brewing beer and getting back into the science of it."

From there, the habit progressed from his kitchen, to his friend's basement, to the garage, to larger and larger batches. In the winter of 2011, that fateful conversation took place—would someone pay us for this? Kocol went back to the numbers he'd run for his previous project, revised them to see what he'd need to do to make it work, found a place in Lansing where they could pay the rent, got the village to give them the go-ahead, and started brewing on a tiny 1 bbl system in May 2012.

"We didn't really tell anybody we were doing something," said Kocol. "The only people who knew we opened were the Village, the Feds, and the state. We didn't tell anybody else. I think I started the Facebook page on the night we opened and no one was there. If the market says that we belong there, we'll get there."

Playing the long game has worked out thus far, as they quickly graduated to a larger space up the road. Since then they've also expanded to an 11 bbl system using repurposed dairy equipment (call it the Two Brothers method of brewhouse creation) with a larger taproom and some room to grow into the growing demand for their beers, which include the equestrian themed **Spotted Saddle** pale ale, **Marsh Tacky** stout, and the **Kisber Felver** black IPA.

Increasingly available outside the taproom on draft around the south suburbs and in various beer-focused establishments around the city, One Trick Pony is gradually making their way into small-release runs of bottles as well.

ONLY CHILD BREWERY

1350 TriState Parkway, Gurnee, IL 60031; (224) 656-5241; onlychildbrewing.com; @onlychildbeer
Founded: 2013 Founders: Ben and Amanda Rossi Brewer: Ben Rossi Seasonal/rotating beers: Attention Hog Rye Pale Ale, Le Perfectionniste French Saison, Don't Tell Mom the Baby Citra's Dead DIPA
Tours: No Taproom Hours: Tues through Thurs, 5 to 10 p.m.; Fri, 4 to 11 p.m.; Sat, 1 to 11 p.m.; Sun, 1 to 7 p.m.

While many homebrewers jump straight into running a brewery, Only Child's Ben Rossi spent years on the other side of the bar, as the beer director of The Grafton in Chicago's Lincoln Square neighborhood. Rossi watched as breweries popped up left and right around him, he worked with distributors and brand representatives, and bought a lot of beer from folks like Begyle, Metropolitan, and Spiteful. And then, one day, while helping brew one of his homebrew recipes at Begyle's brewery, it happened.

"That was when it was like, 'Man, I can't think of anything else other than doing this constantly,'" said Rossi. "That was the catalyst."

Only Child was Rossi's brand even as a homebrewer, which he'd been at for six years before opening the brewery. It emerged from a late night behind the bar when someone recommended he think about something that defined him or his childhood. "Calling it Adopted Only Child was kinda long," he jokes, "but Only Child stuck."

There's a playful, and yes, childlike quality to Rossi's beer names, which include the **Eat Your Damn Vegetables** pale wheat ale, the **Attention Hog** rye, the **Soooo Big,** and the **Don't Tell Mom The Baby Citra's Dead** double IPAs. (Can you tell he's got kids?) Those beers started out being made in Northbrook on a tiny 1 bbl (yes, one single barrel at a time) system starting in September 2013. Rossi cranked out 200 barrels that year in the production-only space, along with selling and distributing the beer.

It quickly became apparent that more space was needed, along with a taproom, so Rossi picked up stakes and found a more long-term space in far-north Gurnee. After going through the state licensing process all over again and graduating up all the way to a 2.5 bbl system, Only Child opened (again) in August 2015.

After starting the business with a "bomber of the week" gameplan, he quickly pivoted to taproom sales and draft accounts along with a move into 16-ounce cans. With a location pretty much smack dab between the beer drinkers of Chicago and Milwaukee, Rossi hopes that Only Child bridges the gap between the two as a must-visit every time you're on your way to one city or the other. And yes, Rossi still visits the Grafton every few weeks—but this time it's to deliver another few kegs of the **Training Wheels** golden ale, the restaurant's always-on house beer.

PENROSE BREWING COMPANY

509 Stevens St., Geneva, IL 60134;(630) 232-2115; penrosebrewing.com; @penrosebrewing
Founded: 2014 **Founders:** Eric Hobbs and Tom Korder **Brewer:** Tom Korder **Year-round beers:** Devoire Saison, P-2 Belgian-Inspired Pale Ale, Desirous Belgian-Inspired White IPA, Fractal Belgian-Inspired IPA **Seasonal/rotating beers:** Wild Series, Spectral Stout Series, Session Sour Series **Tours:** Yes **Taproom Hours:** Tues through Thurs, 1 to 9 p.m.; Fri, 1 to 10 p.m.; Sat, 11 a.m. to 10 p.m.; Sun, 1 to 5 p.m.

By 2013, "Goose Island brewer leaves to start his own company" was a story frequently told in those post-AB-buyout months. But when Eric Hobbs and Tom Korder announced their intention to start a company called Penrose Brewing in March of that year on the Hopcast video blog, there was something different about it.

Hobbs, who brought experience from years spent on Goose's sales team, and Korder, an "innovation brewer" and manager at Goose who also had experience brewing for the consistency-uber-alles Anheuser-Busch, created Penrose to be a finely focused Belgian-inspired brewery in an age where the "we just brew what we like," throw-it-against-the-kettle-and-see-what-sticks ethos was rampant.

That kind of focus alone was refreshing, but knowing they had the experience to back it up, and to do it in the western suburbs, made for a story worth watching. In the months following, social media fans were privy to a parade of teasing buildout photos, including one of Korder (who has a mechanical engineering background) building the brewhouse control system by hand. That kind of stuff had us hardcore beer fans primed.

Their debut a year later in March of 2014 saw the release of their core beers: a Belgian-inspired pale ale called **P-2;** a Belgian-inspired black ale called **Navette;** and a Belgian-inspired single called **Proto Gradus,** which quickly became their most recognizable brew. (Note that Gradus rhymes with "rod," not "ray". This'll spare you some embarassment at their taproom.) Their beers were defined by delicate, precise flavors dialed in to a tightness rarely seen by a new brewery.

Many more beers have since poured from the handful of lines in their Geneva taproom just a couple of blocks from the Fox River, but Korder's series of funky, sour, and tart ales have quickly eclipsed the rest of Penrose's brews as fan favorites. Their **Wild** series, aged in oak wine barrels and bottled in 375 ml corked-and-caged packages and released to early-morning lines outside the brewery have earned them a reputation for a quality in their wild fermentation that few other brewers can approach. Their **Deminimus** "session sour" series with a rotating focus on a variety of different low-ABV (down to 3.2 percent in one case) tart and acidic beers is a notable experiment in what sessionable beers can be once you wander away from maximizing hoppiness in a light pale ale.

An expansive barrel-aging program, experiments with coolship fermentation to grab crazy airborne yeasts floating down the air above the Fox River, and all sorts of fun one-offs like experiments with adjuncts such as black currants, lemongrass, and lingonberry (which speaks to Geneva's Swedish heritage) make Penrose one of the most nerdily fun, and most dependable, breweries in the Chicagoland area.

POLLYANNA BREWING COMPANY

**431 Talcott Ave., Lemont, IL 60439; (630) 914-5834;
pollyannabrewing.com @PollyannaBrewCo
Founded:** 2014 **Founders:** Brian Pawola, Paul Ciciora, Don Ciciora,
Ed Malnar, Ryan Weidner **Brewer:** Brian Pawola **Flagship beer:**
Lexical Gap IPA, Mazzie APA, Eleanor Porter, Full Lemonty Golden Ale
Seasonal beers: Acclamation Belgian Golden Strong with Apricots,
Summerly Raspberry Wheat, Humpenscrump Hefeweizen, Personal
Chain Letter Imperial Stout **Tours:** Yes **Taproom hours:** Tues through
Thurs, 3 to 10 p.m.; Fri, 3 to 11 p.m.; Sat, 12 to 11 p.m.; Sun, 12 to 7 p.m.

Sometime in the future, I envision a world where you can hop on a pontoon boat and sail down the Des Plaines River or the Chicago Sanitary & Ship Canal, hopping off at a dozen breweries and brewpubs along the way for a beer or three. It could be a wonderful and literal cruise for beer. Until that date, Imperial Oak (see page 71) and Pollyanna Brewing Company a little farther south in Lemont will have to tide me over.

After deciding to get out of the health care IT consulting business, Brian Pawola decided making beer would be way more fun. "Getting bitched at by doctors and nurses got old," he said, as you could imagine. Homebrewing passionately and volunteering at breweries like the former Limestone in Plainfield was a good start on getting some experience, but Pawola wanted to do it right, which meant a stint at Siebel.

He studied in Chicago and Germany under professors who'd spent time at Weihenstephan, one of the world's oldest breweries. Pawola felt as if he had a good base to come home and start making beer of his own. Along with some likeminded compatriates, he identified a spot near the I-55 and I-355 intersection in Lemont to set down roots for Pollyanna.

Originally built to be an Italian restaurant, the Pollyanna space overlooks the canal and offers a unique layout most breweries don't have—a mezzanine overlooking the brewery.

"You see everything, you smell everything," said Pawola. "When I'm brewing, you get everything that's going on. It's pretty unique." Opened in September 2014, the brewery features a 15 bbl brewhouse made a few miles away by Crawford in Rock Island. They produced about 1,800 barrels of beer in their first year.

Brewing with a focus on quality and consistency over variety and insanity, Pollyanna (the name represents "irrepressible optimism" as opposed to any sort of appreciation for children's literature from 1913) features four core flagships. Their **Full Lemonty** golden ale and **Mazzie** pale ale are available in cans; the **Lexical Gap** IPA and **Eleanor** porter are on draft but, with expanded fermentation capacity, plan to be in cans soon.

Other less-frequent brews include the **Dr. Pangloss** black IPA, the **Orenda** Belgian-style quad, the GABF bronze medal winning **Fruhauf** Oktoberfest and **Commentator Doppelbock.** "There's not any one style we focus on but as a German-educated brewer, I focus on balance and consistency. That's the way I was trained," says Pawola. Outside the taproom, you can find Pollyanna increasingly available at bars and restaurants in the city and suburbs.

SCORCHED EARTH BREWING COMPANY

203 Berg St., Algonquin, IL 60102; (224) 209-8472; scorchedearthbrewing.com; @ScorchedEarthBr
Founded: 2014 Founders: Michael and Jennifer Dallas Brewer: Dan Payson Flagship beers: Hickster American Cream Ale Year-round beers: Hickster, Rugged Coalminer Porter Seasonal beers: General Resin Imperial IPA, Saint Monty Belgian Dubble, Exiled Angel Blonde, Foraging Swine Smoked Beer, Bitter Chocolatier Oatmeal Stout Tours: Yes, first Saturday of every month Taproom Hours: Thurs and Fri, 3 to 10 p.m.; Sat, 12 to 10 p.m.; Sun, 12 to 7 p.m.

Mike Dallas was well on his way to spending a life in city administration, serving as assistant city manager in Mount Prospect, when a homebrew kit changed everything. After receiving a kit from his in–laws in 2006, "It really took off," Dallas remembers. "I couldn't stop learning."

Dallas and his wife, Jen, had discussed opening their own business over the years, and as he explains, "We never knew what it was going to be. When this thing happened, [Jen] could tell this was my first passion. I'd loved things before, enjoyed things before, but nothing so crazy and so passionate as this." Beer has a way of doing that.

The two are natives of small-town Marengo and noticed a general lack of craft beer options in the McHenry County area; that and a Siebel class the two took convinced them they needed to open a production brewery in their neck of the woods. After doing a deep dive into local history and trying on a variety of names for size relating to their geography, they stumbled across a story about a phenomenon of lightning strikes clearing the prairies of life and allowing for rebirth. They researched and found that Scorched Earth was available and had a nice craft-beer-friendly edge to it.

Dallas works on a 30 bbl system configured to allow him to do step-mash brewing where the wort spends time at multiple temperatures. He has a few normal conical fermenters but also prides himself on making beer using one of the few open fermenters in the area. Made to let the yeast ferment with less stress and release CO_2 more naturally, open fermentation is a more traditional, historic way of making beer that also allows different flavors to develop from the yeast as it creates alcohol.

The taproom pours flagship beers like their **Hickster** cream ale (made with locally grown corn, an adjunct that most brewers eschew) along with brews like the **Base Jumper** IPA, the **Rugged Coalminer** robust porter, and **Foraging Swine** smoked ale. The taproom is unique in that there's no separation between brewery and the bar area—if you're sitting there having a pint and they're making a new batch, you can have a chat with the brewer as he works.

Most Scorched Earth beer is on draft, but growlers and howlers can be taken to go from the taproom. Semi-regular batches of special release beers like a pumpkin porter, an imperial IPA, or an imperial oatmeal stout made with cacao nibs from a local chocolatier occasionally make their way into bottles, be they bombers, six-packs or four-packs. With so many interests across the beer spectrum, Dallas doesn't like to assign any one particular style to the brewery, but the ability to source local fruits and veggies from nearby farms, some just minutes away, make those beers particularly appealing.

SKETCHBOOK BREWING COMPANY

825 Chicago Ave., Evanston, IL 60202; (847) 859-9051; sketchbookbrewing.com; @Sketchbookbrew
Founded: 2013 **Founders:** Cesar Marron and Shawn Decker **Brewer:** Cesar Marron, Shawn Decker **Flagship beer:** Orange Door IPA **Year-round beers:** Orange Door IPA, Snowy Owl Rye Amber, No Parking Session Pale **Seasonal beers:** Lapwing Scotch Ale, Turbulence Imp. Stout, Back Alley Abbey Dubbel **Tours:** Yes **Taproom Hours:** Tues through Fri, 12 to 8 p.m.; Sat, 12 to 6 p.m.; Sun, 12 to 4 p.m.

A homebrew kit, a wedding favor, and a competitive spirit brought Evanston's Sketchbook Brewing into being. Founder Cesar Marron received a homebrewed IPA after attending a wedding ceremony and considered himself able to do better. Marron fell in love with the process of brewing, the tinkering with equipment, the honing of his skills. He began planning to open his own place and joined a local homebrew club, where a few years later he met co-founder Shawn Decker.

"One day Shawn asked me, what do you think it would take to do this commercially?" remembers Marron. "I was looking for a partner and it clicked." They incorporated in 2013 with the intent of starting a subscription-based Community Supported Brewery (CSB). Marron was working in the software management field but wanted to get back to something with direct contact with the community—his folks run a butcher shop in Brazil, and he liked the personal nature of the business. Decker is an artist and teacher at the School of the Art Institute who also works on art installations worldwide. That artistic background led to the Sketchbook name, as the brewery's size allows them to operate creatively, or "sketch" new beers regularly.

The brewery got a nice burst of pre-opening press when one of Marron's beers won a nationwide homebrew contest run by Sam Adams. Marron submitted his **Gratzer,** a smoked wheat beer, to their LongShot American Homebrew competition while the two were getting Sketchbook up and running with a Kickstarter campaign. Marron's beer was selected as one of three winners from a field of a thousand entries and was brewed at Sam Adams for distribution in a mixed six-pack featuring the victor's recipes.

Marron and Decker brew on a 7 bbl system in their brewery, which also has a small taproom. They're in the process of moving the taproom to a more accessible part of the building (currently you enter through an alleyway, in a very speakeasy-esque way), which will free up space for more brewing gear. Their CSB has a few hundred subscribers and they open up new spaces every six months or so. Patrons can sign up for monthly growler fills for six- to twelve-month runs.

In the early days there was no real flagship beer due to the ever-changing nature of the brewery's lineup, but as a year progressed and the customers made their influence known, the **Orange Door** IPA emerged as a crowd favorite. The **Snowy Owl** rye amber made from a recipe Shawn had honed over the years is another favorite.

Most beer is served from their taproom, but some kegs do make their way to restaurants and bars near Evanston; the self-distributing nature of the small brewery makes it tough to get much further at the moment. Packaged beers emerge rarely, as part of their sustainable focus keeps their eyes on growler fills as opposed to being on store shelves, but some small-batch seasonals make their way into bombers on occasion. Canning is their preferred method of packaging, which they hope to move into.

SOLEMN OATH BREWERY

1661 Quincy Ave. #179, Naperville, IL 60540; (630) 995-3062; solemnoathbrewery.com; @solemnoathbeer
Founded: May 2012 **Founders:** John and Joe Barley **Brewers:** Tim Marshall (head brewer), Matt Offerman, Paul Schneider, Lou Waldmeir, Mike Murphy **Seasonal/rotating beers:** Butterfly Flashmob Belgian IPA, Kidnapped By Vikings IPA, Snaggletooth Bandanna IPA, Pain Cave DIPA **Tours:** No **Taproom Hours:** Mon through Thurs, 12 to 9 p.m.; Fri and Sat, 12 to 11 p.m.; Sun, 12 to 7 p.m.

The ascent of this production brewery, camped quietly in an industrial corner of the large and heavily residential conservative suburb of Naperville, has been both rapid and impressive. Were one to walk into Chicago not knowing much of the beer market and look around for the first time, he might think that Solemn Oath was an older, established brewery akin to something like Deschutes—creative and dominant but also mature and quietly (massively) confident. In fact, they only served their first beer in May 2012, but are already well underway to be one of the strongest and largest Chicagoland area breweries.

Solemn Oath began when John Barley visited his brother Joe in that cradle of craft beer magic, San Diego, California. On the return trip, visions of opening a brewery danced in his head like proverbial sugarplums, except these plums needed to be milled, sparged, boiled, hopped, and fermented. After picking the brains of some of his favorite brewers, plans came together and Solemn Oath was born, named for a passage in a Robert Burns poem (who, as a Scot, knew a thing or two about alcohol).

With brewer Tim Marshall (formerly of Rock Bottom) aboard, they began brewing in 2012 with a focus on Belgian styles and barrel aging, releasing

their first beers in May at Beer Under Glass, the kickoff of Chicago Craft Beer Week. The brewery quickly became known for their complex, bitter, aggressive but clean beers. They also are in the running for best-named beers, including offerings like **Snaggletooth Bandanna, Punk Rock for Rich Kids, Butterfly Flashmob,** and **Kidnapped by Vikings.** (Not much chance of a cease-and-desist over any of those.)

Soon enough, the taproom opened with its specific rules (no tips, no food, no cash, and a limit of three pours or flight per person thanks to city regs) and John Barley was soon the president of the state's Craft Brewers Guild, advocating for changes to state laws regulating craft beer. Their Oath Day, similar to other brewery events like Three Floyd's Dark Lord Day and Goose Island's Black Friday, became an annual destination for west-suburban drinkers and beyond.

An expansion was announced in July 2014 nearly doubling their production, with a new brewhouse added (up to a 30 bbl system from the original 15 bbl workhorse) and a canning line. Solemn Oath is well on its way to changing the world, probably. (Their words.) When they announced their presence in 2012, it was near impossible to imagine any sort of worthwhile beer coming out of a place like Naperville. Just a few years later it's impossible to picture the landscape without them.

TEMPERANCE BEER COMPANY

2000 Dempster St., Evanston, IL 60202; (847) 864-1000; temperancebeer.com; @temperancebeer
Founded: 2013 **Founder:** Josh Gilbert **Brewers:** Claudia Jendron (head brewer), Jordan Binder, Dave Gibbons, Mike Van Camp
Flagship beer: Gatecrasher IPA **Year-round beers:** Gatecrasher IPA, Smittytown ESB, Restless Years Pale Ale with Rye, Escapist IPA
Seasonal beers: Greenwood Beach Blonde with Pineapple, Smittytown Tart, Root Down Porter, Might Meets Rights RIS **Tours:** Yes **Taproom Hours:** Tues through Thurs, 4 to 10 p.m.; Fri, 4 to 11 p.m.; Sat, 12 to 11 p.m.; Sun, 12 to 6 p.m.

The craft brewing movement (and American alcohol legislation, for that matter) hit another milestone when Temperance opened up its doors. Anywhere else, naming your brewery after a movement based around total sobriety would just be ironic. In Evanston, it's local history.

The Women's Christian Temperance Movement was founded here in 1873, and their efforts would eventually contribute to the ratification of the 18th Amendment, also known as Prohibition. (For details on the repeal of that amendment, we refer you to San Francisco's 21st Amendment brewery.) Prohibition was enacted in 1919. Evanston was a completely dry town until 1972. Temperance Beer Company opened their doors in 2013. Times change.

Founder Josh Gilbert was an Evanston native, homebrewer, and an architect who started envisioning the brewery during the economic downturn of 2008. He met Claudia Jendron, a microbiologist by schooling. Jendron was working as a brewer at Goose Island; she started there as a receptionist but elbowed her way onto the deck after deciding to follow her grandfather's homebrewing roots and become a brewer. They met at a bowling event held by the Illinois Craft Brewer Guild and eventually plans coalesced into the brewery called Temperance.

Their first breakout offering bucked the trend of hugely hopped American pale ales or double IPAs. It was a delicately hopped, herbal and bready English-style IPA called **Gatecrasher,** which went on to earn them a silver medal at the 2014 GABF; an impressive feat for any brewery, but more so for one in their first year. (Gatecrasher would go on to win Gold at the GABF in 2016.)

Other notable brews include their **Root Down** porter, spiced similarly to a root beer but not quite enough to get lumped in with the other hard root beers that have recently taken the country by storm. Their **Smittytown ESB** follows the English-style line laid down by Gatecrasher; their **Greenwood Beach** blonde with pineapple puts a light twist on the many citrus shandys available during summer.

Their barrel-aged **Might Meets Right** might be the most desired bottle Temperance has on offer. Jendron aged this imperial stout in High West distillery barrels previously used to age cocktails—a Manhattan and a Boulevardier specifically. The Manhattan-aged version took bronze in the experimental beer category at FoBAB 2014. It makes a certain amount of poetic sense for the former Goose brewer to push barrel–aging into new and interesting places.

TEN NINETY BREWING COMPANY

1025 Waukegan Rd., Glenview, IL 60025; no phone;
ten-ninety.com; @Ten90Brewing
Founded: 2012 **Founders:** Brian Schafer, Jamie Hoban, Andy Smith
Brewers: Brian Schafer (brewmaster), Gibbs Lippai (head brewer)
Flagship beer: Imperial Witbier **Year-round beers:** Imperial Witbier,
Half Wit, 90 Feet From Heaven IPA, 72 Hour Work Week Imperial IPA,
Saint Jaggery, Sharp Wit **Seasonal beers:** De Ogen, MPH, Zen,
Apricot, Milk & Cookies, The Closer **Tours:** Yes **Taproom Hours:** Tue
through Fri, 4 to 10 p.m.; Sat and Sun, 12 to 10 p.m.

From contract brewing their food-friendly, high-gravity beers to acquiring the contractor to opening their own brewery, Ten Ninety has carved their own path via their unique brews. If the phrase wasn't already locked down by Dogfish Head, I'd say they were a little off-center, but suffice it to say they're doing their own thing with a very specific viewpoint.

Ten Ninety, named for the original gravity (10.90) of a high-alcohol beer dense in fermentable sugars, began with a band of three friends: Brian Shafer, Jamie Hoban, and Andy Smith. The three were longtime homebrewers together who would compete in the annual Beerfly Alleyfight event, which was a battle of homebrew paired with homemade cuisine and "homegrown art". The team won the competition twice in a row; it was then that they thought maybe they should make a go of this brewing thing.

The original Ten Ninety lineup featured one of those award winners, the **Imperial Wit,** a 10.1 percent ABV Belgian-style witbier brewed with honey, coriander, and orange peel. Other offerings included **Saint Jaggery,** a Belgian tripel made with jaggery sugar from the Asian subcontinent, and **MPH,** their imperial porter with pomegranate juice and cayenne pepper. Sorta weird stuff, but also thoughtful and made with a food-friendly purpose in mind.

Their initial all-imperial outlook, with no original beers under 10 percent alcohol, was a bit of a thumbing of the nose to the growing "sessional" trend of high-flavor/low-alcohol brews, but they also reinforced the idea that these beers should be cracked open at the table and shared among friends, lest any one person be hit too hard with the weight of their strong brews.

They began in May 2013 by brewing their beers on contract with Big Chicago Brewing in Zion. Their first brews were packaged in large, 750 ml bottles and aimed for a higher level of customer. It's fair to say that these were made with an eye on the wine market and the restaurant sommelier who might be looking to pair a meal with a craft brew instead of another bottle of Bordeaux or Pinot Noir.

Not content to have their brews made on contract, the Ten Ninety team had the opportunity to purchase Big Chicago Brewing less than a year later, in March of 2014. While growing their own brand, they continued to help other contract brewers and gradually edged into the more mainstream world of beer, developing a series of witbiers as well as further unique brews, including **Zen,** a pale ale brewed with green tea and lemongrass and **De Ogen,** a pumpkin saison brewed in the fall.

Gradually, the Ten Ninety team wanted to build a community around their brewery and bring their beers closer to their drinking public, so a taproom was required. A space in downtown Glenview was acquired, the Zion space was shut down, and the gear moved south. Finally, in early 2016, the taproom opened to help serve the under-utilized north suburban market of beer drinkers, more used to passing by golf courses and country clubs than craft brewers. (And if you want to serve craft beer to a wine-centric audience, you can't go wrong on the North Shore.)

3 FLOYDS

9750 Indiana Pkwy., Munster IN 46321; (219) 922-3565; 3floyds.com; @3floyds
Founded: 1996 **Founders:** Nick Floyd, Simon Floyd, Mike Floyd
Brewer: Chris Boggess **Flagship beers:** Alpha King, Zombie Dust, Dark Lord Russian Imperial Stout **Year-round beers:** Alpha King, Arctic Panzer Wolf IPA, Backmasking Oatmeal Stout, Dreadnaught IPA, Gumballhead Hoppy Wheat, Jinx Proof Lager, Permanent Funeral Pale Ale, Robert the Bruce Scottish Ale, Yum Yum Session Pale, Zombie Dust APA
Seasonal beers: Alpha Klaus Christmas Porter, Apocalypse Cow DIPA, Moloko Milk Stout **Tours:** Yes **Taproom Hours:** Sun through Thurs, 11 a.m. to 11:15 p.m.; Fri and Sat, 11 a.m. to 1:15 a.m.

F FF. Just three letters symbolize much of the culture from which craft beer came—at least through the early 2010s. 3 Floyds (or Three Floyds, if you're going by AP style and their Facebook page) started as a brewpub in 1996 and was one of the early Chicago area craft beer pioneers along with Goose Island and Two Brothers. Arguments still rage to this day about whether FFF should be counted among the Chicagoland area breweries; there is no doubt as to their influence.

It started in an auto garage when Nick, Simon, and Mike Floyd opened shop with the intention of making hardcore, heavily–hopped beers. They paired those with an anti-authority, thrashmetal attitude; the intensity and the scarcity of their beer quickly made them one of the most sought-after and cultishly adored breweries in the nation.

It helps that their beer is spot on—their **Alpha King** pale ale is basically a perfect example of the style, their hoppy wheat **Gumballhead** is a staple on as many taphandles as beer buyers can get their hands on. Their citra-happy **Zombie Dust** is about as cultish as beers get—at the peak of Zombie fever, bars who could announce they had a barrel were quickly swarmed for it; stores and bottle shops had to ration it to beer fans even more than usual with 3 Floyds beers.

Of course, we have to talk about **Dark Lord** and its accompanying annual event, Dark Lord Day (DLD for short). Started in 2004 when 12+ percent ABV Russian imperial Stouts were rarities, the brewery sold their Dark Lord beer for one day only. Show up, get in line, get the beer, or don't. It became the equivalent of a Mecca trip for beer fans. The brewery's many partnerships with metal bands for collaboration beers quickly turned the event into equal parts concert, bottle share, beer release, and general party.

Every year in late April when the weather could be kindly described as "unfriendly" toward an outdoor event, come rain or shine, thousands line up with tickets in hand for their allotment of stout and the hopes that one of the many variants might make its way into their beer-sticky paws. Versions have been aged in barrels that held bourbon, cognac, aquavit, port, and brandy.

Rumors continue to float around about a Chicago location for a 3 Floyds bar, brewery, or brewpub. While nothing has solidified, there are certainly many hoping that city-based fans won't have to cross state lines (barely over the Illinois line as it is) to drink FFF at the source.

That's not to say that the Floyds are standing still. They recently expanded their brewery, added a distillery, and opened a new brewpub in partnership with gypsy brewer Mikkeller in Copenhagen called WarPigs. All while making some of the world's most sought-after beers and organizing the equivalent of an Woodstock Festival of craft beer. 3 Floyds can basically do whatever they want, and they do. No one would dare ask them to do anything else.

350 BREWING COMPANY

7144 183rd St., Tinley Park, IL 60477; (708) 825-7339;
350brewing.com; @350Brewing
Founded: 2013 **Founders:** Erik Pizer and Todd Randall **Brewer:**
Erik Pizer **Flagship beer:** Crook IPA **Year-round beers:** Crook IPA,
Stupid Kid APA, Heavy Metal Garbage Man DIPA, 350 Porter, Ruckus
Golden Ale, Coolidge Session IPA **Seasonal beers:** Dreamsickle, Hold
Your Horses Irish Red, Gypsy Knuckles Irish Stout **Tours:** No **Taproom
Hours:** Mon through Thurs, 12 to 10 p.m.; Fri and Sat, 12 p.m. to 12 a.m.;
Sun. 12 to 8 p.m.

Many breweries can get a little high-minded when they name their beer or describe their styles. A lot of references to art and science get thrown around, and it can get slightly tiring. What you rarely see is a brewery take the non-pretentious punk-rock route and name themselves after the street address of their college party house.

350 Brewing did just that when they opened in September 2014. Brewer Erik Pizer describes his time at Northern Illinois University as "the best three semesters of [his] life" and when it came time to name the brewery he started with his friend Todd Randall, there was only one thing it could be. "We would always say, 'will I see you at 350? Are you going to 350?' when we were in college . . . it meant something to us." That party continues, just with better beer.

Pizer started brewing in 2008 when a friend came over on New Year's Eve and talked about the homebrew kit he'd received as a Christmas present. His friend brought the kit over for Pizer to help with the first brew, and you can guess what happened from there. "I was 10 minutes in and I was like, this is the best thing ever. My wife said, 'You can just go buy your own kit, you know.' The rest is history."

The brewery lives in a small strip mall in Tinley Park, and creates its brews from a 3 bbl system similar to what breweries like Pipeworks, Begyle, and 18th Street started on. Pizer estimates they put out a little over 300 barrels in their first twelve months, and the smaller size of the system lets them plow through dozens of different beer recipes on their twenty taphandles.

Even though 350 never planned on having a flagship beer, their **Crook County IPA** was by far the favorite of the taproom patrons, so it's been in regular rotation and has even made it to cans. The demand was so high for it that they had to reach out to the community of brewers around them to see who could let them brew it on a larger scale—for a while, they were doing big batches of the IPA at Ale Syndicate and Finch's. A smaller but no less consistent beer tradition exists in their **Sunday Detention** series, where wilder, experimental beers brewed as small as 5 to 10 gallons at a time are released on draft and occasionally in tiny bottle runs.

The punk-rock vibe that runs through 350 extends into their beer names, many of which have a musical origin story. Beer names come from songs by Alkaline Trio and the Descendants, so it should come as little surprise that the brewery hosted a festival (appropriately named 350Fest) in the Tinley Convention Center across the street and booked local and national bands like the Smoking Popes to play while they and other breweries poured some quality beers. Look to this to be an annual feature, and if you happen to hear an aggressive, uptempo song playing at the taproom, ask about it—who knows, maybe 350 will book them to play next year.

TIGHTHEAD BREWING COMPANY

161 N. Archer Ave., Mundelein, IL 60060; (847) 970-9174; tightheadbrewing.com; @TightHeadBrew
Founded: 2011 **Founder:** Bruce Dir **Brewers:** Billy Oaks, Adam Bogac, Bruce Dir **Flagship beers:** Scarlet Fire Red and Irie IPA **Year-round beers:** Scarlet Fire Red Ale, Irie IPA, Chilly Water Pale Ale, Comfortably Blonde Ale, Boxcar Porter **Seasonal beers:** Hat Trick Tripel, Mechanics Grove Maibock, Go Go Witbier, Octoberfest, Reformator Doppelbock **Tours:** Yes **Taproom Hours:** Mon through Thurs, 4 to 10 p.m.; Fri and Sat, 12 to 11 p.m.; Sun, 12 to 6 p.m.

Like a few other breweries in Chicagoland, Tighthead has its origins in the Great Recession. Bruce Dir had been homebrewing for two decades and a Beer Judge Certification Program (BJCP) judge for a dozen years, all while working as an HR professional during the same period of time.

"My wife and I decided that since I hated what I did, I should do what I had a passion for, and not be so grumpy all the time," Dir said. "It helped that I was 'reorganized' out of a job in late 2009."

A business plan was created, a Siebel degree attained, and Tighthead was underway. Dir also worked for a short while at the Flatlander's brewpub to get the hang of working with larger equipment, and opened his doors in September 2011, with the taproom opening in December.

Working on a 15 bbl brewhouse, Tighthead (named for a position played by Dir in his rugby days) produces about 2200 barrels annually, and is growing. They were draft-only for nearly four years, but introduced

22-ounce bombers of their main five brands in early 2015. A line of canned Tightheads is expected in the future as well.

The first three main beers were the **Irie IPA,** the **Scarlet Fire Irish-style Red,** and **Comfortably Blonde.** A pale ale called **Chilly Water** came out shortly after that and quickly became the brewery's largest seller. A robust porter named **Boxcar** rounds out the core offerings and also serves as a base for cask beers and aging experiments.

Tighthead distributes throughout northern Illinois, though taproom patrons get the bulk of the experimental beers Tighthead produces. "We have sixteen beers on tap—all ours—and we've done probably over fifty-five styles . . . we like to turn people on to new things," Dir says. Small-batch offerings include traditional styles like maibock, witbier, doppelbock, and the occasional tripel.

TWO BROTHERS BREWING COMPANY

30W315 Calumet Ave., Warrenville, IL; (630) 393-2337; twobrothersbrewing.com
Founded: 1997 **Founders:** Jim and Jason Ebel **Head Brewer:** Jeremy Bogan **Flagship beer:** Wobble IPA **Year-round beers:** Wobble IPA, Domain Dupage, Prairie Path Golden Ale, Ebel's Weiss, Outlaw IPA, Sidekick Extra Pale, Cane and Ebel Red Rye **Seasonal/occasional beers:** Monarch White Beer, Atom Smasher Oktoberfest, Northwind Imperial Stout, Heavy Handed Harvest IPA, Hopcentric DIPA **Tours:** Yes **Brewery Hours:** Mon through Thurs, 11 a.m. to 11 p.m.; Fri to Sat, 11 to 12 a.m.; Sun, 11 a.m. to 9 p.m. **Roundhouse Hours:** Mon through Thurs, 11 to 12 a.m.; Fri and Sat, 11 to 1 a.m; Sun, 11 a.m. to 11 p.m.

Like so many other breweries, Two Brothers started with a visit to Europe in the late 1990s. Unlike many other breweries, Two Brothers actually survived out of the 90s. Jim and Jason Ebel began their beer ascendency in 1992 with a humble homebrew and winemaking shop in Naperville, but didn't graduate into the brewery business until 1997, when they set up shop in nearby Warrenville.

The original brewpub was distinguished by the brothers' use of old dairy tanks, gifted by their grandfather from his farm, as fermenters and finishing tanks. Hidden in a small industrial park near the intersection of two state roads, Two Brothers quickly emerged as a rare option for locally-produced beer in a time when Goose Island kept to the city and Three Floyds was just something people whispered about.

Their beers skew traditional with the occasional twist. Their **Cain & Ebel** red rye comes with a healthy dose of Thai palm sugar; their wethopped **Heavier Handed** benefits from a bit of age in their oak foudres. The majority of their year-round profile, however, is the kind of easy-drinking, dialed-in, quietly perfect beers that show the decades of work that have gone into making these beers spot-on. Their **Ebel's Weiss** is a creamy, delicious wheat beer that stays true to the phenolic banana and clove flavors familiar from the classic

hefeweiss, and their **Atom Smasher** is a nutty, toffee-happy Oktoberfest enhanced by a spin in the aforementioned foudres.

This is not to say that they can't occasionally get crazy. Their **Hopcentric Double IPA** squeezes out every last bit of of hop bitterness backed up with a healthy dose of hearty malts for a classic yet intense example of the style, and their **Project Opus** sour beers prove an old brewery can learn new tricks—their **Sour Beer #2** took home Gold at the 2014 Great American Beer Festival (GABF) in the wood and barrel-aged sour beer category.

In early 2015 the Ebels expanded their domain over to the sunblasted deserts of Scottsdale, Arizona, with a Two Brothers brewpub as well as a growing distributorship that brings their Chicago-area beer to a city full of Chicago expats (the Phoenix area boasts a Portillo's as well as a number of other hot dog and beef joints to serve the Illinois snowbirds and transplants). The triple-digit temps should treat the sharper, hoppier brews like **Sidekick** and **Wobble IPA** well.

TRIBES BEER COMPANY

11220 W. Lincoln Hwy., Mokena, IL 60448; (815) 464-0248;
tribesalehouse.com @tribesalehouse
Founded: 2015 **Founder:** Niall Freyne **Brewers:** David Kerns (head
brewer), Ben Michaels (assistant brewer) **Flagship beers:** Craft'd
IPA, Big Twin Double IPA **Year-round beers:** Daylight Kolsch, Craft'd
IPA, Tribes Pale Ale, Big Twin Double IPA **Seasonal beers:** Zero to
100 Imperial IPA, Blood Twin Double IPA, Belgo Peach Belgian Style Ale
Tours: Yes **Taproom Hours:** Daily, 11:30 a.m. to 12 p.m.

The leap from owning a bar to opening a brewery isn't a huge one compared to some of the places from which our other area breweries have stemmed, but it's one that very few have taken thus far. One of the few is the family of Tribes Alehouses, with locations in Mokena and Tinley Park. Adding to the beers flowing from the dozens of taphandles between the two were their own beers, released in May 2015 from the Tribes Beer Company and brewed in a space adjacent to the Mokena pub.

Head brewer David Kerns moved over from Haymarket to the helm of the new brewing company, working on a 7 bbl system to crank out hop-forward beers like the **Zero To 100 imperial IPA,** the **Rebel Monk Belgian Style IPA,** and the **Ol' Tango Dark IPA.** They quickly boosted capacity to meet demand in the taproom as well as select restaurants and bars around the city. The benefits of a partnership between a brewery and beer bar can be seen in the regular beer fests hosting dozens of brewers and the all-Illinois beer tap takeovers.

MYTHS AND LEGENDS BREWING COMPANY

1115 Zygunt Circle, Westmont, IL 60559; (630) 442-7864;
urbanlegendbrewing.com; @UrbanLegendBeer
Year-round beers: Hasen Fuss, Scylla's Grasp, Mug Shot, Cooper's
Parachute, Catherine The Great, You Big Dummy, and The Creature
Seasonal beers: The Devil and Jack, Fain's Sword, The King's Tree,
Imperial Mugshot, Nessie's Gnarly Nectar, Otis, Responsibly, Spy's Secret,
Step On It Klaus, Tree Hugger, and Wail of the Banshee **Tours:** Yes
Taproom Hours: Tues through Thurs, 5 to 10 p.m.; Fri, 3 p.m. to 12
a.m.; Sat, 12 p.m. to 12 a.m.; Sun, 12 to 6 p.m.

The brewery first known as Urban Legend started with "a partnership between a homebrewer and a plumber," as Shannon Hancock explains.

Like many partnerships, this one didn't last much beyond the honeymoon stage, and the "divorce" left the plumber's side with a brewery and a taproom, while the homebrewer's party departed with his recipes to start his own brewery, 51st Ward. That's the not fun stuff, but it happens. The fun stuff is that Myths and Legends (a name forced by a trademark dispute in August 2016) is still cranking out fun beers like their **You Big Dummy** imperial red and their **Creature** black IPA.

Working on a 3.5 bbl system, Myths and Legends powers out upwards of 800 barrels a year, with "a focus on the quality, but we don't want all the beers to taste the same. We want people to have a variety of experiences," Hancock says. That task is left to operations manager Dan Rosenberg, who leads the brewing team, along with cellaring and managing inventory. Beers make their way to customers on draft and in bombers; core offerings include the **Scylla's Grasp** mosaic pale ale, the **Hasen Fuss** cream ale, and the **Cooper's Parachute** west coast IPA.

Tucked into a corner of an industrial section of town (the cross street is literally named Vandustrial) alongside a school bus parking lot, M&L considers themselves lucky to have had the support of Westmont since the beginning, going so far as to rewrite ordinances to allow them to open up shop and serve beers and bring locally brewed beers to the masses. "We choose to make a variety of styles, for a broader range of beer experiences," Hancock says. "We're not just catering to sours or IPAs or lagers. We want to help build the public's knowledge and experience. Our goal is to help educate the general public about craft beer."

WERK FORCE BREWING COMPANY

14903 S. Center St. #107, Plainfield, IL 60544; (815) 531-5557; werkforcebrewing.com; @werkforcebrew
Founded: May 2014 **Founders:** Brandon and Amanda Wright
Brewers: Brandon Wright, Steve Woertendyke, and Jake LaDuke
Flagship beer: The Beer Formerly Known As . . . IPA **Year-round beers:** The Beer Formerly Known As . . ., Sleepy Bear, Axis: Bold as Beer brown ale, Bad Polaroid red ale, Oats Made Me Do It oatmeal stout, Super Galactic, Farmhouse Vultures saison **Seasonal beers:** Steve's Going To Helles, Water On Mars saison, Spicy Mullet, Can Your Bagpipes Do This scotch ale, Mandarzilla, Pressure Drop, Wolf of the Henhouse **Tours:** Yes **Taproom hours:** Tues through Fri, 10 a.m. to 7 p.m.; Sat, 10 a.m. to 5 p.m.; Sun, 11 a.m. to 3 p.m.

By now you're surely familar with the "longtime homebrewer gone pro" tale told by so many startups around Chicagoland. Werk Force has its own unique angle on that particular story—not just content to open a place to make some beer, Amanda and Brandon Wright opened their own homebrew store in advance of their taproom and nanobrewery.

Chicago Brew Werks opened in Plainfield in early 2012. Brandon Wright was a homebrewer for a decade-plus and recognized the need for not only some fresh beer in the southwest suburbs, but also a destination for beermaking supplies that didn't require a long drive or waiting for kits to be shipped. The wide array of brewing ingredients they have on–hand also serves to give the Werk Force beers even more experimental creativity, with new hop varieties and experimental malts to play with.

In addition to serving as a homebrew shop and a brewery, Werk Force was also licensed as a tavern for a few months, serving up guest handles so folks could sip a finished product while they shopped for their own brewing needs. Werk Force brews on a system that can brew 1 barrel or 2.5 barrels at a time, depending on what kind of beer output they're looking for. Larger runs go through a few turns to fill the 7 bbl fermenters while smaller batches are reserved for playing with new recipes or ingredients.

The brewery side has been open since 2014 and in that time, Amanda estimates that they've gone through nearly a hundred different recipes. There's no single flagship beer though they do like the farmhouse and saison styles; you can regularly find a variety of Belgian-styled beers, IPAs, stouts, kettle sours, and more. A growing barrel-aging project finds its way into bombers and 750 ml bottles every few months (their tart cherry saison aged in a wine barrel medaled at FoBAB in 2015) though otherwise they're entirely on draft.

If you like something you try at the taproom, there's a good chance you can give it a go yourself—Werk Force also sells both extract and all-grain kits of some of their own beers. Classes are available on everything from extract brewing, kegging your beer, water chemistry, and brew-in-a-bag techniques. From grain to glass, Werk Force literally has everything you need.

WILD ONION BREWERY / THE ONION PUB

22221 N. Pepper Rd., Lake Barrington, IL 60010; (847) 381-7308; onionbrewery.com; @wildonion21
Founded: 1997 as Wild Onion, 2003 as the Onion Pub and Brewery
Founders: Mike, Pat, and John Kainz **Brewmaster:** Mike Kainz
Year-round beers: Paddy Pale Ale, Hefty-Weiss Hefeweiss, Misfit IPA, Hop Slayer DIPA, Phat Chance Blonde Ale **Seasonal beers:** Faux-Pas Session IPA, Jack Stout, Pumpkin Ale, Drago RIS, Otis Wet-Hopped IPA, Bloodline Black IPA **Tours:** Yes **Taproom hours (at The Onion Pub):** Tues through Thu, 11 a.m. to 11 p.m.; Fri and Sat, 11 to 12 a.m.; Sun, 11 a.m. to 8 p.m.

Opened in 1997 at the tail end of the first wave of microbreweries, Wild Onion has gone from production brewery to brewpub and back again. Owner and founding brewmaster Mike Kainz had his eyes opened to great beers during a year studying abroad in Paris. When he returned stateside he started homebrewing "like so many, out of necessity to drink beer with more flavor." He then went and worked in California's wine country for eighteen months learning about fermentation and running a cellar program, then returned home for a stint at Berwyn's Weinkeller alongside other early beer pioneers like a pre-FFF Nick Floyd.

Wild Onion started selling beers made on a system made from converted dairy tanks "scavenged in Northern Wisconsin," as Kainz puts it, and began packaging their beers in 1998. Then, in 2000, something changed the brewery's gameplan significantly—Kainz's dad hit the lottery. That infusion of capital "took us to a completely different level," Kainz said. "It allowed us to buy [a] property and basically build our dream taproom and pub, along with moving the entire brewing operation over. It was nice to not have to deal with the banks for a while."

The new brewpub was created with a 8 bbl system and they focused strictly on what they could sell from there, walking away from packaging entirely. That worked fine for a decade, but as the craft beer scene began heating up again in 2010, Wild Onion decided to re-enter the production world and opened a new 50 bbl brewing facility.

Now, with a foot firmly in both camps, they're rolling out about 3,200 barrels a year of beers like their flagship **Paddy Pale Ale,** their best-selling **Misfit IPA,** a seasonal **Bloodline** black IPA, the **Drago** barrel-aged Russian imperial stout, and a variety of other seasonals like a session pale, a pumpkin, an oatmeal, and even a harvest IPA made from a small patch of hops that grow on their property. As the production side continues to grow, the brewpub serves as a R&D lab for new beers and ciders that may make their way into future large-scale batches.

ZUMBIER

3232 W. Monroe St., Waukegan, IL 60085; (847) 420-7313; zumbier.com; @ZumBierMon
Founded: July 2012 **Founder:** Larry Bloom **Brewers:** Larry Bloom, Jim Buche, Kelly Below **Flagship beers:** Citra-Tasm, Super Chong, Hoppy Time **Tours:** Yes **Taproom Hours:** Wed through Thurs, 4 to 9 p.m.; Fri, 3 to 10 p.m.; Sat, 2 to 10 p.m.; Sun, 1 to 6 p.m.

We would have had one less brewery in this book if owner and brewer Larry Bloom had lived closer to Westmont. Bloom was working to set up a brewery with 51st Ward's Tim Hoerman when the proposed location started moving south. Preferring to keep things closer to home, Bloom split off and started his own small brewery in Waukegan, perhaps depriving western suburbanites of his brewing skills but saving a lot of time on the roads. Today, ZumBier serves up bottles to northern Illinois bars and restaurants as well as the patrons of Bloom's brewery taproom.

The ZumBier name comes from the German word for "destination" or "to the"—the Bier part should be self-explanatory—to celebrate the exploration of the beer experience and the world culture created by beer. Bloom opened a production facility in February 2014 and a taproom in early 2015 for growler fills and bottle sales. Finally, in July 2015, patrons were able to have a pint poured for them onsite.

Brewing on a 1.5 bbl PsychoBrew system, ZumBier is still a true nanobrewery, churning out under a hundred barrels a year of dozens of small-batch options. True to the Germanic origin of the name, there are kolsch, altbiers, and dunkelweiss, but the American side makes itself known through citra-hopped pale ales, a rye black IPA, and a straightforward IPA named **Liberty Call** in tribute to the nearby Great Lakes Naval Station.

ZumBier's philosophy of world citizenship comes through in that mix of international styles. "What we want the beer to be is a meeting point for celebration and bringing people together," he explains. "We use traditional styles when it's appropriate for the beer we're producing, and we're also unafraid to be experimental and try new things." Americans traditionally aren't stifled by rule following, so expect beers to continue to push to the experimental side.

JOHN HALL: THE Q&A

You can look at Chicago craft beer and separate it into two different eras—before Goose Island and after Goose. You can also look at the craft beer business around the nation and separate that even further into two eras—before Goose Island was sold to Anheuser-Busch, and after. To say that John Hall Goose Island's founder created something that influenced the way the entire nation drinks is not an exaggeration.

Hall sat down with me to talk about what the city's beer scene looked like as he was opening his brewery, when he finally felt like Goose was safe, and a little bit about that big sale to A-B.

Karl: Before getting Goose Island off the ground, what did your career look like?

John: I spent twenty years with Container Corporation of America, which is a packaging company that when I joined them, was an independent company. Then I joined with Montgomery Ward to form Marcor, which a couple of years later, Mobil bought.

Karl: The apocryphal story is you on an airplane reading an in-flight magazine about brewing and making the decision to jump into the game. There's gotta be more than that. What else got you into beer?

John: That is exactly correct. I had a series of different jobs, but, a couple of them, took me to Europe. I was amazed at the beers available there. I drank import beers here in the states, but I mean, come on, they were import beers that were, for the most part, look-alikes to American beers just with a little bit more flavor and more traditional names.

I was also exposed to Michael Jackson and his books. The romance of brewing was kind of in me and after twenty years, I basically wanted to do something on my own. Quite frankly, I was researching a couple of things, working on a couple of opportunities to go out and start a company or buy a company. This magazine article came out and . . . wow. I said "Why not brew beer?" Think of the opportunity.

Karl: Talk about something that nobody else was doing at the time; 1988 wasn't a great time for small breweries. Craft beer wasn't even a phrase anyone used.

John: That's right. It was just starting. I grew up when it was hearty burgundy and Chablis, things like that, and there were starting to be all kinds of varietal wines. Something as simple as ice cream, you have thirty-one flavors of ice cream. Starbucks was just starting, all of those things. I said, "Wow, this is an opportunity, maybe."

I didn't want to move from Chicago and I knew Mobil was going to sell our company. I was vice president of Planning at one time and I just knew they were going to do it. The last thing I wanted to do was get involved in another go-around of something. I was ready to go off on my own. It really seemed like a great thing to do at the time. I had a wife who was more than willing to do it. That was a big deal.

Karl: At this point, though, had you ever done any homebrewing or anything like that?

John: No, no I hadn't. I had been through a lot of breweries being in the packaging industry. I knew how to start finance and everything. I had, if anything, a little too much confidence and not a lot of common sense.

Karl: So, in the beginning—what came first?

John: I did several things. First of all, I reached out to the predecessor of the Beer Institute of the Brewer's Association. We were allied members, and I asked them to send me data on beer consumption.

It showed that imports were really growing while the overall beer industry wasn't. More than anything, that gave me a contact. They called me back after they sent me some information because I had told them what I was looking at doing. They said they had an individual who was just starting a consulting firm by the name of Karl Strauss. [Author's Note: This is the same Karl Strauss who, along with his cousin, helped start the brewery and brewpubs in San Diego that carry his name.]

I called Karl. I don't know if I was his first client, but I was pretty close to it. He became my mentor in the brewing business. He came down. He spent time with me. He and I took a couple trips together. We went out to California to see what was going on out there and he introduced me to brewpubs. I had no idea what brewpubs were, really.

Karl: You obviously did a lot of research into the beer industry itself, but tell me what you remember about the beer-drinking world around you at that time.

John: When I started, Sieben's was in the process of starting. We were all trying to open first. Sieben's opened on Ontario Street where Reza's is now, but the first one was Tap & Growler, [which] started over on West Jackson, where Jak's Tap is now. That used an electric brewing system not with hop and malts, but with a pre-made brewing malt extract.

That was really a disaster, but it was the first one by a few months before Sieben's and then we came probably less than six months after that. Sieben's, when they first opened, made some very good beer. They had great trouble with their food, as I recall. We all had trouble with food a little bit, but they had great trouble with food. When they started to have trouble, they also dumbed down their beers a little bit. We stayed true to the beer cause all along.

Karl: When Goose launched, what were the core beers Goose sold?

John: Our first beers were a **Golden Goose Pilsner,** we had **Honkers Ale,** we had an **Old Clybourn Porter,** a maibock, and **Lincoln Park Lager.**

Karl: What kinds of things did you learn about Chicago beer drinkers after you opened?

John: First of all, most every beer that was consumed in Chicago was a light lager and so anything we did either with flavor or color was a little bit out of the ordinary. I mean, ales were really the new thing. Nobody drank ales back then. There might have been a Ballantine Ale but it was one of the few. It had no flavor whatsoever.

That was the big [thing.] We had people who would come in and they wanted something, if it had any color in it they were like, "Whoo, what was that?" If it had any flavor . . . We were looking at IBUs of like thirty, low thirties for Honkers and Maibock, and the Golden Goose Pilsner was low, low thirties. They weren't overly hopped or anything. They were well-balanced.

Our first brewer, Victor Ecimovich, I found at the [Millstream] brewery in Amana, Iowa. Karl recommended him. My son was a student at the University of Iowa in creative writing and he said, "I don't know, Dad, but if you haven't tasted beers out here you oughta talk to this brewer in Amana." He recommended him, too, which is fun. I hired Victor and he was a graduate of Siebel. His grandfather happened to be a brewer at the old Chicago Best Brewery that made Meister Brau, which was located a hundred yards from where we were. That was interesting.

We had great difficulty getting people to try anything other than the lighter beers. We came up with a plan in about 1988 or '89 called the MBA program, Master of Beer Appreciation, which was absolutely the best thing we ever came up with. We had a curriculum. The MBA program was hugely successful in getting people to sample different beers, develop a palate. We were brewing probably thirty beers a year for the first couple of years, and then my son took over and we really started to ramp it up. We started with traditional styles, [and] he started to get creative with so many different things.

Karl: I have an MBA booklet in my wallet as we speak.

John: That was wonderful. The other thing, that we started was the Chicago Beer Society. Of all the homebrewers in the country, Chicago was fortunate to have some of the best and the biggest leaders and the most influential. They became apostles of Goose Island and good beer. We were the only place that was doing this, so that was fabulous.

Karl: Was it a slow build at the beginning, or was it something where there was just so much desire for beers like these and you guys were the first people to do it in awhile?

John: We started out and we did very, very well. We were part of [the Clybourn Mall] project, the project didn't do well and it ran into some very hard times. It was sold in bankruptcy so they tore the place down. That was almost the doom of us. I was fortunate; I could put some money in but if I hadn't had some money that could carry us for like a year and a half, we wouldn't have made it.

Karl: Once you survived that, did you feel like Goose was around for the long haul?

John: We opened the Fulton Street Brewery in '95 and I would say I really started to feel comfortable in probably the late 1990s, '99 to 2000, somewhere in there. When you can see we were going to make it, we didn't have to worry about everything all the time anymore. Not that we didn't have some issues that went forward because it's a capital-intensive business and every time you grow you need a helluva lot more capital.

Karl: In the process of putting this project together, it's a real parade of people who've worked for you, either at the brewpub or at Fulton. Do you know, just ballpark, how many people have brewed for you and gone on to do something else?

John: They've got something over at Fulton where they've made a family tree of Goose Island. There's a great number of them. Quite frankly, at first it bothered me a little bit that people wanted to leave, but people, including my son, have told me everybody makes decisions for their own personal lives and you've got to go ahead and give people the freedom to do that. I think that became one of the hallmarks we have—you learn an awful lot and you grow and you can help your career going forward. There's more than a few who have started their own companies based upon, I think, the experience they gained from us.

Karl: Now we get to the point where we talk about the Anheuser-Busch stuff. I don't think it's overstating things to say that when Goose announced it was going to be purchased by A-B, that really kind of changed everything in the world of beer. Now that it has been a few years and you've been able to get a little bit of distance on it, how do you look back on it? What do you remember about it specifically?

John: A lot of things. I got into this because first of all, there's nothing better than creating something—not just creating a product that everybody likes, but building an organization. That's one of the great, personal accomplishments of seeing people all come together to make something better. That's a great, great feeling and I take great pride in that. I started Goose Island when I was in my mid-forties and I had a son that, I can't tell you the joy of working with your son, who grows in the business, and you see him become accomplished.

Nonetheless, it's a very capital-intensive business. I've personally signed for more notes and everything as I grew the business. I knew that at some point in time there had to come an end to it. Believe it or not, from the beginning I thought my most likely candidate to probably come in and buy us was going to be someone like Heineken. I thought it would be someone from outside the US who would want to protect their footprint in the US by hooking up with a local brewer.

It didn't happen that way; we hooked up with A-B and quite frankly, of all the partners, I don't think there's any question that they're the best, as far as having a strategic partner from an equity holder, but also for our employees. You look at the employees, those who chose to stay, and most of them, have increased their financial and professional responsibilities.

[As] part of growing we had to do some contract brewing. It isn't easy to find a good contract partner and I guarantee you there's not a better brewer in the world to make your beer for you. Once they dial it in they're going to do it better than anybody and they're going to be a better supporter of you. I mean we couldn't keep up with the contract brewer; we had problems with that. That is a big issue.

Karl: What were you having to contract at that time? This was about around 2010—Goose must have been almost entirely 312 at that point?

John: Oh no, 312 was growing like mad but, the craft beer movement was starting to grow. We expanded somewhat but we didn't expand willy-nilly. We tried to expand in an area that we could continue to support. We were growing at 25 percent a year.

We [also] have the most complex mix of just about any brewery in the country from Bourbon County Stout to 312. Bourbon County Stout, it consumes about six times as much brewing time as 312, and so we had to cut back on Bourbon County Stout a little bit and then you're in a couple new markets, so we had to suffer with a couple new markets. We started contract brewing in 2010 with Honkers and IPA. Honkers was our biggest one at that time. Shortly thereafter, 312 surpassed it but that was a big deal. If you can't continue to grow with your wholesalers you might as well forget it.

It's a growth business and we designed the brewery to do a hundred thousand and we were doing 130,000-plus out of that brewery with a very complex mix. [A-B] contacted me, I talked to my management team, and everybody concluded, far and away, this was the one we wanted to do a deal with. It took us less than six months to really finalize the whole thing.

Karl: Another thing I'm curious about is that you retained ownership of the brewpubs, while A-B basically took over Fulton and grew it like crazy from there. How has it been, in terms of a management structure, with you both operating in somewhat of the same world with the same name, but also in two separate worlds at the same time?

John: When A-B acquired us, they had no interest in and no knowledge of brewpubs, and under Illinois law they couldn't own the brewpubs. They obviously have made acquisitions since then that have included brewpubs and they understand the value of brewpubs in marketing, especially with craft beer and everything like that. From that standpoint, that explains why I own the brewpubs.

It does present some complications, but I understand because I'm a retailer now, and so we have to be very careful that we don't violate Illinois state law and get any extra benefits from a brewer. That's a big issue and they're very concerned about it, as am I. It does present some problems but I do know the brand pretty well and we try, to promote the brand as much as ever.

Karl: Since you guys inked the deal, the rules have changed significantly, to the point where breweries and brewpubs can co-mingle a little bit. Revolution, for example, has a production facility and they started in a brewpub. Do you see a day where you're ready to let A-B take over Clybourn as well?

John: I think that is a possibility, without a question. [Author's Note: Hall sold the Clybourn brewpub to A-B in February 2016.]

Karl: Is there any misperception that people have about Goose today that you want to clarify?

John: I mentioned that I take great pride in the organization. Everybody says, "Who's making the decisions?" The people making the decisions are basically people I hired who are running the company now. Ken Stout, whom I recruited from Heineken. He's the General Manager of Goose Island and I couldn't be prouder of him and what he's doing. How he's involved with everything going on that continues Goose Island as I envisioned it, really. I couldn't be more pleased.

We're more innovative now than ever. We've got good people in the company and we continue to support the same institutions here in Chicago that we've always supported.

Karl: I'll also say that Clybourn is still one of the greatest places in the city to have a beer. It's really huge though. It didn't start that size, did it?

John: It wasn't quite that big. We expanded a little bit when they tore everything down. It's a great place—it's kind of my family room. I love to go there and sit at the bar and drink a beer and talk to people.

Karl: Finally, were you surprised by the general response of beer fans, when the sale was announced?

John: Not really. Beer is something people believe in and they think it's their personal product a little bit and when something happens to it they get emotionally involved, so that didn't surprise me.

Some of the people who worked for me [were surprised] when I announced it. I saw it on their faces that they were just absolutely shocked. I said, "Hey, trust us. Just give it a little chance." I think it's proven that it has worked out.

Independent Brewpubs

ANDERSONVILLE BREWING

5402 N. Clark St., Chicago, IL 60640; (773) 784-6969;
http://hamburgermarys.com/chicago/brewing/
@MarysChicago
Founded: 2009 **Brewer:** Brandon Wright **Flagship beers:** Mary
Hoppins Pale Ale, Blonde Bombshell Golden Ale **Year-round beers:**
Gangster Amber, Speakeasy Saison **Tours:** No **Taproom Hours:** Mon
through Wed, 5 p.m. to 12 a.m.; Thurs and Fri, 5 p.m. to 1:30 a.m.; Sat, 12
p.m. to 2:30 a.m.; Sun, 12 p.m. to 12 a.m.

One of those "hidden in plain sight" breweries that dots the city's landscape, Andersonville Brewing is something of a brewpub/ taproom/brewery combo. They have operated out of the bar at Hamburger Mary's, a LGBT-friendly burger joint, serving their handful of beers since 2009. At around 200 barrels a year, they were nano before people knew what nanobreweries were.

Owner and brewer Brandon Wright got into the brewing world via his homebrewing habit, but his story goes a little deeper than a few buckets and a burner in a garage. As an engineer stationed in alcohol-unfriendly Saudi Arabia, Wright essentially brewed prison wine from fruit and yeast and sugar. This is either dedication to a cause, a noble act of quiet rebellion, or an indication that a dude really needs a drink at the end of a Saudi Arabian workday.

Wright brewed out of Mary's Rec Room for years until they rebranded into Andersonville Brewing in 2014, in part to simply alert people that yes, the beer on tap is actually made there. Beers skew from a blonde ale for the lite-drinking portion of the audience, to a rotating IPA and seasonals like a peanut butter porter and a gluten-free rice beer.

The Hamburger Mary's team took their efforts a few miles west and opened a similar setup in Oak Park. The appropriately named Oak Park Brewing Company opened in March of 2016 alongside Hamburger Mary's, adding beers like the **Frank Lloyd Rye** to the rotation.

INDEPENDENT BREWPUBS

BURNT CITY BREWING COMPANY

2747 N. Lincoln Ave., Chicago, IL 60614; (773) 295-1270
Founded: 2012 (as Atlas Brewing), re-founded 2016 as Burnt City
Founders: John Saller, Ben Saller, Steve Soble (CEO/president), Greg
Lamacki (COO and co-founder) **Brewers:** John Saller, Ben Saller,
Christian Burd **Year-round beers:** Dick The Butcher Pale Ale, Face
Melter Hibiscus IPA, Balloon Boy Farmhouse Wheat, Retrofit Lime Radler
Tours: Yes **Hours:** Mon through Thurs, 5 to 11 p.m.; Fri, 5 p.m. to 2
a.m.; Sat, 12 p.m to 2 a.m.; Sun, 12 to 11 p.m.

It's hard not to like a brewery that names its beers after different kinds of dinosaurs and runs a facility attached to a bowling alley. Appropriately enough, Burnt City Brewing has a lot of fun doing what they do. Burnt City started their life as Atlas Brewing, a heritage brand revived from one of the turn-of-the-century Chicago breweries that didn't survive prohibition. Even though they've brought that brand back from the dead, it doesn't mean their beers are stuck in the past. Not even close.

Brothers Ben and John Saller are at the helm of the Burnt City ship; they helped open the brewpub on Lincoln Avenue in late 2012 and are the source of the widely varied and entertaining beers like **Archaeopteryx Dreamcoat, T-rex Hugs,** and **Nanosaurus Slumber Party.** Lest you think they're entirely dino-centric, they also have beers like the **Andromeda** milk stout and **Old Disheveler** barleywine . . . but let's not forget that they also host events like the Prehistoric Beer Prom with inflatable dinos.

The space is an updated tavern with decades-old Atlas advertisements lining the wall facing the bar, and the 7 bbl brewing system at the back of the room. The whole place connects to the Seven Ten Lounge, an eight-lane bowling alley with plenty of house-brewed beers on tap, along with a variety of guest handles (the brewpub side features only Burnt City beers). Early-week bowlers can often find the Illinois Craft Brewers Guild bowling league here battling for brewer bowling supremacy.

In 2015 they opened a production facility in a former Jay's potato chip factory, bringing one former Chicago icon into a space that housed another heritage brand. Cans of their **Diversey Pale Ale, Rookery Rye IPA,** and **Farmhouse Wheat** hit stores in July 2015, though a trademark dispute forced the change of Atlas to Burnt City in early 2016, allowing them to rebrand and expand their core line of beers.

BAND OF BOHEMIA

4710 N. Ravenswood Ave., Chicago, IL 60640; (773) 271-4710; bandofbohemia.com; @bandofbohemia
Founded: 2015 **Founders:** Michael Carroll and Craig Sindelar
Brewer: Michael Carroll **Year-round beer:** Culinary Noble **Seasonal beers:** Orange Chicory Rye, Roasted Beet Thyme, Persimmon Honey Biscuit **Tours:** No **Hours:** Tues through Fri, 4:30 p.m. to 12 a.m.; Sat, 11 to 12 a.m.; Sun, 11 a.m. to 2 p.m.

Very rarely does something come along in the brewery or restaurant world that can be considered "new." When two guys from the finest of Chicago's fine dining world get together and decide they're going to open a brewpub that offers culinary-inspired beers and elevated cuisine, that counts as new in my book. Band of Bohemia was announced in 2011, and finally opened their doors in November 2015, immediately adding a new level to the city's beer and dining landscape. The world's vaunted Michelin Guide apparently agrees with me. The brewpub was awarded a Michelin Star in 2016, about a year after opening—and is the only Michelin-starred brewpub in the world.

Michael Carroll and Craig Sindelar both spent time working at one of the world's greatest restaurants, Alinea, the three-Michelin-star juggernaut of innovative cuisine that brought the phrase "molecular gastronomy" to America's Hog Butcher to the World. Carroll worked front of house and also was the restaurant's first bread baker, while Sindelar served as sommellier. How do a baker and a wine guy end up opening a beer hall in one of the most-brewery-dense neighborhoods in Chicago? Well, Half Acre definitely helped.

After leaving Alinea, Carroll spent three years at Half Acre working with Phil Wymore (who went on to create the critically praised Perennial in St. Louis), with the intention of opening a place for creative beers with a menu to match. Sindelar and Carroll then spent the next few years finding a space and building it out, all while the world's mentality about beer caught up to their ideas. In 2011, a fine dining audience would have rebelled against a tasting menu without an $80 wine pairing; in 2015, the beer scene was ready for higher-end plates paired with avant-garde ales.

The restaurant/brewery (calling it a brewpub just doesn't seem to fit this place) features a huge open kitchen, a wood-fired grill for everything from roasted meats to fire-kissed ingredients for new beers, two bars, and a large high-ceilinged dining room that's not quite a beer hall, but closer to a really large brick-walled living room where fancy beers are made and poured. Also, this may be the only brewpub in the world with a kitchen that doesn't have a fryer.

The 10 bbl system pours five beers at a time from serving tanks directly behind the bar, with each beer matched to a specific piece of glassware. There's no lagers, no IPAs, no hoppy beers here—Carroll's beers are like dishes on a plate, except that one of the ingredients is beer—a beet and thyme ale may pair with salad and goat cheese, an orange, chicory and rye beer may pair with roasted lamb and root vegetables.

For those who don't feel like a beer, there's also wine and cocktails on hand, which is another interesting choice for a brewery to make. Most brewpubs open and serve only their beer, and maybe a couple guest handles; cocktail choices are often relegated to neat pours of a handful of brown spirits. There's also coffee service in the morning for commuters heading to the Metra station right across the street; It's a one-stop shop for train travelers who head to the Loop from the neighborhood. Wake up in the morning, dial back at night. It's as new an idea as it gets, but one thing remains the same—they want this to be a community hub, which is an idea as old as bierhalls.

CORRIDOR BREWERY & PROVISIONS

3446 N. Southport Ave., Chicago, IL 60657; (773) 270-4272; corridorchicago.com; @CorridorChicago
Founded: 2015 **Founders:** Greg Shuff **Brewers:** Brant Dubovick (head brewer) and Danny Monnot (lead brewer) **Flagship beer:** Wizard Fight, 7 percent Lactose IPA **Year-round beers:** Wizard Fight, 7 percent Lactose IPA **Tours:** No **Hours:** Mon, 11 a.m. to 11 p.m.; Tues to Fri, 11 to 12 a.m.; Sat, 10 to 12 a.m.; Sun, 10 a.m. to 11 p.m.

DRYHOP BREWERS

3155 N. Broadway, Chicago, IL 60657; (773) 857-3155; dryhopchicago.com; @Dryhopchicago
Founded: 2013 **Founder:** Greg Shuff **Brewers:** Brant Dubovick (head brewer) and Adrian Vidaurre (lead brewer) **Flagship beer:** Shark Meets Hipster, 6.5 percent Wheat IPA **Year-round beers:** Shark Meets Hipster, 6.5 percent Wheat IPA **Tours:** No **Hours:** Sun through Thurs, 11 to 12 a.m.; Fri and Sat, 11 to 2 a.m.

Corridor and DryHop are combined here because they share a few things in common: a Lakeview address, the ownership of Greg Shuff, and most notably, the beers of brewer Brant Dubovick. This burgeoning brewpub empire shows that just like there's no wrong way to open a brewery, there's also no wrong way to expand a brewery. (Except the ways that eventually lead to closing. That's a wrong way. But other than that . . .)

DryHop opened in June 2013, right in the midst of the huge brewery boom of 2013. It was the brewpub that Lakeview so desperately needed—they had lines down the block the first time they opened to sample beers and fill growlers, even before the kitchen was open. Their hop-friendly and easily drinkable beers with names like **Shark Meets Hipster** and **Head Full of Zombies** flowed freely.

The space was prime for Instagramming, with gleaming serving tanks behind the bar, the brewhouse behind glass facing it. Tiled floors bounced the voices of happy drinkers out the front façade, which opened up completely to the street; tables were set elbow to elbow and nearly always full. Just weeks after opening, word was already spreading that they were thinking of expanding.

DryHop could have contracted some beers to get onto store shelves, or built their own production facility a la Revolution, or broke through a few walls to add some square footage. Instead, they took the restauranteur's approach: if you've opened one good restaurant, don't open the same thing and make a chain. Open a different restaurant with a new concept. Shuff told the *Chicago Tribune*, "We like the idea of doing for craft beer what the great Chicago restaurant groups have done for the food scene...that was the model from the very beginning for me."

They found themselves a few blocks west on Southport Avenue, in a stretch of pavement called the Corridor (hence the name). Whereas other breweries tend to reside next to autobody shops and factories, Corridor counts yoga pants stores, boutique salons, and upscale restaurants as neighbors. Corridor's theme is farmhouse-style beers like saisons and biere de garde; Shuff was inspired by a trip to St. Louis's Midwest Belgian Beer festival.

Corridor opened its doors in October 2015 and the look is similar to those familiar with DryHop—gleaming fermenters and serving tanks, big open-front facade, plenty of brick. The food is paired appropriately to the farmhouse-style brews—instead of fries and burgers, think more rustic sandwiches and stews. Shuff's team plans more brewpubs in the future; every neighborhood should be so lucky to have them move in.

EATALY (LA BIRRERIA)

43 E. Ohio St., Chicago, IL 60611; (312) 521-8700; http://www.eataly.com/us_en/chicago-la-birreria/; @eataly
Founded: 2013 Founders: Mario Batali, Joe Bastianich, Sam Calagione, Teo Musso, Leonardo Di Vincenzo Brewer: Tyler Prokop Seasonal/rotating beers: Marrone Brown Ale, Birramisu Coffee Stout, Mandarina IPA, Go-Zeh Gose Tours: No Hours: Daily, 11 a.m. to 10 p.m.

The Birreria in Chicago's massive Eataly complex isn't so much a traditional brewpub as it is a large walk-in closet where you can drink beer and eat Italian food. But brewpub is the closest category we've got for it, so here we are. Opened in December 2013 along with the rest of the River North superstore, Birreria comes with the heritage of three internationally famous craft breweries—Delaware's Dogfish Head, Italy's Birra del Borgo, and Birreria La Baladin—baked in.

The seeds for Chicago's Birreria were planted in New York when chef Mario Batali and Joe Bastianich brought in brewer Sam Calagione to work alongside Italian brewmasters Teo Musso and Leonardo Di Vincenzo to create cask ales that pair with Eataly's menu. From that groupthink, New York gets a rooftop brewpub in the shadow of the Empire State Building with thyme-infused pale ales and peppercorn witbiers. Chicago has a corner overlooking a bunch of concrete. So it goes. At least we get the same beers.

Birrerra has a nice looking artisinal brewery, featuring a 7 bbl brewhouse and a few 15 bbl copper-clad fermenters behind glass. If you see brewer Tyler Prokop working on his newest project, try not to make him feel too much like a fish in a tank. Prokop started washing kegs and sweeping floors at New York's outpost and worked up from there. When Chicago came onto the horizon, he made the leap to brewer with Calagione's guidance. When Eataly opened the beers were very similar to existing beers at other outlets, but now that Prokop's been given a freer hand, brews like an oyster stout, a gose with grapefruit peel, and a coffee-infused porter are making their way into the world.

There are a number of places within a short walk that aren't slammed with tourists every hour of the weekend. However, between the house beers, the guest brews that skew large-local (Half Acre, Revolution, Three Floyds), and the prime rib sandwiches served just a few feet from the brewery's front door, you can put together quite the satisfying culinarily experience.

FORBIDDEN ROOT RESTAURANT & BREWERY

1746 W. Chicago Ave., Chicago, IL 60622; (312) 929-2202; forbiddenroot.com; @ForbiddenRoot
Founded: 2013, brewpub opened February 2016 **Founder:** Robert Finkel (also "rootmaster") **Brewers:** BJ Pichman (head brewer) and Nick Konwerski (assistant brewer) **Flagship beers:** Forbidden Root Beer, Sublime Ginger, Wildflower Pale Ale, Shady Character Porter **Tours:** Yes **Hours:** Mon through Sat, 4 p.m. to 12 a.m.

Introducing the world to "botanic beers" isn't an easy sell, but the uniquely flavored, spiced, and fruited beers of Forbidden Root became a part of the Chicagoland brewery landscape almost immediately after their initial package release. They've been operating since 2013 in a rather mysterious manner, rolling out slowly and popping up periodically at a few festivals to start. Once bottled, their food-friendly **Forbidden Root** brew and **Sublime Ginger** found their way onto beer lists and restaurant menus around town.

While the core beers are produced out of the 5 Rabbit facility (beer author/recipe formulator/consultant/artist/guru Randy Mosher has a stake in both breweries), their flagship brewpub opened in 2016 after many years of planning and community outreach in an airy former theater space. Working on a 15 bbl system with a custom-crafted "infuser" to help bring the most out of the many varied and rare spices, Pichman was finally allowed to unleash some new and interesting brews.

While Forbidden Root's core array of beers didn't change much since hitting the scene three years prior, the brewpub finally allowed the city to get a taste of their other thoughtful and creative beers, like a cherry-stem amaro brew, a celery radler, and a beer inspired by a gin-and-juice cocktail, paired with menu items like malted hangar steak made with a toasted beer malt rub. If you want a beer you've not even considered before made with ingredients you've likely not heard of let alone considered in a fermented beverage, Forbidden Root is your place.

GINO'S EAST RIVER NORTH / GINO'S BREWING COMPANY

500 N. Lasalle St., Chicago, IL 60654; (312) 988-4200; ginoseast.com; @ginoseast
Founded: 2014 **Brewer:** Kevin McMahon **Year-round beers:** Lasalle St. Lager, Witte Chicks Dig Me, Broken English ESB **Tours:** No **Hours:** Sun through Thurs, 11 a.m. to 10 p.m.; Fri and Sat, 11 a.m. to 11 p.m.

Pizza and beer is such a drop-dead perfect pairing that it's hard to believe it took as long as it did for someone (other than the Piece Brewery team, of course) to pick up on the genius of it. Even considering Piece, they're focused on New Haven–style pizza—life without a Chicago deep-dish pizzeria serving its own beers alongside their pies is just strange to consider. And yet, that was the reality before Gino's East opened their brewery in River North, a couple blocks from the Merchandise Mart.

Finally, in late 2014, there existed an option for classic Chicago deep dish and nice, fresh ale made on site. Plunked into a former nightclub space on the west edges of River North, this Gino's is a far cry from the inked up, graffitti'd, and carved-on space that most longtime Chicagoans would recognize. But the dark booths, tile floors, soaring bar, and glassed-in brewing facility are probably a little more conducive to making nice, clean beers.

It would have been easy to get a small brewery up and running and pound out the expected crowd-friendly gamut of beers—an average amber ale, a middle-of-the-road pale ale, and so on. Instead, Gino's opened with a lineup of some interesting, pizza-friendly brews. The English-style bitter is happily traditional with rich malts and herbal hops, and don't forget the nicely roasty black rye IPA.

True to the collaborative and open-door-policy brewing community, Gino's also creates specialty and one-off beers with the brewers of the CHAOS homebrew club, allowing pro-am brewers to get their beers made on a large scale and in front of a larger audience. Growlers are available to take offsite, and Gino's is one of the few places allowed to pour into 64-ounce containers in the area, making this a really nice option for folks staying in the many nearby hotels.

GOOSE ISLAND CLYBOURN

1800 N. Clybourn Ave., Chicago, IL 60614; (312) 915-0071;
gooseislandbrewpubs.com
Founded: 1988 **Founder:** John Hall **Pub Brewer:** Jon Naghski
Flagship beers: Honkers, 312, Bourbon County Stout **Tours:** Yes
Hours: Sun through Wed, 11 a.m. to 10 p.m.; Thurs through Sat, 11 a.m. to 11 p.m.

If you want to visit the place where Chicago's craft brewing renaissance really started, step inside the doors of the Goose Island Clybourn brewpub, located in a strip-mall-y brick building just off a major Lincoln Park thoroughfare. Within the walls of the Goose Island Clybourn brewpub the craft beer world was changed forever—**Bourbon County Stout** first saw the light of day here, it was here that **312** began its march to nationwide distribution and **Honkers Ale** had its heyday as the city's most recognizable craft beer.

In 1988 John Hall opened the Goose Island brewpub after reading a Delta Sky in-flight magazine article about the growth of "boutique beers." He walked away from a two-decade career with the Container Corporation, and opened his brewpub with a handful of beers available. And so, one of the largest craft beer brands in the nation was born.

Nowadays there are two dozen beers on draft, including mainstays like the **IPA** and **312,** but often extremely innovative and creative brews that never see the light of day outside the brewpub's walls, save for the occasional beer fest. The small batches made in the brewhouse allow for a wide swath of styles to be on hand, so you never know what kind of beers may be available; there's often Belgian styles, stouts, English milds, a selection of hoppy pale ales, and the occasional sour.

Throughout the years many talented brewers have passed through the doors of the Goose brewpub. Original brewer Greg Hall moved on to create Virtue Cider in Michigan; longtime pub brewmaster Jared Rouben left to create his Moody Tongue Brewing Company in Pilsen; Josh Deth served as brewer here before creating Revolution; and Motor Row's Frank Lassandrello started his whole career here, pulling beers behind the bar.

An issue with the landlord threatened the brewpub with relocating or closing in 2008. A few years later a similar issue arose and Clybourn nearly closed near the end of 2013, shortly after the pub's twenty-fifth anniversary. Things were looking dire with the leasing agent going as far as offering to help them find a new space. Thankfully, things were sorted out and the Clybourn brewpub survives to this day.

Since the Anheuser-Busch takeover of the main brewery in 2010 did not include the brewpubs, the brewpub spent a few years needing to purchase things like **Honkers, 312,** and **IPA** from the Bud-owned brewery. These beers are made now in places like Baldwinsville, New York and Fort Collins, Colorado. However, in February of 2015, Anheuser-Busch and Goose Island announced that the brewpub's ownership would be transferred to A-B, which would convert it into a taproom to bring it into line with the state's laws about brewery ownership. (Basically, it means no more wine or spirits—only Goose beers—will pour at Clybourn.)

The Wrigleyville location doesn't have as happy of an ending—the Goose team announced it was closing for good in 2014 . . . and then announced a brief reprieve for the 2015 Cubs season. One more year of Cubby Blue beer was poured before shuttering the location again at the end of the season, which for once made it to October. It was a great place to escape the Bud Light–fueled throngs before and after a game, but a lack of off-season traffic was just too much for the large space to absorb.

Still, stop in the Clybourn space on any night of the week (after a stop at the Marcey Street Binny's just a block away, perhaps) and you can still find dozens of folks enjoying the humble pub that has provided enjoyment and beer enlightenment for thousands of Chicagoans over the decades.

(For more on the story behind Goose Island, see our Q&A with founder John Hall on page 106.)

GREENSTAR BREWING ORGANIC BREWERY / UNCOMMON GROUND

3800 N. Clark St., Chicago, IL 60613; (773) 929-3680; uncommonground.com/greenstar-brewing; @uncommongrd **Founded:** 2014 **Founder:** Michael Cameron **Brewer:** Martin Coad **Seasonal/rotating beers:** Spaceship IPA, Certifiable APA, Mixmaster Mocha Porter **Tours:** Yes **Taproom:** Yes **Hours:** Sun, 9 a.m. to 9 p.m.; Mon through Thurs, 11 a.m. to 10 p.m.; Fri, 11 a.m. to 11 p.m.; Sat, 9 a.m. to 11 p.m.

For years, the Uncommon Ground pair of restaurants built a reputation of ethically sourced food before farm-to-table was cool. They use solar panels and organic ingredients, including herbs and produce grown on their rooftop farm; they have beehives for honey farmed onsite. It should have been no surprise to anyone that they created the first organically certified brewery in the state. It's also one of a handful in the country.

They use organic malts and organic hops (which limits the varieties they can use; hopheads be forewarned). Their yeasts come from Chicago's Omega Yeast Labs and everything is non-GMO. Recipes are bolstered by ingredients from the aforementioned rooftop garden, including coriander and berries for their smooth, flavorful black currant kolsch. The organic rules force them to get a little creative with their beers; most of the organic hops in the world are Cascades, and per the *Chicago Reader*, "organic standards forbid [Greenstar] from adjusting the pH of [the] water with phosphoric acid, which many brewers use, so he relies on lactic acid instead."

Owner Michael Cameron had wanted a brewery to be part of his operation for a long time. It wasn't until they could secure a 1,200-square-foot space next to the restaurant that Greenstar came into being. The 7 bbl brewhouse lives at their Clark Street location, so if you're looking for the closest brewery to Wrigley Field, you can find it a couple blocks north (assuming Goose Island Wrigleyville doesn't magically reappear). Greenstar's beers can be found there and at the Edgewater UG location, in addition to guest handles from other local breweries.

HAYMARKET PUB & BREWERY

737 W. Randolph Ave., Chicago IL 60661; (312) 638-0700; haymarketbrewing.com
Founded: 2010 **Founders:** Peter Crowley and John Neurauter
Brewers: Peter Crowley (head brewer), Eric Morrissey (assistant brewer), and Trevor Hagen (assistant brewer) **Flagship beer:** Speakerswagon® Pilsner **Year-round beers:** Speakerswagon® Pilsner, Mathias® Imperial I.P.A., Oscar's Pardon Belgian Pale, Aleister American I.P.A.
Seasonal beers: Indignant® Imperial Stout aged in bourbon barrels, Last Change Belgo-American I.P.A., Defender American Stout, Clare's Thirsty Imperial Stout aged in bourbon barrels with raspberries
Tours: Yes, Sundays at 12, 2, and 4 p.m. **Hours:** Sun through Friday, 11 to 2 a.m.; Sat, 11 to 3 a.m.

The closer you get to downtown, the less likely you are to find a haven of great, fresh beers. The exception that proves that rule is the Haymarket brewpub, perched precariously between the frantic Loop and the uber-hip restaurant row that is Randolph and Fulton Market just across Halsted and beyond. Owner/brewer Pete Crowley has carved out a little oasis for beer, but his influence goes a lot further than just a brewery near downtown.

Crowley had a ton of experience before opening Haymarket—he spent years keeping Chicago's location of the Rock Bottom chain a step above the rest, and before that plied his trade at a few other Rock Bottoms after a start at the Flying Dog brewpub in Colorado. When setting out on his own, the space near Haymarket Square (of Haymarket Riot infamy) called his name. He told the *Chicago Reader* in 2010, "It just clicked . . .

The history of the square is so rich that it really made the location and the space fit perfectly."

Haymarket is home to dozens of beers brewed onsite as well as a number of guest handles, most notable being the **Defender American Stout.** Brewed roasty, hoppy, and strong, it's a wallop of flavor packed into a reasonable 7.5 percent ABV; it's also one of the world's best beers, winning gold at the World Beer Cup and another gold medal at the Great American Beer Fest nearly back to back. Another reliable part of the Haymarket stable is the **Matthias IIPA,** named for the first Chicago police officer to lose his life at the Haymarket Riot.

Perhaps more impressive than Crowley's beers is the culture he's helped foster throughout the burgeoning years of craft beer growth in Chicago. For years Crowley served as president of the Illinois Craft Brewers Guild, helping build events like FoBAB and Beer Under Glass into top-tier, must-attend annual events that also help fund the organization. He's also helped many a brewer with their own dreams; at least one Chicago brewer calls Crowley their "godfather."

Due to the limitations of being a brewpub, it's hard to get beer beyond the front door, and other newer breweries quickly leapfrogged Haymarket in terms of pure reach, if not status. That was amended in December 2016 when Crowley began brewing at a production facility in Southwest Michigan, where beers will be brewed on a much larger scale than a corner in Chicago will allow. It'll be hard to think of Haymarket as anything other than pure Chicago, though.

HOPVINE BREWING COMPANY

4030 Fox Valley Center Dr., Aurora, IL 60504; (630) 229-6030; hopvinebrewingcompany.com @HopvineBrewing Founded: 2013 **Founders:** Jan and Doug Isley **Brewer:** Ken McMullen **Seasonal/rotating beers:** Mastodon IPA, Brewdacious Blonde, Ruffled Feathers Hoppy American Brown Ale, Aurora Amber **Tours:** Yes **Taproom Hours:** Tues through Weds, 11 a.m. to 11 p.m.; Thurs through Sat, 11 to 12 a.m.; Sun, 11 a.m. to 10 p.m.

Doug Isley and his wife, Jan, like to say the idea to start Hopvine was divine intervention. "We got the idea from talking with [brewmaster] Ken [McMullen] after church," Doug explains. This brewpub housed in a former Enchanted Castle on the outskirts of the Fox Valley Mall isn't quite the same as a house of worship, but you get a certain sense of reverence nevertheless.

Hopvine opened in October 2013 and added a true independent brewpub to the Fox Valley area—other chain options like Gordon Biersch and Rock Bottom are scattered throughout the 'burbs, but Hopvine flies solo. McMullen, who worked just down the road at the former Limestone Brewing Company in Plainfield and the Temecula Brewing Company before that, crafts beers on a 7 bbl system and cranks out about 700 barrels per year of beers that vary from Belgian-style tripels to Russian imperials to a series of **Alpha Mastodon** IPAs with a rotating featured hop.

As a true brewpub with wine and spirits available, Hopvine can also have guest handles, which typically feature other local independent breweries like Flesk, Urban Legend, and Church Street—the biggest brewer you're likely to find is Two Brothers. A full restaurant with menu items like poutine, poblano corn fritters, and a smoked potato with pulled pork is on hand as well. In warmer weather there's a 5,000-square-foot "hopyard," where they are growing their own hops for brewing.

A small pilot system offsite or a tasting room might be in the cards down the road, but for now, other than beer festivals, onsite at Hopvine is the only place you'll be able to try their brews.

HORSE THIEF HOLLOW

10426 S. Western Ave., Chicago, IL 60643; (773) 779-2739; horsethiefbrewing.com; @HTHollow
Founded: 2012 **Founder:** Neil Byers **Brewer:** David Williams **Flagship beer:** Annexation Ale **Year-round beers:** 18th Rebellion, Kitchen Sink, Annexation, Hollow Grounds **Seasonal beers:** Black Currant Milk Stout, Pomegranate Cherry Wheat, Citra Hefeweizen, Sweet Potato Bier De Garde, Peppermint Mocha Cream Stout **Tours:** Yes **Taproom Hours:** Sun through Thurs, 11:30 a.m. to 10 p.m.; Fri and Sat, 11:30 to 12 a.m.

For a very long time, the South Side and far south border neighborhoods were bypassed by the craft beer revolution. The one major South Side brewery for a long time, Argus, was founded in 2009, a little too early and too far away from many folks to really get into the mix with the likes of Half Acre and Metropolitan. There's still a goodish way to go to match the density of the North Side, but Horse Thief Hollow, a brewpub on the main drag of Beverly, has tried to change that.

Housed in a former carpet store on Western Avenue, the brewpub resembles a house of worship more than a House of Rugs. The vaulted wooden ceilings lead down to bright white walls, which contributes to a Germanic bierhall feel; the carved wooden doors with leaded glass evoke the entrance to a Belgian monastery (which certainly doesn't hurt the vibe for beer lovers).

The menu is southern-style with barbecue smoked in-house, shrimp po'boys, and a riff on a downstate Illinois classic, the Springfield specialty horseshoe sandwich. With their taphandles emblazoned with horseshoes themselves, it's a perfect pairing. Flagship beers include the **773** stout (which also makes its way into their barbecue sauce), the **Black Sox** black IPA, **18th Rebellion** kolsch, and the **Annexation IPA.**

Named for the reputation once held by the Beverly neighborhood—it used to be a haven for those prone to fits of equestrian burglarizing—Horse Thief Hollow is more than in the neighborhood, it is of the neighborhood. They support the local Beverly Arts Center with the art on their walls, they use local vendors as part of their menu, and a local coffee roaster just over a mile north makes their coffee beans.

They even helped raise a cow on spent grain from the brewery . . . which then became part of the menu, after they purchased it back from a Chicago agricultural school. It's these things that helped owner Neil Byers earn a citywide leadership award in 2015, with a $25,000 check attached to it. (The prize money immediately went back into expanding the brewery and investing in some more experimental beers.)

This local-first, small-batch approach to things has paid off for the brewpub. In their short history they've taken home medals from the GABF (bronze in 2014 for their **Kellerbier** and bronze in 2016 for their **Prunkel's Dunkel** dark lager) and the World Beer Cup (silver in 2014 for a sweet potato ale).

THE LUCKY MONK

105 Hollywood Blvd., Barrington, IL 60010; (847) 898-0500; theluckymonk.com; @luckymonk
Founded: 2009 **Founders:** Jeremy Samatas and Phil Thiem **Brewer:** Anthony Carollo **Flagship beer:** Fallen Angel Vienna-Style Lager **Year-round beers:** Fallen Angel (Vienna Style Lager), Confessional IPA (IPA), Cardinal Sin (Pilsner), Tritica Wheat (Weiss), and Solitude Stout (Oatmeal Stout) **Seasonal beers:** Oktoberfest Lager, Maibock, Executioner's Stout, Seasonal Barrel Aged Release, Gr'ale (Belgian Abbey Beer), Kolsh, Pal's Porter **Tours:** Yes **Hours:** Sun through Thurs, 11 a.m. to 11 p.m.; Fri and Sat, 11 to 1 a.m.

There seems to be a theme in the suburbs—find a movie theater, throw a chain-style brewpub in near it, pack the menu with burgers and pizzas, and off you go. You can see it in the Warrenville Rock Bottom near the Regal Cantera 30, which has been serving their beers to west suburbanites for many a year, along with the iPic in Bolingbrook near Gordon Biersch. That same strand of DNA weaves its way through the Lucky Monk in Barrington, just steps from the AMC 30 Barrington. (Is it any wonder movie theaters finally got wise and started serving beer in the theaters?)

Opened at the very end of 2009 just minutes north of I-90, the brewpub is named for the trappist monks of Belgium and beyond who have made brewing beers a centuries-long tradition. The Lucky Monk works from a 10 bbl system and serves up the standard gamut of brewpub beers—an amber, a pilsner, an oatmeal stout, an IPA, a weiss. Seasonal brews mix things up a bit for the nerdier palate; saisons, marzens, barrel-aged brews, and malty maibocks make their way into the rotation. Food is praised as highly as the beers; the burgers are served on a cutting board that essentially seats them on their own throne.

MICKEY FINN'S

345 N. Milwaukee Ave., Libertyville, IL 60048; (847) 362-6688; mickeyfinnsbrewery.com; @mickeyfinns
Founded: 1980 as a bar/restaurant, 1994 as a brewpub **Owner:** Brian Grano **Brewer:** Greg Browne **Flagship beer:** 847 Suburban Wheat **Seasonal beers:** Dog Days of Summer, Helles Bells, Marzen Madness, Santa's Magic **Hours:** Tues through Thurs, 11 a.m. to 11:30 p.m.; Fri through Sat, 11 a.m. to 1:15 a.m.; Sun 11 a.m. to 9 p.m.; Mon closed.

The oldest brewpub in Lake County (and one of the oldest in the state), Mickey Finn's opened in 1980 and started serving its own beers in 1994. Brian Grano took ownership in 2004 and expanded the business to a new location in 2015 just up Milwaukee Avenue. Featuring an arched wooden roof, a 60-foot bar, and twenty-six gleaming taps for all that house-made beer, it's an impressive space to showcase what fresh local beer can do through the years.

The brewers of Mickey Finn's got off to a fast start once they began brewing in the mid-'90s, taking bronze at GABF for their German-style Wheat Ale in 1996, silver in the Scotch Strong Ale category in 1997, and both gold and silver in 1998 for beers in the same category, again, German-style Wheat. For a pub named after an Irishman, these guys had a good run on some very un-Guinness-y brews.

Current beers from brewmaster Greg Browne include the flagship **847 Suburban Wheat Ale** (perhaps the most satirical beer name in Chicagoland), the **Amber Ale** (also in cans), and the low-ABV **Sesh** session pale ale brewed with a rotating feature hop and a variety of seasonals, the most popular of which is the **Santa's Magic** spiced up Belgian strong ale.

MOXEE KITCHEN / MAD MOUSE BREWERY

724 W. Maxwell St., Chicago, IL 60607; (312) 243-3660;
moxeerestaurant.com; @Moxee_MadMouse,
@MadMouseBrew
Founded: 2014 Founders: Rob Strom, Gavin Gillian, Phil Zelewsky
Brewer: Phil Zelewsky Flagship beer: Schnickelfritz Kolsch,
Rathmandu Pale Ale Seasonal beers: Backyard Harvest Pale Ale,
Hippie Johnny Cream Ale Hours: Tues through Sat, 11:30 to 1 a.m.; Sun,
10 a.m. to 10 p.m.

The alliterative Moxee Kitchen and Mad Mouse Brewery on Maxwell Street comes from the ownership team behind the beer-friendly Prairie Moon restaurant in Evanston and the Wheatberry Tavern in Buchanan, Michigan. A brewpub was the next natural step for the group, and had been on their to-do list for some time when the space on Maxwell made itself available. They opened in June 2014.

Brewer Phil Zelewsky has about twenty-five years of homebrewing experience, helped build the beer program at Prairie Moon ("I used to joke we had the best beer between Hopleaf and the Wisconsin state line," he says), and helped start a homebrew club out of Prairie Moon, which helped spawn places like Temperance, Sketchbook, and the Smylie Bros. brewpub.

The brewery is a small 3.5 bbl system, which they double-batch into a few 7 bbl fermenters, and skip the kegs to pour from serving tanks. The twenty-four taps behind the bar provide their in-house brews as well as a selection of smaller, local craft options from around the midwest like DryHop and One Trick Pony. Rather than just serve house beers, like some brewpubs opt to do, Zelewsky is happy to showcase the efforts of other brewers as well. "Beer is wonderful and I like to think that I really brew good beer, but I also would never pretend that all I want to drink is my own beer. There's too many great breweries out there to really limit one's self to just one product from one brewery. I like to think my customers feel the same."

What's with the double name, you ask? The intent is to open a separate production facility down the road for the Mad Mouse beer brand while Moxee is its own restaurant, serving a variety of barbecue (including house-smoked pastrami) and Southern-style cajun dishes. The restaurant's name comes from Moxee city in Washington's Yakima valley, home to about 75 percent of the nation's hop trade, while Mad Mouse comes from "the fact that we're so damn small" along with Zelewsky's business partners' mild accusations that he's "a bit of a mad scientist," he explains.

Mad Mouse's main flagships are their **Schnickelfritz** kolsch and the **Rathmandu** pale ale, which they go through so quickly they actually "gypsy" brew them at Michigan's Saugatuck Brewery. Thanks to an arrangement to use some of their fermenter space, Mad Mouse is able to keep up with demand while brewing the smaller experimental beers on site, though the plan to bring all beers back under one roof is part of the long game. The rest of their beers, including the **Hippie Johnny** cream ale and the **Backyard Harvest** pale ale using locally grown Cascade hops from a friend's yard in nearby McKinley Park, round out the selection. Mad Mouse is draft-only, but growlers are available to go.

NEVIN'S BREWING COMPANY

12337 S. Route 59, Plainfield, IL; (815) 436-3900; nevinsbrewing.com; @nevinsbrewing
Founded: 2012 **Brewers:** Marc Wilson (head brewer), Cory Davidson (assistant brewer) **Flagship beers:** Kookie Monster (Bourbon-barrel aged Russian imperial Stout w/ Chocolate Wafer cookies) **Year-round beers:** Pilsner, Quick Witted (Belgian-Style Witbier), Hook & Hatchet (Vienna-style Lager), Southside Stout (Oatmeal Stout on Nitro), & IPA **Seasonal beers:** Wishful Thinking (Belgian-Style Quad - Fall/Winter), Zicke Zacke (Traditional Marzen - Fall) **Tours:** Yes **Taproom Hours:** Closed Mon; Tues through Thurs, 3 p.m. to 12 p.m.; Fri, 3 p.m. to 2 a.m.; Sat, 11:30 a.m. to 2 a.m.; Sun, 11:30 a.m. to 10 p.m.

Just a little south of the sprawling conglomorate of big box stores, strip malls, chain restaurants, retail spaces, car dealerships, and the Fox Valley shopping mall, sits an unassuming little spot that's been churning out its own brews since February 2013. An extension of the Tommy Nevin's line of pubs with locations in Naperville (just under 3 miles north) as well as Evanston and Frankfort, this spot sits on the former site of the Limestone Brewing Company.

Around a dozen house beers are usually available on tap from brewmaster Marc Wilson, including reliable offerings like the **Southside Stout,** the **Contentious** Belgian-style IPA (also their first beer brewed) and **YOLO!,** a light, easy drinking blonde ale that certainly has discerning Napervillians hollering its name regularly on the weekends. Guest handles from brewers around the midwest include breweries like Revolution, Boulevard, and Two Brothers.

In addition to regular live music (if you've ever wanted to drink at a brewpub that's hosted a Vanilla Ice show, Nevin's is your place) they also host events like their annual 21 Beer Salute, with one-off specialty beers flavored with all manner of things like donuts, Oreo cookies, or pineapple released every twenty minutes or so; they also host a similar OneDer event where other breweries can introduce their one-off beers to the public.

PECKISH PIG

623 Howard St., Evanston, IL 60202; (847) 491-6778;
thepeckishpig.com; @PeckishPig
Founded: 2014 **Founders:** Debbie and Jamie Evans and Tom Fogarty
Brewer: Tom Fogarty (brewmaster), Eric Plata (assistant) **Seasonal/
rotating beers:** Fogarty's Garage American Wheat, Gobsmacked
Kolsch, Purely Medicinal Porter, Solstice Spice, Toffeenose IPA **Tours:**
Yes **Hours:** Tues through Thurs, 4 to 11 p.m.; Fri, 4 p.m. to 12 a.m.; Sat,
11 to 12 a.m.; Sun, 11 a.m. to 10 p.m.

This brewpub, just a few feet inside the Evanston border, sprang up in March 2014 and is the city's first official brewpub. Peckish Pig is part of the Evanston brewing renaissance, which had an extremely busy twelve months—first Temperance kicked off in December 2013, followed by Peckish Pig, and then Smylie Bros. in June. Sketchbook opened nearly a year later in November 2014, marking the busiest twelve months in Evanston's alcohol history for about a century.

Opened by the same family that opened the Celtic Knot Public House, Peckish Pig has co-owner Debbie Evans, who also worked in the kitchen at the nearby Tommy Nevins location. You'd be within your rights to expect some fish and chips and a proper fryup at breakfast, but the menu goes deeper than that—think gastropubby options like an open-faced roast duck sandwich and short rib ragu tacos.

As for the beer, brewer Tom Fogarty works on a 3.5 bbl system with a couple 7 bbl fermenters to turn out beers like the **Purely Medicinal Porter,** the **Scallywag Pilsner** made with flaked corn, and the **Fogarty's Garage American** wheat. In addition to finally offering the city a place for a meal and a beer brewed onsite, they also host a number of guest handles for other nearby brewers including Temperance, Begyle, and Penrose.

PIECE PIZZERIA & BREWERY

1927 W. North Ave., Chicago, IL 60622; (773) 722-4422; piecechicago.com; @piecechicago
Founded: 2001 Founder: Bill Jacobs Brewer: Jonathan Cutler
Flagship beers: The Weight APA, Dark & Curvy Dunkelweizen
Seasonal/rotating beers: Swingin' Single, Golden Arm Kolsch, Top Heavy Hefeweizen Tours: No Hours: Mon through Weds, 11 a.m. to 10:30 p.m.; Thurs, 11 a.m. to 11 p.m.; Fri and Sat, 11 a.m. to 12:30 p.m.; Sun, 11 a.m. to 10 p.m.

In many ways, Piece has flown under the radar of the craft beer masses. They've been making and pouring their beers out of their Wicker Park brewpub since way back in 2001, when there was still some lingering alt-rock grit to the neighborhood. If they opened within the last three years, people would be falling all over themselves to proclaim it one of the best places in town.

And yet, Piece just keeps doing what they do—making award-winning beers and serving New Haven–style pizza. It's a formula that needs no adjustments. Good luck finding another place like Piece—it's been named a World Beer Cup champion brewery, Independent Pizzeria of the Year, and is partly owned by a rock star (Cheap Trick's Rick Nielsen). As much as we love our Chicago pizzerias, none of them have this kind of cred.

Brewmaster Jonathan Cutler has been at the helm of the 7 bbl system since the get-go, and although he basically had the benefit of having the craft beer market to himself for most of Piece's existence, they've won medals for their beers at the World Beer Cup and the Great American Beer Fest as recently as 2015 for a variety of beers. Their award-winning American Pale Ale, **The Weight,** is reliably on tap; they also excel at German styles. If they have their hefeweizen or their dunkelweizen on hand, get it.

The pizza, as we mentioned, is not part of the eternal battle between Chicago-style and everything else—it's New Haven–style through and through, wholly foreign to most local palates and characterized by a thin, malty odd-shaped oblong crust topped with olive oil or just red sauce without cheese. Toppings run the gamut from the standard pepperoni and sausage to apples, mashed potatoes, or "atomic sausage" provided by local encased-meats hero, Hot Doug. It's damn hard to pass up anything called chocolate pizza for dessert, topped with chocolate-hazelnut sauce and mascarpone cheese.

Be warned—as they've been earning their fan base one pizza and pitcher at a time for well over a decade, waits can be long and reservations are not taken for small groups. Pop in for a few beers and a bite and if it's a madhouse (or if live-band karaoke is crushing your eardrums), avail yourself of one of the many other bars in the nearby area.

REVOLUTION BREWING (BREWPUB LOCATION)

2323 N. Milwaukee Ave.; Chicago, IL 60647; (773) 227-2739; revbrew.com/brewpub; @RevBrewChicago
Founded: 2010 Founder: Josh Deth Brewer: Wil Turner Flagship beer: Anti-Hero IPA Hours: Mon through Fri, 11 to 1 a.m.; Sat and Sun, 10 to 1 a.m.

If you want to see where craft beer in Chicago really kicked into high gear, walk into Revolution and order yourself an **Anti-Hero** while you marvel at the surroundings. There were a handful of great breweries in Chicago before Revolution, but the team at RevBrew hit the ground running in 2010 and have hardly looked back. Their aggressive but accessible beers, marked by a "political socialism with a healthy dose of irreverent fun vibe," quickly made them the largest independent craft brewery in Chicago.

The space itself is beautiful—a massive wooden bar dominates the room with carved fists holding aloft the "ceiling" of the structure. Sixteen taps pour Rev brews from their iconic fist-upraised taphandles, from flagships like **Bottoms Up Wit** and **Eugene Porter** to brewpub-only small batch brews like barleywines, herbed and spiced ales, and probably the next big pale ale Chicago will fall in love with.

The rest of the room features huge high ceilings that illuminate a beer-hall type room with a view into the kitchen and the brewing area. The menu offers traditional American bar food that's neither too fancy nor too basic—it's in the Goldilocks zone of elevated, but not priced to match. Think bacon-fat popcorn, smoked chicken wings, and always a selection of vegetarian/vegan options.

Upstairs, a private bar and meeting space is one of the best places to get married in the city. (I've been lucky enough to witness one; it's great.) Riding in on two wheels? You're in luck, preferred bike parking on their own rack is right outside the front door. They pack a lot into a small space. So much so that Rev quickly outgrew the brewpub and moved the bulk of their production to their brewery on Kedzie in May 2012.

That huge production facility (see page 26) is where most of the action happens these days, with a massive field of fermenters and a canning line that used to belong to the RC Cola company. This brewpub, though, is not just a place where beers are made and meals are consumed, it's an anchor for a neighborhood that didn't begin emerging until RevBrew opened its doors. Join them for a meal and a few pints and keep the party—and the Party—going.

SMYLIE BROTHERS BREWING COMPANY

1615 Oak Ave., Evanston, IL 60201; (224) 999-7320; smyliebros.com; @SmylieBros
Founded: 2014 **Founder:** Mike Smylie **Brewer:** Brad Pulver **Year-round beers:** Cali Common, Farmhouse, IPA, Pale Ale **Seasonal/rotating beers:** Purple Line Hefeweizen, Irish Red Rye, Midnight Wheat **Tours:** Yes **Hours:** Sun through Thurs, 11 a.m. to 9 p.m.; Fri and Sat, 11 a.m. to 10 p.m.

Similar to the Gino's East plan of pairing freshly brewed beer with a pizza restaurant, Smylie Brothers combines barbecue and beer. It's a little astonishing that no one in town tried it until this space came along. Opened in June 2014, this brewpub added some much-needed taphandles for house beers and guest drafts to downtown Evanston.

The brewpub, helmed by longtime homebrewer and owner Mike Smylie and head brewer Brad Pulver, churns out beers on a 10 bbl system that range from mild to wild for all kinds of beer drinkers. Brews like a house pale ale and a weissbeer share tap space with beers like a coffee-infused **California Common,** a double dryhopped IPA, and a traditional steinbier brewed with real rocks heated over an open fire.

Many brewpubs seem to value beer as an accompaniment to the food, but Pulver's background working at Michigan's Arcadia Brewing ensures that the beers come with a strong heritage of beermaking experience; their **Purple Line** fruit wheat beer took bronze at the 2015 GABF. In addition to the housemade beers, there are also brews from locals like Tighthead, Miskatonic, and Half Acre.

The barbecue-centric menu features sandwiches and pizzas; if you thought Kaiser Tiger and Paddy Longs were the only ones able to make a bacon sausage you might be surprised to find a bacon hot link smoked and served with homemade sauerkraut here (fermenting apparently extends to cabbage in addition to wort.)

Contract and Alternating Proprietorship Brewers

Even though contract brewing has helped countless breweries get off the ground, the practice still has a bit of a nasty connotation to it, and depending on who you ask, it's an outright sin. For many, it's one thing to open up your own brewery, sign your name to a long lease and get down to work shoveling grain and cleaning stainless. Paying someone else to work on their system can be seen as an easy way into the beer industry—you start making money, you get to build your brand, but you don't have to jump through as many of the governmental and financial hoops along the way.

But consider the other side of the coin. Half Acre famously started brewing their lager on contract, which led to their now-dominant lineup of awesome beers; this alone should earn contracting a pass from most people. 5 Rabbit started brewing on contract as well, and shortly thereafter earned some GABF hardware for their **5 Lizard** beer. Good things can be done in the realm of contract.

Another solution is an alternating proprietorship, where you get to maintain some space in someone else's already-existing brewery but you do the work on their system. Many breweries contract or alt-prop to start getting their name out there while finding a spot for their own brewery, which is probably the best case scenario.

For an increasing number of brewers, contracting allows them to add capacity and keep up with demand when they're otherwise unable to add square footage to their brewery or drop in a few more dozen fermenters. And yes, there are others out there happy to simply send a recipe off to a contract facility and pick it up when it's ready.

Some of these contract/alt-prop breweries have been covered more thoroughly elsewhere in this book because they've got a cool story, they're an impassioned part of the beer community, or they're well on their way to owning their own space. For the sake of completeness of the record, I wanted to include here the wide array of folks putting beer on the shelves, even if they haven't written a check for their own stainless yet.

51ST WARD

www.facebook.com/51stWardBrewing

Owner and brewer Tim Hoerman started out at Westmont's Myths and Legends (originally Urban Legend) but parted ways to start this brewing company on the hunt for its own distinctive space for a brewery. They're currently turning out a variety of different beers like their award-winning flagship **Krispy Karl** stout.

AROUND THE BEND

atbbeerco.com

Launched in May 2015 by owner Dan Schedler, a homebrewer for two decades, with initial offerings of a kolsch and an impressive pale ale flavored with ginger-like galangal root. ATB operates as an alt-prop out of the Burnt City production space with plans to open their own brewery.

BANGING GAVEL

bangingavel.com

Brewmaster Walter Ornelas, along with co-founders/beer lovers Jim and Ed Richert, kicked off Banging Gavel in May 2014 and followed up with a Kickstarter campaign in June to keep things rolling. Beers include the **Chicanery RIS** and **La Ley,** a fruit beer with mango and peppers.

BERGHOFF BEER

berghoffbeer.com

Berghoff's origins as a beer company date back to the late 1800s, and their role as a storied beerhall in downtown Chicago goes back even further. Berghoff beers had devolved to a boring set of basic beers when Ben Minkoff revived the brand in June 2013. Minkoff worked with beer experts like author Randy Mosher and brewing consultant John Hannafan to create a fresh line of more craft-friendly brews.

BIG SHOULDERS BEER COMPANY

bigshouldersbeer.com

Not to be confused with former contract brewer Big Chicago (which was purchased by Ten Ninety) or Broad Shoulders (the original name of Motor Row Brewing), the Big Shoulders line of beers from owner Rich Szydlo has a few packaged options in the market, including the **Crosstown Wheat** and **Hopapalooza IPA.**

CAHOOTS

cahootsbrewing.com

Launched in January 2014 by founder Dustin Atkinson with the intent of being a community-based, crowd-sourced brewery, everything from recipes to labels to names are up for vote. Cahoots produces mostly high-strength beers as they search for their own space, and are most well known for their **No'Smore** imperial stout in both regular and barrel-aged varieties.

CHICAGO BEER COMPANY

cbcchitown.com

Sixers of Chicago Beer Company's brews emblazoned with images of the city's skyline can be found at liquor stores and grocery store beer sections in a half-dozen different states and the list is growing. Beers include their **Windy City Wheat, Pier Pale Ale, Lake Shore Lager,** and **Mag Mile Pilsner.**

HOPOTHESIS

hopothesis.com

Launched in August 2012 with their namesake IPA, this beer company also produces a **Drafty Window** farmhouse and their **Fallin' Oats** oatmeal amber; they even produced a special **Flying Buttress** stout to pour on the Seadog speedboats as part of a series of craft beer cruises on the Chicago River.

HOPOTHESIS™
BEER COMPANY

TWISTED HIPPO

twistedhippo.com

Beers originally hit the streets under the Rude Hippo name, created when two nacent beer companies, Rude Boy and Twisted Hippo, joined forces. The Hippo went back to being Twisted in June 2016. Brews include their **Wooden Nickel IPA** and their **Beeting Heart** kolsch, a light pinkish brew made with (you guessed it) beets.

HOP BUTCHER (FOR THE WORLD)

hopbutcher.com

The Hop Butcher team (Jeremiah Zimmer, Jude La Rose, and Jason Maxwell) started as the South Loop Brewing Company and had their eyes on an eventual address a few miles south (bet you can't guess where), but a trademark dispute forced their name change to their current Carl Sandburg-inspired moniker. They're fully a part of the craft beer community including popular collaborations with DryHop, whose **Milkstachio** collab hit cans in December 2015 and was named one of the top 25 beers in the nation by *Draft Magazine* in 2016; they also produce popular sports-y beers like **Good Ryes Wear Black.**

VETERAN BEER COMPANY

veteranbeercompany.com

Veteran has offices in River North but views their beer-selling mission on a much larger scale than just Chicago. Launched as a way to help the chronic unemployment faced by veterans once they return stateside, founder Paul Jenkins helps by exclusively employing former military members as part of their sales team, and a percentage of every sale goes to a veteran-centric charity. Beers include the **Blonde Bomber** and the **Freedom Road** amber.

Chain-style Brewpubs

THERE ARE A NUMBER OF BREWPUB "CHAINS" AROUND THE CHICAGOLAND AREA, MANY OF WHOM STARTED ELSEWHERE AND HAVE EXISTED FOR YEARS OUTSIDE MALLS AND MOVIE THEATERS. WHETHER OR NOT THEY ACTUALLY BREW ON SITE IS OFTEN IN QUESTION; SOME CHAINS ARE KNOWN TO BREW THEIR WORT IN LARGE QUANTITIES IN ANOTHER LOCATION, THEN TRUCK IT TO THEIR VARIOUS OUTLETS TO FERMENT AND CONDITION ON SITE FOR SERVING. IT'S CLOSE TO BREWING, BUT NOT EXACTLY THE SAME. STILL, THEY'RE WORTH MENTIONING HERE.

MOST OF THESE CHAIN-STYLE BREWPUBS FIT THE SAME MOLD. THEY'LL HAVE ABOUT A HALF-DOZEN OR SO BEERS AVAILABLE; GENERALLY A LIGHT AMERICAN LAGER FOR THE "WHAT'S CLOSEST TO MILLER LITE" CROWD, AN AMBER, A BROWN ALE, AN OATMEAL OR IRISH STOUT, A PALE ALE, AN IPA, AND A SEASONAL OF SOME SORT—A HEFE IN SPRING, AN OKTOBERFEST OR A PUMPKIN IN FALL, MAYBE AN IMPERIAL BEER OF SOME SORT IN THE DEPTH OF WINTER. IT'S A LITTLE COLOR-BY-NUMBERS, AND MANY INDEPENDENT BREWPUBS FALL INTO THE SAME KIND OF STYLE, AND IT'S FINE, IF THAT'S WHAT YOU'RE LOOKING FOR.

THE MOST SIGNIFICANT IS THE ROCK BOTTOM CHAIN OF BREWER-IES, WHICH ORIGINATED IN DENVER BUT HAVE HAD A PLACE IN THE CITY AND SUBURBS FOR DECADES. ROCK BOTTOM ALSO REPRESENTS THE FIRST PLACE MANY RESIDENTS OF A CERTAIN AGE HAD THEIR FIRST TRULY LOCAL BREWED-ON-SITE CRAFT BEER. (I MAY SPEAK FROM PERSONAL EXPERIENCE, HAVING DRANK THROUGH A FEW FLIGHTS AT THE WARRENVILLE LOCATION IN MY EARLY TWENTIES.)

Rock Bottom actually has brewhouses onsite at their restaurants and many local brewers have spent time working through the ranks of the different locations. Haymarket's Pete Crowley cut his teeth at a couple RBs, as did Barnaby Struve of Three Floyds and Tim Marshall at Solemn Oath. The current brewmaster at the Chicago Rock Bottom, Hayley Shine, earned multiple FoBAB medals between 2013 and 2014, and took Gold at the 2016 World Beer Cup for her Snowcat White IPA.

One spot that straddles the line between independent brewpub and chain operation is the Hofbrauhaus in conventioneer-friendly Rosemont. This massive complex sits near a country-themed bar and grill, a hockey rink, and a movie theater (why do brewpubs and movies seem so closely intertwined?) It's part of a global chain of German bierstubes cranking out schnitzel by the ton and pretzels for days; they make their own lagers, dunkels, and hefeweisses on gear imported from Germany. It's a bit of a theme park, with the requisite lederhosen-clad tuba players on hand and serving staff in dirndls, but if you're aching for a Munich vibe surrounded by hundreds of fellow stein-wavers, Hofbrauhaus will scratch that itch.

We'll not go into detail about the different locations of all these various brewpubs as there aren't a ton of variations once you get into each of the brands—they serve beer-friendly food like burgers and pretzels, they have lots of beer, they have bright, shiny stainless tanks for people to enjoy looking at while sampling flights or quaffing pints. The local mini-chain of brewpubs, Emmett's, has its roots in West Dundee, whereas Gordon Biersch's restaurants originated in California. Granite City kicked off in Minnesota and the RAM Restaurant & Brewery chain began in Washington. (Also worth noting—all of these got started brewing in the first wave of microbrewery ascendence in the mid- to late '90s.)

It's a good formula, and even if many of their beers aren't as adventurous as a modern independent Chicago brewery, one has to recognize that they have their place in the grand scheme of things. It's not the 100+ IBU imperial IPA or Habanero Stout that's winning converts from the Silver Bullet, it's these guys—approachable, enjoyable, uncomplicated places that just want you to enjoy a beer. Nothing wrong there.

EMMETT'S BREWING COMPANY

emmettsbrewingco.com
@EmmettsBeer
5200 Main St. Downers Grove, IL 60515
(630) 434-8500
110 N. Brockway St. Palatine, IL 60067
(847) 359-1533
128 West Main St. West Dundee, IL 60118
(847) 428-4500
121 W. Front St. Wheaton, IL 60187
(630) 480-7181

GORDON BIERSCH

gordonbiersch.com
@Gordon_Biersch
639 E. Boughton Rd., Suite 100 Bolingbrook, IL 60440
(630) 739-6036

GRANITE CITY

www.gcfb.com
@gcfb
1828 Abriter Court Naperville, IL 60563
(630) 544-3700
14035 South La Grange Rd. Orland Park, IL 60462
(708) 364-1212
801 Plaza Dr. Schaumburg, IL 60173
(630) 523-5700

RAM RESTAURANTS

www.theram.com
@theRAM
9520 Higgins Rd. Rosemont, IL 60018
(847) 692-4426
1901 McConnor Pkwy. Schaumburg, IL 60173
(847) 517-8791
700 N. Milwaukee Ave. Wheeling, IL 60090
(847) 520-1222

ROCK BOTTOM

www.rockbottom.com
@rockbottom
1 West Grand Ave.Chicago, IL 60654
(312) 755-9339
94 Yorktown Center Lombard, IL 60148
(630) 424-1550
16156 S. La Grange Rd. Orland Park, IL 60467
(708) 226-0021
28256 Diehl Rd. Warrenville, IL 60555
(630) 836-1380

CHAIN-STYLE BREWPUBS

METRA RAIL'S UNION PACIFIC-WEST SUBURBAN "CRAWL"

When you're embarking on a bar crawl, the decision to not drive is often the best one you make. In the suburbs, that can be a bit tough if you want to hit more than a couple of places safely. Thankfully, a number of breweries have popped up in close proximity to train stations in recent years and a weekend pass is just $8 for all you can ride. Grab a schedule and hit as many of these places along the Union Pacific–West line as you feel is appropriate, from the city all the way out to Elburn.

Chicago: Haymarket Brewpub, 737 W. Randolph St., Chicago IL 60661; 312-638-0700; haymarketbrewing.com.

Haymarket Brewpub is a 10-minute walk from Ogilvie Station and home to some really top-notch hop-forward beers like the award-winning **Defender Stout.** Fortify yourself onsite with housemade sausages, burgers, or pizza, or walk over to the train station's French Market and grab something at one of the many food kiosks for the ride (see also, page 126).

From the Ogilvie Station, hop on a UP-W train to the River Forest stop for...

River Forest: Exit Strategy, 7700 Madison St., Forest Park IL, 60130; 708-689-8771; exitstrategybrewing.com.

A bit of an oasis of brewing in the western suburbs, Exit Strategy is the single option between the 20-mile stretch of track from the city to Villa Park. (Things get a little more close-knit beyond here.) Exit Strategy is a 20-minute walk from the River Forest stop. Once you arrive you'll find yourself beneath a large skylight and growler-glass lighting perusing a menu with empanadas and Thai chicken nachos. Beer selections run the gamut of styles, but how can you not love a double IPA called **Judgmental Dick** (see also, page 64).

Hop another train and head down the line to the Villa Park stop for a trip to...

Villa Park: Lunar Brewing, 54 E. St. Charles Rd., Villa Park IL, 60181; 630-530-2077.

A 10-minute walk south of the train station, Lunar Brewing can happily please anyone ready for a brewery or a bar—it's both. Featuring a handful of brews made on site, along with a bar full of other top-quality guest handles, Lunar offers something for everyone, in one of the oldest and least pretentious brewery settings you'll find around. (See also, page 76.)

Head another stop down the line to the Lombard stop and arrange a ride to...

Lombard: Noon Whistle Brewing Company, 800 E Roosevelt Rd., Lombard IL, 60148; 630-376-6895; noonwhistlebrewing.com.

Okay, you'll have to call an Uber or bring your bikes for this one, as the stop isn't exactly super close to Roosevelt Road, but I throw it in just because it's conceivable at this point you could use a brief break for transit. Noon Whistle's 4 percent ABV **Face Smack Berliner** weiss would make a good choice as a nice tart pick-me-up as well as offering a low alcohol content to keep you up for the trek back to the train. (See also, page 81.)

Back to the train you go and head to the Wheaton stop for...

Wheaton: Dry City Brew Works, 120B N. Main St., Wheaton IL, 60187; 630-456-4787; drycitybrewworks.com.

It's less of a haul to Dry City, just a couple blocks down Wheaton's quaint-as-it-gets Front Street and up Main to where this brewery hides. You may actually have to do some hunting to find Dry City, as they don't actually face the street—you have to head back along the side of a building housing a coffee roaster, or wander through a parking lot to find it. Remember that the tasting room rules keep you to just three pours or flights, so grab a growler if you need anything beyond that. (See also, page 62.)

Back down to the train station and hop another ride over to the Geneva stop for a quick walk to...

Geneva: Penrose Brewing Company, 509 Stevens St., Geneva IL 60134; 630-232-2115; penrosebrewing.com.

Hopefully you've maintained some semblance of a palate at this point, because Penrose's generally sessionable lighter beers benefit from an unfatigued set of taste buds. The taproom is just a 15-minute hike through residential streets up into downtown via the most direct route, but since you're on an adventure, might as well backtrack a touch and take a walk next to the Fox River. Bonus points if you want to stop at Stockholm's on the way back, as they've got a selection of housemade beers as well. (See also, page 85.)

One more train trip, if you can fit it into your schedule. Take it to the end of the line and get off at Elburn for one more at...

Elburn: Eddie Gaedel Pub and Grill, 117 N. Main St., Elburn IL, 60119; 630-365-9938; eddiegaedelpubandgrill.com.

This stop is the end of the road for the Metra line, and no, it's not a brewery, but people have been known to . . . shall we say, relax a little too much on the Metra and miss their stop. Should you need a final destination along the line, you can probably find an **Anti-Hero** or a **Two Hearted** on hand here to finish you off.

ONE WORD: SIEBEL

If you read this book cover to cover or talk to the brewers, you're likely to see a name emerge over and over again. Siebel. As in, "So then I went to Siebel." "Of course, I had to go to Siebel." "I knew I had to go to Siebel." Certainly the explosion of craft brewing has a lot to do with things like creativity, experimentation, passion, and dedication, but you can find people with those traits everywhere. Chicago has something other markets don't—a school dedicated to brewing that's been churning out beer experts for nearly 150 years.

Here is the CliffsNotes version of the school's history: John E. Siebel, a German immigrant (of course) and scholar of physics and chemistry, came to Chicago in 1866 where he opened a chemical laboratory. Siebel worked for decades in the field of brewing research and started a school for brewers in 1882. The school continued to grow and expand its courses over the years and added lessons in baking and refrigeration, among other things, when Prohibition kicked in.

Then Prohibition ended. Yay! But Dr. Siebel had passed away just a few weeks prior. Boo. His family was there to continue the Siebel name, though, and the fourth generation of Siebels continue to work at the school. They ditched the non-beer classes and continued to train folks for another few decades, at which point they moved to a space on the city's Northwest side, on Peterson Avenue. In 2002 they moved again and in 2014, Alarmist Brewing moved into that space. Ain't life funny?

From their new space at the Kendall College, the Siebel Institute of Technology continues to be the go-to place for beer education for anyone wanting to get into the industry. They offer shorter classes, like the three-day Start Your Own Brewery course, to the two-week Concise Course in Brewing Technology, to the full-on, three-month International Diploma in Brewing Technology and the five-month Master Brewers Program, both of which include class time in Chicago and Germany, brewing at Munich's Doemens Academy.

Other courses include more accessible options like Advanced Homebrewing, Beer and Food: A Hands-On Encounter, quality control and professional beer tasting guidance. In addition to classroom training, you can take classes online and they offer products like yeast and sensory training kits. They'll even consult on your brewery if you need a hand with anything. And all of this is basically a few blocks from River North, literally on Goose Island.

Much like the Culinary Institute of America isn't the only way to be a great chef, Siebel isn't the only way to be a great brewer. But look around Chicago at all the people who have passed through their doors on their way to careers in the world of brewing, and you can't help but think it sure helps a hell of a lot. There's other brewing schools in the US and many colleges are starting to offer brewing curriculua, but really, let's be honest. There's only one Siebel.

Beer Bars & Restaurants

BAD APPLE

4300 N. Lincoln Ave.; (773) 360-8406; badapplebar.com

When the Bad Apple opened, it was awash in a sea of burger-and-beer places, one of the thousands of sons and daughters of nationally renowned Kuma's Corner. It would be easy to look at the wide variety of craft beers and the menu of creatively topped hamburgers and write it off as another clone. Look closer, and you'll see that it tops Kuma's in a lot of ways.

For starters, they actually have what the beer menu says they do. If they don't, the out-of-stock beers are the first things the staff will tell you about—ridiculously important if your eyes go to the weirdest, rarest beers they're pouring that day. Second, the beer selection may be one of the most thoughtfully curated selections in the city.

This isn't really a tap-takeover kind of place, but rather one where nearly every style and region is represented on tap. I can't remember a time when I've gone to Bad Apple and not said something to the effect of, "How the hell did they get a barrel of that?"

Unique one-offs, crazy beers from far-flung destinations like Japan and various Eastern European locales, special releases from your favorite West Coast brewery, and more are often just hiding in plain site on the draft list. Of course, there's pretty much always fresh Half Acre on as well, seeing as how the original brewery and taproom is kitty corner to the restaurant.

The food? Well, you're shortchanging yourself if you don't order the Wisconsin fried cheese curds, the best in the city. Airy puffs of gooey breaded cheesy glory paired with a ranch dipping sauce, it hits high points that mozzarella sticks could only dream of. Burgers range from really good to great—the Elvis' Last Supper, topped with bacon and fresh-ground peanut butter made in house, may sound weird in theory but trust me, once you have it, it's hard to order anything else.

You can trust them to nail a medium rare. All the beef is provided by New York's famed butcher Pat LaFrieda and well taken care of. In a beefcentric steakhouse town like Chicago, we try not to hold their NYC sourcing against them; the end result makes up for its provenance.

Perhaps the most interesting part of the menu is their variety of unique and surprisingly well-considered beer cocktails. Mixing beer and spirits is a trend that comes around every three years or so depending on any given magazine's editorial schedule, but the combination has been on the Bad Apple's menu from the get-go and works astonishingly well. Get the **Apple**

Pie—a mix of pear cider and gin—and you may have a hard time ordering either without the other ever again.

BANGERS & LACE

1670 W. Division St.; Chicago, IL 60622; (773) 252-6499 and 810 Grove St.; Evanston, IL 60201; (847) 905-0854; bangersandlacebar.com; @bangersandlace

The first Bangers & Lace outpost opened in 2010 on Division Street in Wicker Park, right as that part of the neighborhood was transitioning from divey bars and clubs to more elevated offerings. It was pretty novel back then to open a bar focused on beer and sausages and not have it be some sort of Germanic bierstube, steins a-swingin'. It was in fact a more demure, sophisticated kind of tavern, a sort of Publican Lite.

The lodge-y vibe with wood-paneled walls and taxidermy trophies partnered well with tunes spinning on a record player, and the bar itself is a thing of beauty. Rather than a parade of random taphandles from breweries far and wide, the thirty-two draft lines have the same wooden handles emerging from an exposed-brick wall, making a singular consistent lineup that appeals to my organized OCD side. One could just look at the room and think, "Yeah, of course this deserves to be named Best New Bar in 2011 by *Time Out Chicago* and regularly honored as one of the nation's best beer bars by *Draft Magazine*." The lineup often includes rarities that other spots don't even get their hands on, including crafty imports from abroad that many US–based beer geeks haven't gotten into yet.

Despite the influence of B&L, Division has split the difference between more upmarket places—think boozy lassi drinks at Brit-Indian Pub Royale or fancy tacos at Takito Kitchen—and a "Wrigleyville West" sort of area with sportsy joints like Fatpour, Smoke Daddy, and Fifty/50. The loss of longtime craft beer stalwarts like SmallBar Division and Division in recent years-adjacent classic taverns like Club Foot (both closed in November 2014) make a good beer program like B&L that much more valuable in this part of town.

An Evanston outpost opened in 2015, taking their array of good beers and encased meats up to Northwestern University students, who no doubt could use a drink. The Evanston location took over a former bar called The Keg that catered to a, shall we say, more "undergrad" crowd.

BAR ON BUENA

910 W. Buena Ave., Chicago, IL 60613; baronbuena.com;
@thebaronbuena

If you want something off the beaten path but still within a reasonable walk to either Wrigley Field or the Green Mill, your destination is the Bar on Buena. Tucked into a little stretch of residential Buena Avenue bookended by a branch of the Chicago Library and a Chinese restaurant claiming the throne of the Egg Roll King, this tiny brick-walled pub has served upscale burgers and fancy beers since well before it was the thing to do.

Two old-school brass towers pour more than eighteen beers ranging from unique small-batch local brewers like Illuminated Brew Works and Noon Whistle to German classics like Stiegl Pils and BBK. Here, as in other places, there's a beer of the month selection, but BoB extends that out to a style of the month as well. You can expect an array of Oktoberfests and harvest ales in autumn, winter warmers and stouts in January, and radlers and lagers through the warmer months.

The Bar on Buena is part of the family of bars and restaurants that includes the Fountainhead, the Northman cider bar, and the Montrose Saloon, so if you like drinking at any of those places, you'll enjoy a beer here. The BoB menu got a revamp in 2014, adding a new cantina-style flair with dishes like carnitas chilaquiles and chicken pozole in the mix while keeping the burgers and sweet potato fries the locals love. On winter nights, the dark room with candlelight dancing off the wooden bar defines the word cozy. There's patio seating in the summer, but they often bring the outdoors in—the garage-style glass doors roll up to make a fully open-air bar. It's like one big beer garden for neighbors in the know.

BEER BISTRO

1061 W. Madison Ave., Chicago, IL 60607; (312) 433-0013;
@Thebeerbistro

After having his eyes opened to craft beer while working for Goose Island Clybourn, Bob McDermott opened the Beer Bistro in the West Loop in September 2005. The Madison Avenue bar was just the right space for a neighborhood that was then fairly underserved for drinking establishments aiming higher than a shot and a beer—(the explosion of the West Randolph/Fulton Market neighborhood was still a few years off). As such, the Beer Bistro is the kind of place where you can sample a flight of 3 Floyds and

Founders or just have a can of PBR before heading down the street to a 'Hawks game at the United Center.

The bar is textbook Chicago tavern, which I mean in the best possible way—a long, slender room with a lengthy wooden bar, a towering arched mahogany back bar, exposed brick and mirrors, and an awesome cable-run fan system overhead. Food stays true to the crowd-friendly pub grub side of things, with burgers, pizza, sandwiches, and salads.

BEER HOUSE

322 Yorktown Center; Lombard, IL 60148; beerhousechicago.com; @beerhousechgo

Standout suburban beer bars can be a hard thing to find—generally, if a place has a great list there's a good chance they're brewing most of it themselves. Beer House offers up an oasis of good beer on the outskirts of one of the area's largest shopping destinations. Cruising around retail outlets can be thirsty work.

The beer list here skews heavily local with brews from Flesk, BuckleDown, 350 Brewing, and Noon Whistle regularly available, though heavy-duty craft options from the likes of Goose Island and Ballast Point are also onhand. Beer House also covers options for your own house—they offer package goods to go.

With five dozen beers on tap and a selection of massive televisions, it's a little shocking that Beer House doesn't have its own kitchen to crank out chicken wings and quesadillas, though they do have a few bar snacks and you can bring in food from nearby restaurants (including, it should be noted, the Rock Bottom brewpub a short walk away).

BEER GEEKS

3030 45th St., Highland, IN 46322; beergeekspub.com; @beergeekspub

Snob. Dork. Nerd. Afficionado. Geek. All are terms that can be used to describe folks (like myself) who are seriously into better beers. There's just one place, though, that grabs the term geek with both hands and slaps it on the door as a badge of honor, complete with glasses taped at the bridge. (As the word craft becomes more and more meaningless, I often prefer a less-specific phrase like "drinker of good beer" as a catchall for folks who like this kind of stuff. Geek generally works too, though.)

Northwest Indiana continues to grow as a beer destination, and as such, it needed a bar where you could drink lots of options from the region. Beer Geeks is located in a small strip mall just over 5 minutes from the downtown Griffith area, which boasts the trio of New Oberpfalz Brewing, Pokro Brewing, and Wildrose Brewing Company, 10 minutes from the 3 Floyds brewpub, 15 minutes from One Trick Pony, and about a half hour from 18th Street in Gary. There's lots going on, so someone's gotta pour it all.

Twenty different ever-changing draft options offer a well-curated list of beers from many of those area breweries, along with a cask option on the beer engine and an astonishingly deep cider and mead menu. Spirits included distilled options from breweries like Rogue and Breckenridge, and there's regular live music that skews bluesy.

BRIXIE'S

9526 Ogden Ave, Brookfield, IL 60513; brixies.com; @brixies

A family-run taproom along sprawling Ogden Avenue that can stay in business for about 80 years must be doing something right. Since the turn of the millennium or so, craft beer has been the draw to Brixie's. Chris DiBraccio runs Brixie's and helped transition the bar into a southwest-suburban beer destination. He also hosts a homebrew club at the bar and even helped open nearby Imperial Oak Brewing in 2014. That's a full-service beer lover.

With nearly three dozen drafts, the bar regularly pours beers from nearby BuckleDown and Exit Strategy Brewing, along with beers that are hard to find in the city, including brews from Pipeworks and 3 Floyds. Beer art lines the walls, there's pinball and video games, as well as a handful of video poker games to give you a chance to win back your beer tab.

And how can you not love a place that offers free bacon on Mondays?

BEERMISCUOUS

2812 N. Lincoln Ave.; (855) 450-2337; beermiscuous.com

Okay, it took a while for most of us to get over the name. Once the beer community got over the idea of the iffy portmanteau and saw Beermiscuous for what it was, we all became a lot more accepting. Beermiscuous is a self-described craft beer cafe that feels like a coffee shop, sounds like a beer hall, and provides one of the best damn pick-your-six-ers you can find.

Their unique setup allows them to sell beers one at a time for on-site consumption, or to go as part of a six-pack; pricing varies depending on whether you're drinking there or elsewhere. It serves as both a bar and a market, but doesn't feel like either. It's almost like a group office space during the day and a community meeting center at night.

The space has a serenely European feel—good lighting, high ceilings, and wood paneling that leads into whitewashed walls give it an airy, churchlike setting that doesn't lend to the inebriation of a tavern but contributes the thoughtfulness of a reading room. There's a main level with a communal table amongst other regular seating and a fireplace and a downstairs level for events and groups. Wi-Fi is free.

It's not just cans and bottles you can pick and choose through (though they do boast a selection of over three hundred): They have twelve draft lines pouring almost exclusively locally produced beer or beers from around the Midwest. Through those lines you can get short three- to four-ounce pours of anything they have. It's an excellent way to indulge in the cafe's motto, "Drink around."

It's a great place to launch an exploration of your new favorite style, introduce a friend to new brews with the help of one of their "beeristas" (and we're still not really over that designation), or just launch a good ol' fashioned bar crawl—Delilah's, Atlas Brewpub, and Rose's Lounge are all easily within stumbling distance.

CLARK STREET ALE HOUSE

742 N. Clark St.; Chicago, IL 60610; (312) 961-3738; clarkstreetalehouse.com

If you ever want to feel like you're in a 1940s-era noir film while drinking a good beer at the same time, doff your fedora, grab some cash, and make Clark Street Ale House your first stop. The red neon sign imploring you to Stop & Drink (the name of the pub before CSAH took over in 1994) glowing above the door is as much of a landmark as you can get in this part of the city, a small, relatively quiet no-mans-land of River North while the mad bustle of commerce cranks away just a few blocks east.

With two dozen beers on draft and a cask option as well, Clark Street has served as a beer oasis to untold numbers of brew enthusiasts over the past couple of decades, not the least of which was legendary beer writer Michael Jackson who namechecked them as one of the great American beer destinations in 1999. There's also dozens of whiskey and scotch options, you can bring your own food and they're dog friendly (the *Reader* named them the Best Place to Get Drunk With Your Dog in 2010). There's a patio/beer garden in the back, though you may find it tough to escape the pull of the room. Clark Street feels blessedly dark even during the day.

It may also be the best place in the city to get a great beer late at night, as the bar is open until 4 a.m. six days a week, and 5 a.m. on Saturdays— though many seasoned drinkers maintain that very few good things occur after last call at the usual 2 a.m. bars. A management group responsible for a couple bottle-servicey clubs took over the Ale House in November 2015, but have seen fit to leave the place pretty much alone. For example, the pretzels are still free.

EMPORIUM ARCADE BAR

1366 N. Milwaukee Ave., Chicago, IL 60622; (773) 697-7922; emporiumchicago.com; @EmporiumChicago

When the barcade concept hit Chicago, the city embraced it in a big way. The spot that kicked it all off was this Wicker Park taproom, opened in June 2012. Emporium (the portmanteau fan in me really wants it to be Empourium—get it? pour?— but hey, not my business) brought nearly 40 videogames and a couple dozen new taps to a neighborhood already quite packed with quality drinking establishments.

Prior to Emporium, video games in Chicago bars generally meant a sorta-legal video poker console or a touchscreen setup for a rousing game of "find what's different between these two pictures of girls in bikinis." Emporium's combination of classic games and good beers was an immediate hit—the pairing of games like Ms. Pac Man and Mortal Kombat II along with a locally focused craft beer list hit the sweet spot for the neighborhood's population of extended-adolescense twenty- to thirty-somethings. The jingle of tokens and the rattle of pinball machines all of a sudden echoed down Milwaukee, and brought the city's arcade scene back to life.

It helped that the beers were great, too. Besides a whiskey-focused spirits list, you can reliably grab beers from Chicago and around the midwest; Half Acre, Penrose, Metropolitan, and Off Color are all regularly represented. (PBR is also on hand, for the traditionally minded bike messengers not yet priced out of the neighborhood.) If you want to grab a canned option from Pipeworks, Emporium is the place to be—each of the brewery's can releases has held a kickoff party here, starting with their Ninja Vs. Unicorn rollout in July 2015.

Emporium quickly expanded, taking over an adjoining storefront in June 2013 and adding a Logan Square location in July 2014, adding no new draft options but featuring a full list of bottles and cans alongside videogames and an expanded selection of table games like foosball, shuffleboard, and air hockey. They placed this location a straight shot up Milwaukee Avenue on the same block as places like modern-day beerhall The Radler, Chicago Distilling Company, and the original Revolution brewpub, making for a heck of a one-block beer crawl.

FIRST DRAFT

649 S. Clark St., Chicago, IL 60605; (312)461-1062; firstdraftchicago.com; @FirstDraftChi

One of a handful of places to get a great beer in the South Loop, First Draft runs the risk of being not first-in-mind when it comes to drinking south of Congress. Want a classic old-school joint? You want Kasey's. Want a brewery taproom? Vice District or Motor Row are your picks. Want an elevated dining and craft beer experience? Villains, just down the street, is calling your name. Don't sleep on First Draft, though, because it is what few places are comfortable enough, nay, bold enough, to be these days—a fine bar and grill.

First Draft opened in June 2014, bringing life back to the space vacated by the original incarnation of Villains back in October 2012. It checks off all your must-haves for a quality spot to sit and have a beer in a Chicago drinking establishment—warm wooden arched bar with classic architecture, exposed brick walls, a tin ceiling, sports memorabilia backed up by plenty of sports on the televisions. A wall of glass doors opens on warmer days to bathe the bar in sunlight, though the view only affords you a look at the parking lot next door.

Don't be thrown by the sports-bar-ness of this place; just cast your eyes on the fifty-odd draft beers available to you at any given time, with the requisite local/midwestern options and a reliable variety of Belgians, Germans, and other imports. Not content to only have beer in liquid form, they infuse beer into their recipes as well, including IPA aioli and gravy bolstered by a hefty stout.

FOUR MOON TAVERN

1847 W. Roscoe Ave., Chicago, IL 60657; (773) 929-6666;
fourmoontavern.com; @4MoonTavern

Another of the neighborhood taverns akin to the likes of Bar on Buena and Kasey's, Four Moon offers a fine but tightly curated selection of beers to the residents of Roscoe Village. The immediately comfortable wood-paneled (and ceilinged!) bar room is wall-to-wall with breweriana, various stickers, and bric-a-brac, and just under a dozen taps with beers from Surly to Perennial to Allagash White.

One of the few Northside holdouts that survived the late 1990s/early 2000s purge of bars in residential areas, Four Moon's sign is one of the few external hints that a bar hides in plain sight (though the patio seating is admittedly more of a dead giveaway in warmer weather). Located among the single-family homes and multi-tier condo units that surround it, it's halfway between the Paulina Brown Line stop and the main Roscoe Village drag that runs from Damen to Western. Even though there are some decent establishments past Four Moon, it's best to save the calories you'd burn walking the few extra blocks and just stop in here for a beer.

Food is also better than it needs to be, with stick-to-your-ribs options like pot roast and sloppy joes; brunch is available on Sunday as well. There's a pool table, some couch seating, and the general warmth of the place will have you looking for the fireplace—though that's one thing that Four Moon doesn't have. The glow afforded by a couple higher-ABV beers will have to suffice.

FOUNTAINHEAD

1970 W. Montrose Ave., Chicago, IL 60613; (773) 697-8204;
fountainheadchicago.com

Fountainhead has gone through a number of changes in its relatively short lifetime, but one thing has remained unchanged—its nonstop dedication to pouring really great beers. When Fountainhead opened in 2011, the Lincoln Square neighborhood only knew that its intent was to be a solid local beer bar from the team that ran the equally solid but off-the-radar Bar on Buena (see page 151) over in no-mans land between Uptown and Wrigleyville.

The original focus was actually beer and whiskey, with beer selections split between American craft and German imports to reflect the Germanic nature of the Lincoln Square neighborhood. Food was made for sharing or for more selfish pursuits (which I always liked to think was a nod to the Objectivist philosophy of Ayn Rand, author of a book called The Fountainhead, but that might just be my wishful thinking) and all was well.

Two things happened after they opened that pushed Fountainhead from really good to great.

First: City Provisions, the nearby hyperlocally focused deli and market a few blocks away run by chef Cleetus Friedman, closed. For a brief moment of time, the foodgnoscenti mourned. Just six weeks later, Fountainhead announced that Friedman was taking over the kitchen and remaking the menu to match his slow-food-centric vision, and there was much rejoicing. The fit was like a glove, if the hand going into the glove was also really good at making making collaboration beers with midwestern brewers. That partnership lasted until February 2016, when Friedman left the Fountainhead group, leaving the restaurant in the hands of Sean Sanders, former owner of the nearby Michelin-praised farm-to-table restaurant Browntrout.

Second: They opened their rooftop bar. Promised from the outset, it took a couple years to finally get everything set for folks to hang out a story above Montrose & Damen, but it was worth the wait. Featuring a kitchen, covered and open seating, a full bar with another great draft selection, and an even-better canned-beer list, the rooftop took a great program and essentially doubled it during the city's warmer months.

Most rooftop bars are about view first, drinks second, and service third. The rooftop at Fountainhead is a 180 degrees from that. There's basically no view, other than sky, a few plants and a fireplace—walls and garden cover the rest, but who cares, because there's not much to look at in that intersection anyways. Rather, it's just a place to hang out in the sun on a nice day, have a few really good beers, maybe get a sandwich, maybe watch the game on their two TVs. It's a biergarden twenty feet higher than most. And I defy you to find more than three places better to drink outside than there.

Which is not to say that fall and winter visits are any worse. Once the rooftop closes and cold weather kicks in, it becomes a dim, warm, raucous pub. Day in and day out, Fountainhead just works. I've heard stories of someone who had a broken leg and had become homebound for weeks on end, and his first good beer back in society brought him to Fountainhead. I have heard these stories because that person was me.

THE GREEN LADY

3328 N. Lincoln Ave., Chicago, IL 60657; (773) 525-5571;
thegreenlady-chicago.com

Restaurants open all the time in Chicago. The bar-and-grill concept? There's a new one in every neighborhood about once a quarter. The neighborhood tavern with elevated American comfort food? The gourmet burger bar with a local craft beer focus? Everywhere. It's extremely rare these days for someone to just open a straight-up bar. Just a bar. No kitchen. No deep-fryer. No charcuterie board. No house-made pickles. Just a BAR. With, you know, beer and stuff. Maybe some bourbon.

When Melani Domingues opened The Green Lady in 2011 on an undertravelled stretch of Paulina in Lakeview, she did just that—she opened a bar. And it's one of the most underrated craft beer bars in the city. Dominguez came to the city after time served as director of operations at one of Manhattan's heralded beer bars—The Ginger Man, in a similarly undertravelled section of Midtown East.

At The Green Lady (named for the mythical Scottish spirit that's either benign protector or antagonistic demon) you'll find two dozen handles that offer nothing but finely–curated craft beer. Long-developed relationships with area craft breweries means Domingues can offer draft options available nowhere else in the city—nearby Spiteful Brewing is reliably on tap here when it's only in bottles and cans everywhere else. You'll also find a reliable selection of interesting and rare imports from Germany and Belgium.

You want sours? You can find at least one on tap here, as Domingues is a noted devotee of tart, wild, and funky beers. In fact, during one Chicago Craft Beer Week event, every single draft line was dedicated to nothing but sour beers, and I've never seen the place more packed—obviously there are more than a few fellow sour lovers in the city.

Perhaps as important as the beer selection is the atmosphere of the bar. It's as welcoming as they come, no small feat in Lakeview, where bars range from cooler-than-thou to brotastic beyond belief. Dogs are welcome, you can order in food from nearby restaurants, and the TVs feature classic movies nonstop, a welcome break from every other screen tuned to Sportscenter up and down Lincoln. They host bar trivia, and notably for Michigan expats (of which Domingues is one), a weekly Euchre night.

I take it back—it'd be easy to say The Green Lady is just a bar. It's a whole lot more than just that, though.

THE GRAFTON

4530 N. Lincoln Ave., Chicago, IL 60625; (773) 271-9000; thegrafton.com; @TheGrafton

You would be forgiven for thinking that The Grafton was another Irish pub in a city full of bars paying homage to the Auld Sod, especially if you were to walk by on one of the many times they host an open session for Irish musicians and hear the fiddle, mandolin, and tin whistle jamming away. You would likely assume that the draft list would range from Guinness to Magners to Killians and back again. You would also be missing out on a list of some very-well-curated local craft beers.

Indeed, the Grafton did start out as your run of the mill Irish joint, which is fine—every neighborhood in Chicago has a couple. However, as the Lincoln Square neighborhood transitioned into the beer-loving and beer-producing spot it is today, the Grafton's staff wisely decided to run with it and add several Chicago craft beers, as well as other midwestern selections, to their taplist.

The Grafton was the first account of nearby Begyle Brewing, and you can almost always find a beer or two from them on hand. Onetime beer buyer and bar manager Ben Rossi simultaneously worked the bar and opened his own brewery, Only Child of Gurnee, which you can also reliably find on draft here. It's one of the rare places in the city to find it outside of a bottle format other than their own taproom. The Grafton has also been in the game long enough to get rare releases from 3 Floyds, one-offs from Half Acre, and regular deliveries of barrels from many other small, upstart local breweries.

The menu ranges from Brit-centric options like a proper fry-up at breakfast to a beef & Guinness stew or BLT with Irish rasher bacon; their burger remains one of the more underrated in the city. In winter, there are few bars in the city with a warmer back room than The Grafton when you sit alongside the fireplace while students and teachers from the nearby Old Town School of Folk Music play folk tunes, classic jigs, or whatever the spirit moves them to. Speaking of spirits, The Grafton's got a good whiskey list, too.

THE HOPLEAF

5148 N. Clark St., Chicago, IL 60640; (773) 334-9851;
hopleafbar.com

When Michael Roper took a seedy taproom on Chicago's north side in 1992 and built a haven for some of the world's best beers, calling it a transformation isn't accurate enough—it was more like transubstantiation. In a world where a dozen handles of high-quality beer are available on nearly every surrounding block, it's easy to forget just how much impact The Hopleaf has had on Chicago, and continues to have.

From day one, The Hopleaf was one of the places to find a variety of Trappist and imported beers, back when "good beer" was mostly just shorthand for "Belgian." Over the years as craft grew, Hopleaf was one of a handful of places in the city to find Sierra Nevada, Goose Island, 3 Floyds, and Bells—and I defy you to find another bar in the world that took it upon themselves to have their own Bells neon sign made.

Gradually the Belgian influence shone through from the kitchen as well. To go to Hopleaf and not order mussels and frites is a cardinal sin; if they were to take those or the pan-fried CB&J sandwich (cashew butter & fig jam) off the menu, Andersonville would riot. The kitchen reportedly goes through a half a ton of mussels a week. Before "elevated bar food" was a trend three times over, Hopleaf was serving duck Reubens and Montreal pastrami sandwiches left and right.

As the craft beer world exploded in recent years, Hopleaf has evolved along with it, adding a back patio and a second dining room, which doubled the draft handles but didn't change the feel a bit. The Belgian and Belgian-style side of the menu is easily equalled by American craft beers from nearby and across the country. Brewers in Chicago consider it a point of honor to be served at The Hopleaf.

The Hopleaf is one of the few must-visits of the city's craft beer scene, as it's equally a fixture of where it used to be as well as where it's going. For a city whose culture was mostly uninitiated to good beer throughout much of Hopleaf's existence, a trip here could at one point literally change your life.

HOWELLS & HOOD

435 N. Michigan Ave., Chicago, IL 60611; (312) 262-5310; howellsandhood.com

Take one of the most notable architectural icons in the city, on its most recognizable street. Carve out a huge chunk of the first floor, taking square footage away from one of the city's oldest radio stations and one of the country's largest newspapers. Add a restaurant with 360 draft lines spread between three bars, almost entirely dedicated to craft beer. Stir, and see what happens.

That's the huge gamble the Bottleneck Management team undertook in early 2013, and even if it hadn't paid off, you have to respect the amount of cajones it took to drop one of the country's biggest craft beer bars smack dab in the heart of tourist central. Most best beer bar lists ignore H&H in favor of the cooler, smaller places with non–Michigan Avenue addresses, but this place is bringing craft beer to the masses and creating converts, as opposed to the many places preaching to the craft beer choir.

Who's bringing more people to try new craft beers? The Division Street beer bar playing obscure vinyl records and offering choices ranging from hoppy to hoppier? Or the place where families from out of town stop for a burger and find themselves sipping on a midwestern craft brew instead of an industrial lager?

To be sure, it's a slick, gleaming, stylish space—you don't spend a few million on a buildout and try to fake a dive inside the *Tribune* Tower. It's a massive room, with another massive room behind it that also serves as a private function space; quotes about alcohol are hammered into the marble walls. The outdoor patio is a fantastic summer lunchtime destination if you can get in; drinking during lunch isn't terribly in vogue these days, but most folks should take time to relax with a 3 percent radler or shandy at noon on Tuesday at least once in their life.

The service can be conveyor-belt-esque at times, with an emphasis on maximizing that patio during summertime (the hunt for your beer among all those taps can take some time as well), but it's worth at least one or two trips to take in the marathon-length wall of handles . . . and then checking out another, and then another.

The beer list has plenty of bottles, but if you're here and you can't find something to try on draft, you should probably head to the wine bar in the InterContinental a few doors north. The food is better than it needs to be with fun riffs on bar food like pierogi poutine and gourmet tater tots. If you've got an event to plan and expense budget to burn, reserve a night on the twenty-fifth-floor terrace of the Trib Tower, known as The Crown. Featuring 360-degree views of River North from beneath the stone terraces atop the building, no other rooftop bar in the city can compete.

JAKE MELNICK'S CORNER TAP

41 E. Superior St., Chicago, IL 60611; (312) 266-0400; jakemelnicks.com; @jakemelnicks

There's not a ton of great beer-drinking options in River North. In this neighborhood if you're not serving $17 glasses of wine at a high-end restaurant, you're serving fishbowls full of colored liquor at one of the many bars geared toward bachelorette parties and tourists. One of the much-welcomed exceptions to this is Jake Melnick's, just a couple blocks from the heart of the city's ritzy Mag Mile.

Evoking a northwoods cabin tavern on the inside, this wood-paneled sports bar escape from the relative urban insanity outside has no doubt saved many a traveler from a near breakdown induced by too many shoppers, too many cabs, and too much sales tax. The menu skews to burgers, barbeque, and their famed chicken wings (one level of spice requires you sign a waiver; they serve them to you with a plastic fireman's hat to wear) but really, you're here for a beer.

A long bar runs the length of the dining room and behind it is poured a refreshingly vast selection of local-leaning selections. Random barrels of small-batch Off Color, 3 Floyds, and Penrose regularly pop up alongside midwestern favorites like Wisconsin's Tyranena, Michigan's Brewery Vivant, and Missouri's Perennial. When Surly pulled themselves out of the market briefly between late 2010 and 2013, one of the few places it would occasionally pop up (mostly to tease us) would be Jake's.

It's close enough to many hotels to be a great nightcap, it's near public transit for a post-work drink, and if you're along for a Michigan Avenue expedition you could do worse than starting at Howells & Hood and ending at Jake's.

JERRY'S SANDWICHES

5419 N. Clark St., Chicago, IL 60640; (773) 796-3777; and
4739 N. Lincoln Ave., Chicago, IL 60625; (872) 208-6264;
jerryssandwiches.com; @WithHotSauce

Naming your business as an homage to the Grateful Dead's Jerry Garcia may, in future years become more prevalent at a dispensary than a sandwich joint known for their great beer selection. After opening on Madison Avenue in 2002, they added their flagship location in Wicker Park. The original spot closed in 2012 while the Andersonville location opened up shop in November of that year. A long-awaited Lincoln Square spot opened its doors in February 2016 while the Division Street stalwart shuttered in September 2016.

Jerry's features dozens of sandwich options, hundreds if you want to go deep and consider every bread/filling combination—if it were ever possible to tire of burgers and beer, Jerry's would be your new home (though they have burgers too). All of these options add up to a reliably great dining experience explicitly focused on what's between two pieces of bread. They've been named Best Sandwich for five years running in the *Reader*'s annual "Best Of" poll.

Their beer selection feels nearly as deep as the sandwich selection, with thirty taps at Lincoln Square and fifty taps in Andersonville, split between regular lines and a couple special options on cask. The special bottle list in both locations also offers an impressive list of cellared options. Annual events include their Dark Harvest celebration of beers that skew to the blacker side of the SRM Scale and the Oak & Iron barrel-aged beer celebrations.

KAISER TIGER

1415 W. Randolph St., Chicago, IL 60601; (312) 243-3000;
kaisertiger.com; @KaiserTigerChic

Opened in May 2014 by the owners of Paddy Long's in Lincoln Park, Kaiser Tiger can be viewed as a physical manifestation of the city's beer dominance over wine. Previously it was the location of The Tasting Room, where one could sip flights of wine, enjoy a cheese plate, or peruse the many bottles at the market to find one worth taking home. When they closed in November 2013 and this loud, open-space beer hall took over, it was one more reminder of the ascendance of the beer scene in Chicago.

Located on the far west end of Chicago's Restaurant Row on Randolph and butting up right next to Union Park, Kaiser Tiger bookends the stretch of road that houses heavy hitters like Girl & The Goat, Au Cheval, Belly Q, and City Winery Chicago. If you're heading out from the Loop, the whole street starts with the Haymarket Brewpub, and I like that you can't enter the city's most heralded culinary area from either end without passing by two beer powerhouses.

Kaiser Tiger is beer first, meat second, all other things way back in third. The dozens of taps on two floors hold a finely curated list run by owner Pat Berger, a BJCP judge with decades of beer-drinking and evaluating experience. When he tells you a beer is good or bad, you listen. As if the great list of beers wasn't enough, Berger also occasionally collaborates with breweries on specialty one-off beers just for his bars. Those bars include a great brick & wood main room with a bar in the round, and a bar at an upstairs event space with an impressive West Loop view of the city's skyline.

The beer goes great with the wide variety of house-made sausages and bacon-centric dishes like bacon "grenades" (deep-fried, bacon-wrapped meatballs), bacon-wrapped dates or shrimp, or bacon flights.

For larger groups (or for those looking to help send their cardiologist to Hawaii this winter) should indulge in the famed Whole Bomb, a massive, five-pound beast of meat and bacon. It's also available at Paddy Long's (see page 174), but you'll want the extra floor space at Kaiser Tiger to spread out afterward and maybe unbuckle your belt.

The indoor experience at Kaiser Tiger is assuredly great, but don't sleep on the beer garden right outside. There's a bocce court in high demand during warmer months, and in winter they freeze that thing over and turn it into a curling rink (if you think curling isn't a drinking sport, you don't know many Scandinavians). Very few bars in Chicago are all-season outdoor destinations; Kaiser Tiger counts itself among a rare breed who can get Chicagoans to happily drink outdoors in February.

KASEY'S TAVERN

701 S Dearborn St, Chicago, IL 60605; (312) 427-7992; kaseystavern.com; @kaseystavern

The first thing you should know about Kasey's is their claim on ownership of the second-oldest liquor license in the city of Chicago. The second thing you should know is that even though they could use that to coast on historic coattails, they don't. Instead, it's as vital a neighborhood bar as you can find in the area today, with creaky wooden floors, a classic brass-rail bar, and charm to spare.

Kasey's pours over 100 different beers with over two dozen on tap, which skew toward crowd-favorite crafts like 3 Floyds' **Gumballhead,** Goose Island **Green Line,** and **Allagash White.** Traditionalists can also get a pour of Miller Lite or PBR, which shows a relative equanimity to all comers, beer snob or macro-indifferent.

Kasey's has been a bar "in one form or another," as they put it, for over a century, and if you look back at Chicago's history, their Printer's Row spot was pretty close to ground zero for brothels, bucket-o-blood bars, and even the infamous Lone Star Saloon run by one Mickey Finn from the late 1800s through 1903.

With a century's worth of distance, it's fun to imagine that kind of vice and villainy while putting your boots on the rail and sipping a fresh beer on a calm, sunny afternoon in the South Loop. Nowadays it's significantly more lowkey, attracting condo residents and students from the nearby Columbia College, Roosevelt and Depaul downtown campuses. A few newer beer bars have sprung up nearby, but Kasey's Tavern is still certainly well worth a stop.

KUMA'S CORNER (ORIGINAL LOCATION)

2900 W. Belmont Ave., Chicago, IL 60618; (773) 604-8769; kumascorner.com; @kumascorner

You can call and ask, but they won't give you a wait time at this bar that launched a thousand burger/beer joints. The place that somehow made a high-decibel doom metal soundtrack appropriate background music for families; the home of burgers that redefined what you thought ground beef and pretzel buns could be; the only place where people wait three to four hours for a $12 hamburger and are happy about it; a place where you could reliably order three different beers and the waitstaff will most likely return to tell you they only have one of them in stock.

Kuma's is many things, but above all, it is legend.

Of course, there are the burgers. They are awesome in the literal sense of the word—the first time one is set in front of you, your mind reels. I'm going to eat all of that? you ask yourself. Yes. You will eat all of that. Happily.

The menu is a testament to the power of a simple idea executed well. Big hamburgers with interesting toppings named for metal bands. That's all it is at its core. But it works, doesn't it?

So much ink has been spilled about the burgers that it's easy to bypass the fact that Kuma's is a really good place to drink beer. From day one the menus trumpeted their dedication to quality independent beer and a no-Miller, no-Bud pledge. It was reliably a place to find beers from 3 Floyds and Lagunitas on tap, before Lagunitas was Lagunitas.

Who knows how many people were introduced to beers from Anderson Valley and Dark Horse and Great Lakes just because they wanted to have the monster burgers everyone was talking about?

The subsequent locations in Lincoln Park, Indianapolis, and Schaumburg didn't do much to bolster the Kuma's brand, though short of opening in a barren Detroit field, a factory in Cleveland, or a literal warzone, I'm not sure what options they had in terms of gritty real estate that would fit the brand of the first spot. None of this takes away from the real magic that the original Kuma's created. Great burgers. Great beer. And still, a great amount of time spent waiting in line.

LINKS TAPROOM

1559 N. Milwaukee Ave., Chicago, IL 60622; (773) 360-7692; linkstaproom.com; @LinksTaproom

Another solid drinking option in Wicker Park near the massive North/Damen/Milwaukee intersection, Links Taproom offers a crowd-pleasing selection of house-made sausages, hand-cut fries, and dozens of beers on draft, cask, or package. The industry vets who opened Links in January 2014 knew what the neighborhood needed, and it wasn't another cocktail spot or upscale taco joint—it was a place for a good beer and an encased meat product.

The most fun part of Links is their all-digital draft menu, which shows you the brewery, the beer name, the style and the serving vessel, the ABV, IBUs, and even how much is left in each particular keg. All that information is also translated onto the website, so if you spot something you want and you know it's about to kick, you can haul your ass to the bar ASAP and accelerate your ordering plans accordingly. More fun: updating your various social media feeds might get you a spot on the screen as well.

LOCAL OPTION

1102 W. Webster Ave., Chicago, IL 60614; (773) 348-2008; localoptionbier.com; @LocalOption

A craft-centric beer bar with a crazy selection, a doom and thrash metal soundtrack, and a Louisiana-centric food menu may seem slightly insane, but when you consider the fact that it's smack-dab in the middle of a residential stretch of street in fancy-pantsy Lincoln Park, it strikes one as damn near off the charts—and yet it completely works. The phrase "greater than the sum of its parts" comes to mind.

Not just content to serve beer, they create it, too. Local Option is one of the few beer bars that is as hands–on as you can get with the brewing process—no boring amber "house beer" made on contract by some out-of-state outfit here. They brew about a dozen different beers at various breweries around the country, primarily for purchase on their own lines but are also available around the city on tap and in bottles. You can regularly find their brews like their **Mourning Wood,** an oak-aged amber with Dark Matter coffee; the **Voku Hila** helles bock; or their **Blood Ov The Kings** hoppy red wheat ale.

Local Option also hosts some of the craziest beer events in town, including their Catalina Wine Mixer featuring a guitar shred-off contest, an Ass Makeover (not to be confused with a tap takeover), and the annual The Day After, held on the day following the final "official" Chicago Craft Beer Week events as if to tell the world that the previous week or so of craft beer debauchery can't stop them from having one more shindig. (Like those television professionals tell you, don't try this at home.) If you want to find rare barrels from breweries like Pipeworks, Against the Grain, Dark Horse, Central Waters, and Bourbon County variants, a Local Option event is a good . . . well, option.

Casual fans beware—their events have no tickets, just a seething mass of humanity all hovered around the taphandles in the hopes of getting their hands on some very rare beers. Imagine a zombie horde staggering around to a doom-metal sountrack, getting slowly drunk on exceedingly hard-to-find beers, and you've got a good feel for a Local Option event. (It's fun though, trust me.)

LONG ROOM

1612 W. Irving Park Ave., Chicago, IL 60613; (773) 665-4500;
longroomchicago.com; @LongRoomChicago

Long Room is true to its name—it is a room, and it is long. So is the 60-foot bar within. It is also dark and has excellent beer. Long Room is a weird sort of pioneer in a neighborhood that's otherwise ridiculously affluent, yet the little slice of Lakeview at Ashland and Irving always seems just a bit grittier than the blocks of huge single-family homes that surround it. Regardless, it is a very tightly edited bar that offers beer, seats, and a small patio. That's about it. No televisions, and (until recently) no food.

Opened in January 2000, Long Room has served as a reliable destination for quality beer for years in a subsection of Lakeview that's strangely underserved by bars (maybe that has something to do with Lake View High School around the corner). Long Room became a little bit of a wider room in June 2015 when their Sidecar concept opened with a rotating mix of pop-up-style restaurants. Purveyors of biscuit sandwiches and naan-wiches hand off to a new crew offering burgers and chili at night.

The Long Room also opened for coffee service in the morning, making this otherwise late-night joint an all day affair for the neighborhood, similar to the Map Room's longstanding coffee and pastry program in the mornings. Long Room's cocktail list skews traditional, but even if you're there for a mixed drink, take a look at the beer menu—they've got some of the best descriptions in town. It's almost like word jazz.

LONGMAN & EAGLE

2657 N Kedzie Ave, Chicago, IL 60647; (773) 276-7110;
longmandandeagle.com; @longmanandeagle

Longman & Eagle is more celebrated among the general population for their nationally praised food menu, and for offering a new take on the old tradition of taverns and inns offering both libations and rooms for the night in which you can sleep them off. L&E may have been named one of the best new restaurants in America by *Esquire Magazine* and earned a Michelin star since they started awarding them in Chicago, but they're also a pretty damn good place to get a beer, too.

With a beer menu that ranges into the hundreds of options, you can reliably find some of the more interesting beers in the city on one of their sixteen draft lines. You can also find a line for Old Style, a nod to the tradition of its branding as the longtime Chicago beer. It's the only macro on tap, but you can get a can of Lite or Old Milwaukee if you need to be completely contrarian and hipster about things.

Longman & Eagle's menu plays great with beer, too, with elevated riffs on the sloppy joe and fried chicken while also leaving room for steak, seafood, and charcuterie. L&E has partnered with a couple breweries for their own one-off collaborations, including the **Ram Eagle** bourbon-barrel-aged baltic porter made with Moody Tongue's Jared Rouben, and a riff on a Manhattan cocktail made with Pipeworks—the **Brown & Stirred** is made with rye, corn, bitters, cherry puree, and a bit of lemon peel.

MAP ROOM

1949 N. Hoyne Ave., Chicago, IL 60647; (773) 252-7636; maproom.com

It's a funny thing how the neighborhoods in Chicago that house its top beer bars have all perked up as craft beer expands by leaps and bounds. At the same time, the city has spent years working to decimate the small, family-owned neighborhood taverns that used to dot the landscape like dry cleaners and hot dog joints.

Map Room straddles the line between both—it's certainly a beer destination and has been for a long time, but it almost hides itself on an unassuming corner in a mostly residential neighborhood. It serves some of the best beers in the world, but it opens at 6:30 a.m. to serve coffee, pastries, and sandwiches to locals headed to work. Map Room catches customers coming and going.

This traveler-themed spot isn't the biggest bar in town. It doesn't have the most taphandles or bottles in the cooler. It doesn't have a charcuterie menu or a $14 burger or even a kitchen at all. What it does have is a neighborhood feel that the trendiest new places couldn't buy with a seven-figure check. From the collection of *National Geographics* and other books that line the walls, to the required selection of weekly alt-periodicals at the front door, to the regular Beer School discussions that have been going on for two decades, Map Room is one part bar, one part community center, one part reading room, all good.

Those interested in some higher beer learnings should schedule a visit to their regular Beer School events. Led for two decades by the brewmaster for Mickey Finn's, Greg Browne, the classes have moved to feature the teachings of a rotating gallery of local brewers. Made to embody the concept of the "third place" for people away from home and work, the

Map Room is a great place to drink alone, because you're never more than a beer away from a conversation with someone.

MARIA'S PACKAGED GOODS & COMMUNITY BAR

960 W. 31st St., Chicago, IL 60808; (773) 890-0588; community-bar.com; @Marias_Bar

Every neighborhood deserves a really good craft beer bar, right? Sadly, many places in Chicago are still pretty much deserts when it comes to solid beer options. But Bridgeport was a better place the day that Maria's opened on 31st Street, offering drinkers a great place to purchase their favorite craft beers, as well as sit and have a beer.

Originally a traditional Chicago taproom called Kaplan's, Maria's was taken over in October 2010 by the brothers Marzewski. Their mother, Maria, had run it pretty much as-is since the mid-1980s. The brothers refurbished the bar, the coolers, and the tables, and added chandeliers made from brown glass bombers that any beer dork would be proud to have lighting his home bar (and bonus points if you have a classic tin ceiling like Maria's, too). The upgrades earned Maria's a number of accolades, including an inclusion in 2011's Best of Chicago list from *Chicago Magazine*, saying that "Bridgeport never felt more exotic."

They also added a few hundred new beer options to Bridgeport, in bottles, cans, and eighteen draft lines. It's no exaggeration to say that this is easily one of the best beer lists on the whole of the south side; they do have a natural advantage, though—after helping jumpstart Maria's, Ed Marzewski (more commonly known as EdMar) handed off the bar duties to his brother Mike in order to start Marz Community Brewing.

The "community" part of the Community Bar isn't just lip service—EdMar has been at the forefront of artistic endeavors like *Lumpen Magazine* as well as the Co-Prosperity Sphere, an art gallery and events space just a short walk south that also houses EdMar's Lumpen Radio, a low power FM signal that hosts specialty programming (including, of course, a beer-centric weekly talk show from the Beer Temple's Chris Quinn). Maria's is perhaps the most visible part of the Marzewski's efforts toward community building, as taverns have traditionally been a central part of the city's gathering places since its inception.

MONK'S PUB

205 W. Lake St., Chicago, IL 60606; (312) 357-6665;
monkspubchicago.com; @monkspubchicago

This monastic-styled tavern is planted right at the northwest corner of the Loop; the kind of decades-old hypercasual place where your peanut shells go right on the floor and you're equally likely to be elbow-to-elbow with a law student or city worker. It's a great dark-in-the-day kind of place, with candelabra-style chandelier lighting, books and shelves lining the walls, barrels in the rafters, and nook-like booths for more private conversations.

For such an everyman kind of place, the beer selection skews exceptionally crafty. Manager Melissa Shary curates a list that stacks up with much fancier places just a few blocks north. Small-batch breweries share space with Trappist Belgian stalwarts (much to the presumed pleasure of the namesake Monk). The menu is simple but effective, with over a dozen burger options available.

Events are also a regular occurrence, with tap takeovers, featured beers, new beer releases, or vertical tastings of cellared beers through the years. Monk's also opens at 9 a.m., for lingering third-shifters or folks who want to start the day the way many others finish it.

NORSE BAR

6334 N. Clark St., Chicago, IL 60660; (773) 942-6344;
norsebar.com; @NorseBar

One might expect a bar named for Norwegians to find a home in Scandinavian Andersonville, but as owner and beer buyer Ben Buhr explained to *Chicago Magazine* shortly after their opening in October 2011, "Our friends thought this location was so far north, and one of them was like, 'How about Norse? Sounds like north.'" Good enough for me.

Located way up Clark Street at Devon in Edgewater/Rogers Park, Norse offers a dozen drafts of quality beer and a few dozen more bottles and cans with which to live out their mission statement: craft beer deliciousness without the craft beer arrogance. You can reliably find some Boulevard on draft as well as local selections like Temperance and Metropolitan.

To complement the "neighborhood" side of this neighborhood pub, they're dog-friendly during the week, their Tuesday Trivia is a big draw, and guests are welcome to hang out and grab a board game to pass the time.

OLD TOWN POUR HOUSE

1419 N. Wells St., Chicago, IL 60610; (312) 477-2800; @ OTPourHouse and 8 Oak Brook Center, Oak Brook, IL 60523; (630) 601-1440; @OTPHOakbrook; oldtownpourhouse.com

The Bottleneck Management team may run one of the biggest draft programs in the country at Howells & Hood about a mile or so south, but they really cut their craft beer teeth at the Old Town Pour House, opened in March 2012. The huge bar features ninety different draft options at any one time, and the expansive space clad in dark woods looks like it's made for captains of industry seated in leather wingback chairs, puffing away on cigars. Only the dozens of thirsty patrons get in the way of that.

OTPH earned a nod as one of the best beer bars in the nation by *Draft Magazine* in 2013, which called them "more upscale and less neighborhoody than Chicago's other beer bars but just as beer-heavy." They went on to open a second location in the suburbs outside the Oak Brook Center mall, with another ninety handles for parched shoppers, and a third location brought Chicago dogs to the DC area in Maryland in March 2015, the group's first spot outside the Chicago area.

OWEN & ENGINE

2700 N Western Ave, Chicago, IL 60647; (773) 235-2930; owenandengine.com; @OwenandEngine

The term gastropub is often thrown around in a disdainful manner, with the word used to caustically damn a place as a fancy-ass bar with overpriced and self-important bar cuisine. Owen & Engine dares you to take that phrase back and use it to refer glowingly to this Anglophile's dream of a tavern. Chef Bo Fowler, who ran Fat Willy's Rib Shack next door since 2002, took advantage of the two-story space when it became available and opened O&E in 2011.

Across the street from a Burger King and a movie megaplex might not be where you'd expect a bastion of Brit-centric cuisine and twenty taps of great beer, but the Western Avenue location in Logan Square splits the distance between the food-friendly crowds in Wicker Park and Lincoln Square. Fowler's kitchen produces squared-away versions of fish and chips, bangers and mash, bubble and squeak, and one of the city's best burgers. Along with the regular handles, beer director Elliot Baier brings one of the largest cask operations in the city, with four everchanging selections on the hand-pulled beer engine. Touches like these earned O&E a Bib Gourmand award from the Michelin team for a few years.

In early 2015, the O&E team announced they were expanding on their love of good beer and joining the world of making it. A brewpub project called Bixi will mash together a brewery focused on the melding of beer and tea with a menu focused on the flavors of Southeast Asia. Chicago doesn't need another brewpub serving up more wings and burgers, so the prospect of slurping some noodles or dipping dumplings in spicy sambal oelek while pouring a pitcher of complexly flavored pilsner comes highly anticipated.

PADDY LONG'S

1028 W. Diversey Ave., Chicago, IL 60614; (773) 290-6988; paddylongs.com; @PaddyLongs

Paddy Long's is another one of those fun Chicago bar anomalies. It's a neighborhood joint in a mostly residential chunk of Lincoln Park, surviving in a city that wants its bars and taverns on main thoroughfares if at all possible. It's an Irish-style pub that thrives on its passion for craft beer and bacon and Malort. Owners Chris Latchford and Pat Berger also run Kaiser Tiger in the West Loop (see page 164), but it was opening this small one-room bar in 2007 that put them on the beer drinker's map.

Berger, a restaurant and bar veteran of many years, joined forces with the advertising-minded (and Irish) Latchford after a friendship blossomed over beer and rugby games. They expected to be your normal Guinness-pouring bar, but the other great beers and devotion to cured pork belly quickly gained them a non-Celt following. The eighteen drafts regularly feature locals like 3 Floyds and Solemn Oath as well as barrels of the collaboration brews Berger creates with various area breweries. A nod to the Irish nature is generally maintained with a handle of Murphy's Irish Stout.

Paddy's timing was pretty spot on—they were able to carve out a reputation for quality beers in the early part of the beer craze, and the nation went absolutely apeshit for bacon between 2008 and 2010, which few locations have been able to keep feeling fresh, but the beer and bacon pairings at Paddy's fit the bill. They're perhaps most notable nationwide for The Bomb, a five-pound monster of ground pork and beef sausage stuffed with bacon, wrapped with more bacon, and then slowsmoked and served with fries, cheese, and barbecue sauce. Paddy Long's has also been kind to the cardiologists of the world.

PLANK ROAD TAP ROOM

39W149 Plank Rd, Elgin, IL 60124; (224) 238-3527;
plankroadtaproom.com; @PlankRdTapRoom

No booze. No wine. No televisions. No kitchen—just great, fresh beer and a space to drink it in.

If you open that in Wicker Park, that kind of concept will get you written up in Chicago publications for being awesomely dedicated and single-mindedly pure to the support of beer. In the suburbs, however, it's especially radical—and certainly appreciated by the surrounding Elgin-ites who flock to Plank Road regularly for special beer releases, tap takeovers, and food truck dining.

Sitting in a log-cabin style space on seven acres of land (good luck finding that surrounding a taproom in the city) PRTR opened their doors in August 2014 after owners Breanne and Alan Moreno returned from a trip to Colorado. Inspired by the breweries they visited there, the Morenos decided that a pure taproom was their best bet. By the nature of their focus, Plank Road is already a destination for hard-to-find beers like Bourbon County Stout, Perennial's Abraxas, and Surly Darkness.

The taproom tries not to repeat beers too often, and the regular variety keeps folks coming back to try more. There's plenty to look at from the patio, and a fire pit keeps things warm when the sun goes down. If you find that you like the place and you'd like to tell someone about it, you can buy a friend a beer remotely—their First Round's On Me gets you a postcard to send to a pal letting them know they've got a beer waiting for them whenever they show up.

THE PUBLICAN

837 W. Fulton Market, Chicago, IL 60607; (312) 733-9555;
thepublicanrestaurant.com; @publicanchicago

For a long time in Chicago, it seemed like The Publican was never going to be anything more than a good idea. Chef Paul Kahan's followup to Blackbird and Avec—two standout restaurants in a city of great eating—was discussed, talked about, pushed back, teased, and otherwise covered for literally years before it opened in 2008. Then, bang, Chicago had its new favorite beer hall, and one that immediately put quality beer on the radar of a whole new audience.

Pork, oysters, and beer seems like such a perfect combination that it's hard to believe it ever seemed radical at the outset, but such a downscale, rustic ethos from an otherwise fine-dining team seemed revolutionary at the time. The first time the city got their hands on the plates of expertly shucked Kumamotos and the immediately copied-everywhere pork rinds, communal-table dining like this instantly became second nature.

One thing that took Chicagoans some time to wrap their brains around was the idea of a "beer sommelier," a role filled by Michael McAvena for years. Helming the beverage program of a top-tier Chicago restaurant notably devoted to beer was something akin to a culinary highwire act, and even with just a dozen handles available to him behind the bar, there was always a nice mix of Belgian beers, sour and tart wild ales and saisons, tight crisp pilsners, and the occasional cider. You quickly learned you didn't go to Publican for the crazy new stuff, you went because they found excellent beers that went great with the excellent food, and vice versa.

Nowadays the idea of a beer sommellier isn't such a crazy thing, though now the role is generally referred to as a Cicerone. Michelin-starred restaurants with a well-developed beer program are no longer rare, communal seating briefly became the norm, and as mentioned above, fried chicharrones went from Atkins snack to de rigeur drinking appetizer. The Publican was worth the wait, and its contributions to beer and dining may in fact last for decades.

SHEFFIELD'S

3258 N. Sheffield Ave., Chicago, IL 60657; (773) 281-4989; sheffieldschicago.com

In Sheffield's we find another fine example of bar slyly infusing a neighborhood with great beer. Off the beaten Clark Street path of faux-Irish pubs, sports bars, and beer-pong places catering to those still indulging in undergraduate lifestyles is a brick-clad Chicago tavern that is deceptively large, righteously comfortable, and full of fantastic beers on draft.

Sheffield's started in 1980, and gradually transformed itself from a neighborhood taproom to a craft-beer-centric destination with the purchase of the bar by Ric Hess in 1992. Hess pushed beers like Goose Island and Bells when most other bars considered Amstel Light their most interesting import. Between the rebirth of Sheffield's and the opening of the Hopleaf just up Clark Street, 1992 was a good year for Chicago beer drinkers. Hess passed away in 2011, but as credit to the place he built, Sheffield's hasn't lost a step.

Featuring a front bar that's as classic Chicago neighborhood tavern as can be, Sheffield's features twenty-four taps up front with reliable mainstream craft options for the masses. Once you move back into the Beer School Bar, things get more progressive with a well-curated bottle list of fun, funky bombers of beer and more obscure taps. There's even a third bar in back with a fireplace that can host private events but is generally open to the masses on high-traffic evenings and weekends.

The beer garden at Sheffield's is a must-visit during warmer months. Some outdoor beer drinking spaces aim for that feel of someone's backyard or patio. Sheffield's does them one better and gives you the vibe of an open-air beer hall with the loftiest ceilings on Earth. If the three indoor bars weren't enough, there's one final bar outside with taps coming straight out of the exterior brick wall with just the right fruit beers, kolsches, and pilsners for outdoor imbibing.

Garden drinkers hide beneath the branches of a huge cottonwood tree with the leaves blocking some of the sun. The natural rotation of the earth does the rest of the work—stuck between two big buildings, there's only a short window of time where the patio is in full blast brightness. When it gets there on a hot summer afternoon, with the energy and foot traffic of a nearby baseball game, there's hardly a better place to be on the North Side. *Food & Wine Magazine* has named it one of America's Best Beer Gardens; this on top of earning a nod from *Esquire Magazine* in 2009 as one of the nation's best beer bars.

The food is pretty good too—a nice plate of smoked meats like brisket, sausage, and pulled pork pairs really well with a sharp, crisp pale ale or IPA; those hops clear through the rich meaty fat like a squeegee. If you ever hear someone ask, "Where's the best place for a good beer near Wrigley Field?" the immediate response need only be "Sheffield's."

TWISTED SPOKE

501 N. Odgen Ave., Chicago, IL 60642; (312) 666-1500; twistedspoke.com; @twisted_spoke

There are a lot of bars with "themes" in this city—Irish bars, sports bars, video game bars, blues bars. Very rarely do you find an actual biker bar in Chicago. (Leather bars, sure, biker bars, not so much.) West Town's Twisted Spoke has basically owned the city's market on beer, bikes, and bar cuisine since 1995, and there's no one on the horizon even close to taking the crown from them.

Brothers Cliff and Mitch Einhorn opened Twisted Spoke with the theme of "eat, drink, ride," and most patrons here are good for the first two. The restaurant provides enough biker attitude for pretty much everyone, from the multiple motorcycle frames "planted" vertically out front, to Skelly the skeleton riding a black bike mounted and spinning above the bar's entrance.

If, at this point, you're imagining something akin to the place where Pee-Wee Herman dances "Tequila" on the bar, don't be concerned—the Spoke pushes their beer and whiskeys harder than they do the attitude. Spend a morning sipping a (very good) bloody mary on the rooftop patio some spring and you'll see what I mean. As a biker-place goes, it's pretty family friendly. Except for Saturday nights when Smut & Eggs takes over—more on that in a second.

The Spoke is a truly underrated place to get a great beer. Twisted Spoke has always been more of a whiskey bar (literally hundreds of options await you), but the Einhorn brothers are also beer guys, so much so that they started a beer brand called Nomad so they could gypsy brew when the desire struck them. Back in 2010, it was one of the first places to pour beers from Stone Brewing when they entered the market for the first time. They've always had a wide variety of excellent beers, including rarities from Brewdog and Dogfish Head.

The menu is straightforward—bar food, burgers, and a solid brunch, but a longstanding Chicago tradition of some infamy is the Saturday night Smut & Eggs. At the stroke of midnight, the brunch menu kicks in, as do some films of a shall-we-say adult nature, generally of the 1970s-era stag film nature. I'd love to be a fly on the wall to watch the first-date couple that lingers too long over a couple beers when this kicks in. Porn & pancakes. You wouldn't think that pairing would work, but like a biker bar on the near West Side of Chicago, it does.

QUENCHERS

2401 N. Western Ave., Chicago, IL 60647; (773) 276-9730; quenchers.com; @QuenchersSaloon

Quenchers has always seemed to be a little bit in conflict with itself. On one hand, you have a divey bar in a classic tavern setting on a relatively anonymous corner of urban Chicago. You have a popcorn machine, you have a single TV in the corner with the game on, and you have a band playing in a room next door. And on the other hand, you have literally hundreds of bottled beers from dozens of countries to explore; a sort of Around The World in Eighty Beers.

The claim to fame for Quenchers (other than being an oasis of quality beer in an otherwise desolate section of town) was always the chalkboard listing beers from countries some might not even be able to locate on a map—Tusker from Kenya, Xingu from Brazil, Sinebrychoff from Finland. Drinking at Quenchers was always a good way to feel well-traveled with just a $20 bill.

It's a dark-ish place, even at 3 p.m. on a Saturday afternoon, and a recent addition that installed a glass door to an outside patio only mitigated that slightly. It's never exactly been a congenial place, which means it more than fits its surroundings, but that doesn't mean it's uninviting—you just sorta have to earn your stripes. That said, nothing is more comforting than walking into Quenchers on a February evening with the wind blasting down Western Avenue, stripping off eight layers, and having the bartender open a bottle of whatever's dark, rich, malty, and high ABV.

Even though smoking has long since been banned, it still feels smoky. Quenchers was never a beer bar that happened to be in a dive; it's a classic tavern that just happens to have been one of the city's best beer destinations for decades.

A couple dozen tap handles now populate the wall in one corner of the bar, and you can get a hot dog or a sandwich if the kitchen is open. Bands play regularly in the second room, more often than not, the cover is free. You can get a rare Belgian import, any manner of crazy American craft beer, or you can get a $3 PBR on special. Quenchers isn't trying to be all things to all people, it just is. It's one of those rare places you can distill into four words: a damn good bar. Bring cash.

VILLAINS CHICAGO

730 S. Clark St., Chicago, IL 60605; (312) 583-0283; villainschicago.com; @VillainsCHI

The first incarnation of Villains was your average burger-and-beer joint. It was nice for the South Loop to have, especially early in its run when the 2007-era area had a couple of bluecollar pubs and a few fast food joints to service the college crowd at Columbia and Depaul's nearby downtown campus. When it closed in 2012, and the South Loop was bummed, but life pretty much moved on.

Then the plans for the reincarnated Villians emerged, and folks started to get a little more interested. The idea of dozens of craft beer lines and unique distribution agreements for special beers only available there was tossed around. There would be two coolers for two different temperatures of beers—a warmer pour for stouts, porters, and heftier beers to let their flavors shine through, and a standard chilled cooler for the IPAs, pilsners, and the like. Elevated American cuisine from an alum of well-known kitchens like Big Star, Longman & Eagle, and Hot Chocolate would be available. All of this added up to a much-anticipated new spot.

Then the neighborhood waited. Paper covered the windows for longer than anticipated. The grinning skull and the "black market craft" tagline teased residents for months, thirsty Sloopers gained places like First Draft and Vice District. They waited.

Finally in May 2015, Villains threw open their doors with dozens of geek-friendly Mikkeller beers on draft and a rustic interior decked out in concrete, wood, and steel. A wall glassed in with empty bombers of lusted-after rare beers from floor to vaulted ceiling, and some really impressive food came out of the kitchen. Villains wasn't your run-of-the-mill beer joint any more. It was a dining destination that paired wicked good beers with refined plates of pork belly, sirloin steak, roasted chicken, and grilled trout.

Service is fine-dining-level attentive and knows what pairs well with every part of the menu. The beer list has evolved to something much more than just a parade of American IPAs and pale ales peppered with a few weird stouts and barrel-aged options. It runs the gamut from Belgian specialties to Spanish and French brews you rarely see on other lists.

Villains elevated the level of dining in the neighborhood and the idea of what a craft beer bar and restaurant could be. Chicago finally had a place that took food as seriously as beer, and vice versa. It's a great addition to the city, and still a bit of a hidden gem.

Q&A WITH THE HOPLEAF'S MICHAEL ROPER

It's not just breweries that change people's minds about the beers we drink, it's the places in which we discover them as well. I first wandered into the Hopleaf in the mid-2000s and immediately fell in love with the place. It's a love letter to the talented individuals making the greatest beers in the world, from here to Belgium and back again.

Michael Roper has been at the helm of The Hopleaf since opening its doors in 1992, a time when Zima still ran rampant. The nation's most famous bar, Cheers, was still a year away from ending its run on NBC, and beer from craft breweries—then just microbreweries—barely crossed sales of 1 million barrels a year.

You wouldn't expect a beer bar focused on obscure European imports and experimental breweries from Michigan and California (and one or two from Chicago) to make it. But The Hopleaf did. Michael Roper sat down with me to talk about what things were like in the world of beer at The Hopleaf's start, and what has made it change so dramatically since then.

Karl: Talk to me about the first time you walked into the space that would become the Hopleaf. What it was like?

Michael: This was an old man bar. Chicago used to have a lot these liquor store/tap rooms. There's not very many of them left, but this was one of them. You could buy packaged goods, a six-pack of tall boys of Old Style, and then sit down at the counter and have a beer.

It was not pretty. It was mostly old Swedish guys, a lot of gambling. There were three poker machines and a craps game almost all the time. They had a TV built into the back wall where they showed porno movies. There were virtually no women in here.

Karl: It sounds almost like a private club.

Michael: They had a buzzer on the door at night. It was because they didn't want blacks and Hispanics in. If you rang the bell and put your face up in the little window and you were white they buzzed you in; if you weren't they didn't. That was a very common thing. They had covered all the windows so you couldn't see in.

They had two draft lines, Old Style and Special Export. They weren't even aware that there were any other things going on in the beer world. It was not a place anyone would look at and think it had any potential at all. I actually had looked at it the year before it was on the market. It was so ugly and was not doing any business.

In 1991 this neighborhood was not a happening neighborhood. It was not a neighborhood that anyone was coming to for anything like what we wanted to offer. People said, when I was considering it, "God, that's awfully far north." Lakeview, Lincoln Park, at that time Bucktown and Wicker Park, were still kind of gang–infested. There wasn't much happening.

Someone else did buy this place. In the meantime we had looked at a couple of places and gone as far as having architectural drawings made. Then we went to the aldermen, who were saying, "I don't really want another bar in my neighborhood. My constituents don't want anymore bars." So we didn't do that.

After a year this place came on the market again. The guy who bought it completely failed. He was doing even worse business than the old Swede. It had the advantage [that] it was turnkey. The licence was incorporated. It's very very important in Illinois that the licences not have a person's name on it. If on the licence it has a corporation, that means you can take it over just by doing a change of corporate officers so that there's a consistent ownership.

Karl: You knew that you always wanted to do something that offered an elevated beer experience. Is that because no one was doing it at the time, or was that because this has always been something you gravitated to?

Michael: I had worked in music venues and owned a bar that had live music and I knew I didn't really want to do that anymore. I was familiar with a couple of other places that were doing kind of this concept.

Karl: Here in Chicago?

Michael: I came out of Detroit. I wanted to do the food thing and I wanted the food thing to lean toward Belgian stuff. There was a bar in the east side of Detroit near where I grew up that was the oldest Belgian bar in America. They'd been open since 1919. They had mussels and frites, they had the little bit of Belgian burgers available. I thought that was a really cool atmosphere. I liked everything about it. I [thought] I [could] do something like that here.

I rented from a landlord and my hope was that eventually I could buy the building and make my real concept happen. It was a leap of faith because, what if she never sold to me? What if she sold to somebody else? As it turned out, in 2000 she did sell me the building, and I was able to do the food and sort of realize my concept. The first few years we were just a beer bar, no food. We sold bags of peanuts and stuff like that.

Karl: What other beer bars were around in the early to mid-90s?

Michael: Sheffield's always had a really good beer list and they predated us by about five years. There was Quenchers, which had also been around for about five years longer. They had a different concept. They wanted to have the beers from the most countries, which doesn't really make sense because they have beers from Vietnam and the Philippines ...

By the time you buy it here, it's old and it's not going to bring that [exotic flavor] back to you—you're still in Chicago.

There was a place out in Berwyn that had a huge selection of bottled beers. A couple other places like The Ginger Man near Wrigley Field. You have to understand, a very good selection of beer then is not like a very good selection of beer now.

You had a lot of import beer that now we would think is not special at all.

We did have some local breweries then that have fallen by the wayside. We had Chicago Brewing Company, they made Big Shoulders Porter and they had a lager, which was pretty good. We had Golden Prairie and they actually had some very good beer; they were run very poorly. The original Baderbräu, which was a far cry from any of the other people who've used that name since then. We had River West Brewing Company; they were short-lived.

We also carried some craft from other cities that doesn't exist anymore. We have a neon in our window for New Amsterdam Brewing Company from upstate New York, a microbrewery that doesn't exist anymore. There was a Cincinnati brewery called Duesseldorfer, long gone. If you looked at our beer list back then you would see a lot of names that you don't recognize, that don't exist anymore.

Karl: Do you still have some of those lists hanging around? Like a Hopleaf archive?

Michael: I do have a list of old menus some place. I did save a lot of stuff. I have photographs of the old blackboard. It's very interesting to see where we were at then compared to where we are now.

When we first opened we were actually running the place as it was before and we morphed into [this]. We didn't have our official grand opening until a year after we took over.

What I did was get rid of one of those [Bud and Miller] brands every couple of weeks . . . we used to keep a dollar beer, we had Huber in long neck returnables. That was the last thing that we kept for the few old timers who still came here from the old days. At a certain point pretty early on, it wasn't relevant.

Karl: You were starting to find your people.

Michael: We found our people really quickly. Most of the holdovers didn't really like us because we didn't allow gambling anymore, we took the porno movies away, we took the poker machines away, we put windows in.

Karl: All they could do was smoke cigarettes and drink beer.

Michael: Also these guys, for a long time felt very comfortable using language and racial epitaphs that we found offensive. I had to go and talk to these guys and say, "I can't change the way you feel, but we welcome all kinds of people here, so you can't use that kind of language." Some of those people said, "F— you." We got rid of that stuff pretty quickly.

Karl: So in the beginning, when you were getting rid of the mainstream beer brand, was there ever any push back from distributors saying, "I'm not going to get you the fancy stuff if you don't have a handle of Budweiser here," or anything like that?

Michael: Frankly they were happy to find someone who wanted some of this stuff. They were having trouble selling it. They'd taken on these obscure imports or some of these American microbreweries and were like, "Oh my god, well at least Hopleaf will take them." And that was our advantage.

The most important beer for us in the early days, the one that actually kept our doors open and distinguished us, was Bell's. It was a cult beer in Chicago. They didn't really come into Chicago with any presence until 1992. At that time there were a lot of Detroit diaspora, people who left Detroit because it was such a terrible mess, and other Michigan people who had come here from Flint and Saginaw and Port Huron and all the other cities that were kind of in a tailspin.

Those people were loyal to Bell's. Bell's also caught on with a very small group of homebrewers and beer fans who really recognized that this beer was not like any of the other microbreweries we had. It was something special. Bars that had Bell's became kind of like . . .

Karl: A beacon in the night?

Michael: We were kind of desperate to find people to come way up here. I talked to Larry Bell and I said, "You guys don't have a neon do you?" [He says] "We don't have a neon." I said "Would you mind if I scanned your logo and I made a neon?" [He says] "No, it'd be great!" So I did.

We put that thing in the window and people were going on the Clark Street bus from downtown on their way to Rogers Park, or going through this dead zone where they never even looked out the window and then they saw this Bell's neon. And they just got off the bus and came in. It was really that dramatic.

Having Bell's was so unusual. At that time Bell's Amber, Kalamazoo Stout, Porter—those early brands for them and Solsun, which later became Oberon, were huge draws to have on draft.

Karl: Did you find that to be at odds with your intention of opening a Belgian-focused place?

Michael: Not so much because there really wasn't much Belgian beer available on draft. The first Belgian beer we had on draft was Grimbergen. That was because Grimbergen's national importer was some little company out in Wheaton.

Later on there were things like Hoegaarden and Leffe, but in the early days, Grimbergen was it. If we were going to have draft beer it was not going to be Belgian. We did have a little selection of Belgian beers in bottles. At that time, Duvel, Chimay was pretty new in the country then, Westmalle had been around a while. We actually had Westvleteren, which is now...

Karl: The white whale of white whales. The "best beer in the world."

Michael: Yes. It was available then. Hardly anybody carried it because it was so expensive. They were under the moniker of Saint Sixtus. They were readily available. They were imported through a wine importer. We carried those things, but it was really Bell's that kept our doors open and made us a destination for people looking for better, more interesting beers.

Karl: Then things sort of tailed off again at the end of the '90s and into the beginning of the 2000s.

Michael: A lot of breweries started going under because they were run by old hippies [and] passionate homebrewers who were not good business people. They had won a very small portion of the beer consumer market. At best, in the mid-90s, 2 or 3 percent of people were choosing those beers. The big beer companies didn't have much to worry about.

Karl: I'm sure they weren't even on their radar.

Michael: The big beer companies had new brands like Miller Genuine Draft, Bud Light, Bud Dry . . . and there were new imports coming in. It was slowly growing, but not a very big part of the total beer scene. There weren't that many bars that really felt like they were ready to buy into it. A lot of bars, sales guys would go in and they'd say, "You know I've got this Bell's beer from Kalamazoo. It's really cool." Owners would ask, "Well how much is it?" and [distributors] would say, "It's $27 a case." The response would be, "$27 a case! Jesus Christ, who's going to buy that beer?"

Because at that time they were buying Bud or Miller for eleven bucks a case. You're telling them to sell this beer that they've never heard of for twice as much money. A lot of people were not buying it. I should mention that some of the success of Bell's and some of these other brands had a lot to do with certain sales people on the street who really evangelized for them. There was a guy John Barabus and Terry Whiteside. They went out there and they evangelized. They were selling salvation.

They were with the distributor. They had big portfolios, but they themselves drank this beer and recognized these few breweries were doing something very different. They were going out and putting their reputations on the line and really pushing it, giving away free samples to the owners and saying, "Really drink this." They made believers. It is the same today if you don't have some feet on the streets, but if you get the right person, someone who people know and trust, who really invests in your brand and your concept, you can succeed.

I think the draft beer revolution that is happening now has a lot to do with the fact that draft beer is so much better than it was. There's still some old man bars that don't clean their lines, or don't clean their lines very frequently. Now I would say that for the last few years we are state of the art.

Karl: You've been watching the city's beer culture progress for a long time, but it's really exploded in the last five years or so. What do you think is the reason that all of this started happening when it did?

Michael: We were behind. Chicago was behind the rest of the country. New York, San Francisco, Colorado, California, Washington, Michigan all seemed to be having a lot more success with the new craft beer movement than we did. There are two reasons, one is a national phenomenon, and one's a local phenomenon that changed things.

The local phenomenon was that in the first twelve years of the Daley administration, we had a liquor commissioner named Winston Mardis. During his twelve years, not one tavern license was issued in the city of Chicago, and 750 taverns were closed down. It became a goal of the Daley administration to get taverns out of neighborhoods. [They wanted to] concentrate nightlife into districts, and to turn down applications for things like breweries and distilleries. My feeling is that 3 Floyd's would have been in Chicago. Everyone who works there, who's involved in it lives in Chicago. But they couldn't open here.

Karl: How did Goose get in?

Michael: They were before that. They beat it. A lot of the people who wanted to open breweries in Chicago were told by the city, you can open, but we're going to find some sites for you. They were all abandoned industrial sites.

They sent them down to South Shore where the steel mills were. In the case of the Clybourn corridor, at that time it was a derelict old industrial district with abandoned rail spurs. They sent them there. They said, "You can open here, because nobody else gives a shit. Nobody lives around here." There were no neighbors. They just beat it out.

After that time it was impossible for somebody to open a brewery, a distillery, or even a tavern in Chicago. You could open a restaurant with liquor, but you couldn't open a bar. That twelve-year period was a disaster for us. We got so far behind. It was really hard for us to expand. They put us through so many hoops. They didn't want us here. They did not want us to expand.

Karl: They just wanted people to go to the grocery store, and go home, and drink beer there, and not get into trouble.

Michael: Right. Daley had, for an Irishman, some very conservative ideas about the place of alcohol in society. Considering that his father's career started in Bridgeport, you would never know that by his feeling about it. He actually wrote a guest editorial in the *Tribune* after I opened here in which he said that his administration would help neighborhoods, in any way possible, close taverns because taverns are where criminals congregate.

Here I am, I'm investing everything I've got in [this] place. . . We are not a tavern where criminals congregate. He made us into this dark, evil place. Toward the end of Daley's era, they got rid of Winston Mardis. The next liquor commissioner was much more enlightened. Daley had also come around. Bars, brewpubs, wine bars, places like that fill storefronts, pay taxes, hire Chicagoans.

We got really behind because of this political clampdown on anything involving alcohol. When the light started shining, we did a big catch up.

You'll notice that the other thing is that so many of the breweries here are spawns of Goose Island. You cannot overestimate the value [of Goose]. A lot of people are very negative about Goose Island these days. Our beer scene would be completely different. The national beer scene would be very different. The head brewer at Firestone Walker is from Goose Island. Their brewers are everywhere. That's because of the close relationship between the Siebel Institute and Goose Island. It's a very important step for us.

Things got better in this regard . . . Rahm Emanuel drinks craft beer. He comes here. He looks at our beer menu, and he knows the brands. He came here before he was mayor. When he was a congressman, he came here. He and his administration, they have been very supportive of brewers, distillers, places that make wine on premise. We have some cider makers here in the city. He wants all that. He understands that it's an economic engine.

Look at what it's done for Portland, Oregon. It's a big part of their economy. It's a big part of the tourist draw. He gets it. Daley did not get it. That's the micro reason, the local reason that we are in this boom now, after not so many years passed.

The other part of it that's more national, is that there's a lot of money sitting around right now. Some people after the real estate crash were afraid to invest in real estate. Some people didn't trust the stock market anymore. There's no reason to buy bonds, the interest rate is so low. There's a lot of cash sitting with some pretty big investors. Week after week they read *Crane Chicago Business*, the read the *Wall Street Journal*, and what do the you see? *Forbes, Fortune*, everybody says 35 percent growth last year in craft beer. Craft beer profit, it's booming. These people want to get in on that, and they are.

There's a lot of money funneling into craft beer. It's also funneling into star chef restaurants and stuff like that. The press has convinced people that this is where they should put their money. On a positive side [for me], it means that a lot more breweries are opening. On a negative side, people are opening breweries for the wrong reason. They are not passionate beer people. Some of these people don't know anything about beer. They just see dollar signs. Some of the breweries are making uninspired beers.

I can make this comparison to expansion baseball. You have too many teams, and there are not enough good pitchers and catchers around. What's happening now is that there are not enough great brewers.

Karl: Like anything, there's a lot of average ones, and there are some who are really good, and there are some that are . . .

Michael: Inspirational. Some are really great. The problem is that there are a lot of competent technicians who are available to these money guys. They can say, "I can nail this style, that style." But they don't have any creativity.

Karl: It's a unique type of brain that can make a beer really well. You have to be equal parts artist and scientist; be a creative person and also basically a chemical and mechanical engineer. Those two things don't live in the same brain very often.

Michael: Sometimes you have to have two or three people at the same brewery. You have the scientist who runs the lab and then you have the creative person, and then you have the businesses guy. Those people have to all get together. Sometimes magic happens, where everything falls into place. 3 Floyd's is a great example of that. It's this overall aesthetic that they have. It has to do with the label, the branding, the names; it has to do with Nick Floyd, his personality; it has to do with lots of things like that, but the beer is pretty damn good.

We have some really good breweries here. We have some people who are doing very experimental things and succeeding. We have some people who put the classics out and do it well.

These days the new craft breweries are not biting into Miller, Coors, or Bud that much anymore. They still have their solid market, they're still selling a lot of beer. Who's really getting killed are the mainstream imports. Go up and down the street, try to find a Bass line, try to find a Becks draft handle, or Heineken—they're gone. They are getting killed, because they're not special.

Why would I order that when I can get a Firestone Walker Pils, or a Victory Pils? Great stuff. Pony Pils, from Half Acre. Fantastic, fresh, delicious.

Find a location that is underserved, make a good bar, serve the beer you brew in-house, and offer good service and good food, and you've got something that's lasting.

Karl: The DryHop model. Don't build a brewery and keep expanding all the time—build a series of brewpubs.

Michael: Absolutely. That's a great example. Sometimes after a while, maybe you will grow into a situation where you can sell your beer elsewhere.

My favorite example in Chicago is Piece. Jonathan Cutler is one of the best brewers in the country. He, year after year, [at the] Great American Beer Fest wins all kinds of medals. He gets offers, I'm sure, all the time to go with much bigger brewers, but he's content with his life. He sells his beer there. I'm not even that huge of a fan of the pizza there, but I will go there just to drink the beer, because his beer is fantastic, and you can only get it there.

Karl: You don't have it on draft.

Michael: I wish I did.

Karl: I have to imagine that there are lots of people lately who have opened a brewery and have had their eyes opened to craft beer here. I bet they really want a handle at The Hopleaf, as a kind of "I've made it" sort of moment.

Michael: A lot of people are really desperate to get in here, and they're desperate to get into Map Room, as symbolic . . . It also opens doors for them. They go to some bar that may be half craft, and they're still carrying macro's and stuff. The guy goes in and says, "Hopleaf has my beer. The Map Room carries my beer." They say, "Well, maybe I should taste your beer."

There are people I like, they're earnest, they're working hard, their beer just isn't there yet, or they're brewing styles that have been done so many times before. If you come in here and say, "I have the IPA to end all IPAs," well . . .

Karl: Good luck.

Michael: I also think it's important to sometimes give somebody a shot. The one thing that won't get you in here is offering me a free keg or something. I don't want a free keg. I'm going to buy it. I don't want to owe anybody anything. I'll pay you a fair price, so that you make your money, and I'll put it out there. As much as I am sort of the grim reaper in saying yes or no, the real arbiter of taste is the customer. You've got to win them over from the get go. It's really hard if they've had a beer they didn't like. They are not going to spend $6 or $7 on it again.

Karl: People remember that stuff.

Michael: They remember a long time afterwards. "I had this beer and it sucked." Then you see it on the menu again, and say, "I'm not going to order that, because there are these beers that I have great experience with that are on the menu, too. They've got this new sour beer, but Perennial has got a beer here, and every time I've had a Perennial beer I really like it."

The customer really makes that choice. I don't want to ever have anything on tap that I'm embarrassed to have on tap, but we'll give some things a go and see what the customer thinks. Sometimes it's amazing. Our customers are very good at sniffing out good stuff.

Karl: It's a turnaround from those guys that would come in, and sell you on Bells, that were evangelizing for them. Something comes in that really excites you guys, and then you can evangelize for it.

Michael: Yes. There are some other breweries in the larger region that have done this too. Perennial is a great example of somebody we have a great relationship with. Dark Horse is another really cool brewery.

Karl: I evangelize for Dark Horse all the time.

Michael: They're cool people. I still consider that kind of local, very good beer. My customers like them. There are some [other] beers that we've put on tap that we notice really quickly . . . they drink one pint and they say, "I'll have a Zombie Dust now." Or they just go, "eh." The worst thing is, and this happens in the dining room more than at the bar, that people finish eating and there's a half a pint of unfinished beer, or they order another thing and say, "You can take that, I'm not going to finish it." I try to keep my ear close to that reaction. My servers and bartenders can tell me, "Eh, people aren't liking that." Then I'm not going to order that anymore.

Karl: Watching Hopleaf progress through the years, it's been a real evolution. It's grown from the front room, to a back room with a kitchen, to the back patio, to a new space, with the new kitchen. At this point, are you content with the way this is now?

Michael: We have realized our vision. In spite of the fact that I've been approached by some of those same kind of money people who want me to open a Hopleaf in Naperville, a Hopleaf at the airport, a Hopleaf in . . .

Karl: There's the Hop Cat line of beer bars that started in Grand Rapids. Everybody loved it, and they were there for years, now every six months they're announcing a new one.

Michael: I'm not into that. I live in the neighborhood, I don't need any more money. By growing slowly over twenty-four years, I've been able to maintain complete control, without taking on partners, or investors. I don't need anything else. I like my life the way it is. I think that you water down brands, it's really hard to open a second place and be as vested in it.

A lot of places that do this become lesser places. Like Jonathan Cutler at Piece, Hopleaf is going to be a single location. If you like what we do, this is where it is. You're not going to find it anywhere else. I'm going to be sixty-two in January. Do I want to go through that trauma of opening another place?

I would warn anybody, don't get too big. I wouldn't want to ever have somebody who used to come here years ago come in, or read about me in an interview or something, and ask "Is Michael here today?" If the bartender said, "He's never here." I would never want that to happen.

Bottle Shops

ARCHER LIQUORS

5996 S. Archer Ave., Chicago, IL 60638; (773) 582-4767;
archerliquors.com; @archerliquors

Bringing a vast array of bombers, bottles, and cans of craft brew to the public since 1993, Archer Liquors offers up more than just beer, wine, and spirits. This spot, located on the Southwest Side with planes screaming overhead into nearby Midway Airport, also features a monthly food truck gathering, a small selection of homebrew supplies, and a unique customer rewards system that comes into play for special releases that should be replicated across alcohol sales locations throughout the land.

Their dedication to freshness can be delivered every week in the form of the Fresh Report, an update that tells drinkers what's good right now, in designations of mileage from the local (under 20 miles for beers like Spiteful, Pipeworks, and Lagunitas) to the regional (20 to 200 miles for Michigan, Indiana, and Wisconsin brews), and beyond (California and Colorado beers, for example). With best-by dates and even dates when the beer was canned or bottled, it's a must for aficionados dedicated to maximum hop flavor.

In a world where small-batch beer releases can get hyped to the point of people changing clothes in their car to receive a double allotment or hiring "mules" to stand in line for top beers, it's their points system, concocted to reward loyal customers and not folks swooping in for a couple of beers a year, that deserves some attention. Customers can amass points by purchasing beer throughout the year, and redeem them for small batch, special event, or high-demand beers like 3 Floyd's **Zombie Dust** or the annual **Bourbon County Stout** release.

Stand in line overnight or just support a neighborhood business for my yearly BCS? Easy choice.

THE BEER CELLAR

488 Crescent Blvd., Glen Ellyn, IL 60137; (630) 315-5060;
beercellarchicago.com; @beercellarchi

A bottle of New Belgium's La Folie got proprietor Dave Hawley into the world of craft beer in 2007, and rather than grab a homebrew kit and start a hobby that would lead to a brewery, he went the other direction— moving it from his shelves into your fridge. Opened in January 2014, the Beer Cellar is the first true craft bottle shop in the western suburbs, located in quaint-as-hell downtown Glen Ellyn.

It was the lack of any other shop nearby paired with ongoing growth of breweries around the area that gave Hawley the idea to open the Cellar, which is literally what it started as —the original store sat beneath a clothing store, though a move down the block in 2016 made the "cellar" part of the name more of a euphemism. Centrally located amongst breweries like Noon Whistle, Pollyanna, Miskatonic, and Solemn Oath, the Cellar is the go-to for hyperlocal beer as well as hard-to-find outfits from the city like Spiteful, Pipeworks, and Marz.

BEERSHOP

1026 North Blvd., Oak Park, IL 60302; (847) 946-4164; beershophq.com; @BeerShopHQ

THE OPEN BOTTLE

7101 W. 183rd St., Unit 105, Tinley Park, IL 60477; (708) 263-0449; theopenbottle.com; @theopenbottleco

After Beermiscuous kicked things off in June 2014, the rise of the "craft beer cafe" continued in 2015, that being a place where you can shop for beer while sampling a few things on draft or just having a pint before or after making your purchases. Beershop and the Open Bottle have a couple things in common—they're both split concepts of a bottle shop and a taproom, and both offer a wide variety of top-notch craft beer to communities that really needed them.

Beershop opened in Oak Park in April 2015. Other than a couple other taverns and the Exit Strategy brewery in nearby Forest Park, it's a shining beacon of craft beer quality in a desert of average beer that extends for miles around. Owner Tony Compaglia worked for a similar setup on the west coast before coming back to Chicago to start his space. The Village had to adjust its license structure so he would be able to open and sell beer without also selling food.

Similarly, owners Julia and Patrick Bisch opened The Open Bottle in November 2015 with eight draft lines to sip on while you shop, along with a few hundred package selections for folks to take home when they're done. Tinley Park isn't quite the beer desert that Oak Park has traditionally been—Flossmoor Station and Tribes Beer Company are a short drive away. Hailstorm is just down the street and 350 Brewing is literally across it. But for packaged goods, The Open Bottle provided a much needed better place to pick up a six-pack than the nearby grocery store.

From the combination liquor stores and taprooms in the city some call "slashies," to tiny neighborhood bottle shops, to beverage superstores like Binny's, to small cafes with a few taps and package offerings to go, it's not just breweries that are adding to the rich tapestry of beer options in Chicagoland.

THE BEER TEMPLE

3185 N. Elston Ave., Chicago, IL 60618; (773) 754-0907; craftbeertemple.com; @thebeertemple

The name is The Beer Temple. The slogan is "Beers to revere." Setting craft beer on a quasi-religious level sets a high bar, but proprietor Chris Quinn meets it readily. Talk to Quinn for more than a minute about anything beer–related—styles, hop varietals, up-and-coming breweries, consolidations and buyouts, and especially freshness—and you get an idea about how seriously he loves beer.

You can see it in the dedication to quality, such as LED lights in the coolers specifically to keep the beer from getting lightstruck and skunky to hosting beer events and inviting brewers to talk to people about their beers on a level beyond the usual "beer is made of four ingredients" intro-level conversations. Quinn is so hardcore about selling the best beer to his patrons that if a beer isn't up to his standards, it may get pitched into the dumpster.

You can see it in the two podcasts he hosts about beer. One is a video review podcast, often a discussion on beers in a certain style, varieties of beer from one brewery, an examination of beers new to the market, or just stuff that's currently in season. The other is a weekly roundtable conversation about beer with market insiders—unsurprisingly called the Insiders Roundtable—that is free-flowing, ridiculously informative, occasionally combative, but always interesting.

And we haven't even talked about the selection yet. At this point, do I need to tell you it's good? That there's more excellent beer in a few hundred feet of shelf space and cooler racks than some entire states likely have? (Looking at you, Mississippi.) That on any given day, you can walk in and sample beers that you can't even buy in this state just because Quinn wants his patrons to have a chance to try them? That he measures the freshness of his just-in beers in *hours*, not days or weeks?

Yeah. All of that. Oh, and it's a few minutes off the Kennedy for folks coming in from the suburbs or out of state, and there's free parking. What else could you ask for?

BINNY'S

Multiple locations; binnys.com; @binnysbev

If you are in the Chicagoland area, there is a very good chance you're within about a half-hour drive of a Binny's right now. Binny's motto is, "If it's not here, it's not worth drinking," which is a nice thought but completely antiquated in a world of limited bottle counts and beers made to sell out in a single day. That said, Binny's was always more of a wine place anyways.

Okay, to be fair, Binny's has advanced its craft beer efforts by leaps and bounds over what it stocked not even a few years ago. Wisely catching onto the rising tide of craft beer, they've expanded from a couple shelves and coolers into entire departments, even going so far as to add a taproom to their flagship Marcey Street location in Lincoln Park.

In existence since the late 1940s, Binny's expanded to nearly thirty locations around the Chicagoland area over the years, with varying focuses on wine, spirits, cigars, and even cheese depending on the market. A takeover of a competing brand, Sam's Wine & Spirits in 2009, cemented their dominance as the go-to major alcohol vendor with nothing but corner stores and single-location independents in their competitive wake.

The collection of stores is such a force in Chicago that Goose Island (briefly) made Binny's the only place to be on the day after Thanksgiving for the release of Bourbon County Stout, making Black Friday a whole different thing for beer geeks. Since Goose took BCBS national, Binny's can no longer be the only retailer to release the beer on that date, but they remain ground zero for the biggest sales of the day—lines start the night before for variants like Barleywine, Proprietors, and Rare.

If Binny's doesn't have it, it may very well be worth drinking, but even in "its" absence, you'll still be able to find a reliable replacement.

BOTTLES & CANS

4109 N. Lincoln Ave., Chicago, IL 60618; (773) 857-2270; bottlesandcanschicago.com; @BTLSandCANS

For as much craft beer is made and poured in Lincoln Square, Ravenswood, and North Center, it's a little astonishing that there's just one serious bottle shop serving all three neighborhoods (as well as nearby Lakeview and Albany Park). That could be because proprietors Joe and Carly Katz have created such a friendly little shop that no one with a conscience would be able to open nearby and compete.

As part of the initial move to make a craft-beer-friendly neighborhood by Alderman Ameya Pawar, Bottles & Cans started like so many other businesses in Chicago—politically. The Katzes had to get a moratorium on alcohol sales lifted, because for a long time the only thing people would be interested in selling or buying on that stretch of Lincoln would be a $1.89 bottle of King Cobra. After community meetings and many conversations, the zoning was changed, and the "Nicest Little Bottle Shop in North Center" (their words) was ready to roll.

They opened in 2012 and immediately became the place to get package versions of the myriad beers coming out of the nearby breweries—Begyle, Spiteful, Metropolitan, and Pipeworks can reliably be found on the shelves dedicated to local beer. Beyond that, the offerings are designated by state— looking for an all-Michigan selection? A Wisconsin, Missouri or Kansas City sixer? Or maybe something from the West Coast? Belgium? The UK? Crazy gypsy stuff? All available.

Maybe you'd like to taste a few beers from a nearby or regional brewery before you visit it? Beer, wine, and spirits tastings are scheduled regularly, usually involving reps directly from the brewery—especially if that brewery is within a bike ride away.

Perhaps the most notable thing that Bottles & Cans offers is the city's best pick-your-six variety. Want to try just one beer? Go ahead and break that six-pack up. Take just one of those tallboys. Leave the rest for them to shelve and then someone else can try 'em too. You can make a six-pack of just about anything in the store, as long as it's 16 ounces or less.

Sure, there's a price for that kind of variety, but consider that at most other stores, the pick-your-six varieties are nothing more than nearly-out-of-date beers in a selection ranging from Sam Adams to Leinenkugels. For superdorks like myself, that kind of freedom is invaluable when you want to try a series of session beers, a parade of pumpkin ales, or an octet of Oktoberfests. (Alliteration!)

PUERTO RICO FOOD & LIQUOR

2559 W. Augusta Ave., Chicago, IL 60622; (773) 342-2678; no website; @prfl2559

This little corner store is the Millennium Falcon of Chicago craft beer providers—she may not look like much, but she's got it where it counts, kid. There has to be a whole bunch of Humboldt Park beer lovers within close proximity to Puerto Rico Food & Liquor, because this place stocks a whole lot of great beer in not a lot of space, and keeps it moving with no problem at all.

From the outside, it's no more than your average bodega, a small storefront that in hundreds of other places around the city is good for things like cigarettes, candy, and maybe a cooler of your run-of-the-mill six-packs. Here, though, it's transitioned from a family store into a true destination for great beers, and has perhaps one of the greatest beer-variety-to-square-footage ratios on the planet. Check out their BeerMenus page to get a feel for just how much beer they've got.

Stacked deep onto racks of shelves and a row of coolers is a tightly packed array of top beers from around the nation. Bombers of special release beers, hyperlocal nanobrewed beers, and old standbys all have a home at PRFL.

WEST LAKEVIEW LIQUORS

2156 W. Addison Ave., Chicago, IL 60618; (773) 525-1916; wlvliquors.com; @wlvliquors

For quite a long time, West Lakeview Liquors (or WLL for short) was the bottle shop in Chicago. Not because it was the best—though it was—but because it was kinda the only one. This little corner shop in an unassuming brick storefront opened in 1988 with a highly curated selection of great beers, spirits, and wines, with a major focus on beers (at that time) from abroad and increasingly produced here in the States.

Proprietor Kristina Bozic doesn't just sell alcohol, though. Relationships with brewers across Europe and scattered throughout the US allow her to be on hand to help brew with the likes of Jester King in Austin, Texas, De Molen in the Netherlands, and Chicago's Off Color. Getting exclusive access to these beers, along with all the other specialty releases, is part of what makes WLL the destination it's become.

Voters at RateBeer agree, they've named West Lakeview the best bottle shop in the city for eight straight years. Voters at RateBeer also have West Lakeview to thank for another of their favorites—Beejay Oslon and Gerritt Lewis, co-founders of Pipeworks, met at West Lakeview and hatched their plans to start a brewery behind the counter as they checked out customers. RateBeer voters named Pipeworks the best new brewery in the world in 2013.

WLL's biggest claim to fame may be as one of the few sites selected to participate in Zwanze Day, an annual celebration by one of Belgium's most acclaimed beer producers, Brasserie Cantillon. Just fifty-six locations in the entire world are allowed to sell a unique one-off beer made only for the Zwanze Day celebration. When you consider that even the regular stuff from Cantillon gets snatched up as soon as it hits the shelves, you can only imagine at the intensity that goes into getting one's hands on a super-limited release.

The other 364 days of the year, however, West Lakeview is home to great beers, hand-picked single-barrel spirits, and tastings from breweries around the world including many not even distributed in the States. As if that's not something to be proud of every damn day.

THE BEST BEER FESTIVALS

The Chicago area is, for lack of a better term, infested with festivals celebrating craft beer. In warmer months, you can hit a beer festival every weekend if you wanted to, and help do your share to support the neighborhood organizations, churches, chambers of commerce, VFWs, and other groups who put them on. But if you've only got a few days to get away for a beery event (and probably a day or two to recover), here are your best bets:

The first and foremost among all Chicago area beer events is the **Festival of Barrel Aged Beers,** affectionately known as FoBAB. Started in 2002 outside of Goose Island's Wrigleyville location, this festival has grown into the world's greatest assemblage of some of the best and most creative beers on earth, all pitched into barrels to see what comes out. It's fitting that this has grown from Chicago, home of the foremost bourbon-barrel-aged beer on the planet, Goose Island's Bourbon County Stout.

Growing from an outdoor space in a northside neighborhood to a union hall in the West Loop, to a beautiful events center in Bridgeport, to smack dab in the city center at the UIC Forum, FoBAB keeps getting bigger and better. The festival grows larger with each iteration; with hundreds of different beers and breweries. Often small breweries will have a barrel-aging program of just one or two barrels, but they know that there are a lot of eyes on FoBAB and it's a good way to earn some quick attention if you take a medal in one of the many categories.

FoBAB attendees throughout the years can tell you that it really, really helps if you like bourbon or whiskey, as the vast majority of barrel-aged beers typically rested for a few months in casks once used by the likes of Heaven Hill, Elijah Craig, Jim Beam, or the occasional Pappy Van Winkle. In recent years, however, beermakers have blown out the margins on these hyper-experimental styles, bringing beers aged in wood that has held tequila, port wine, aquavit, and absinthe. (A beer or two aged in a tabasco barrel have even surfaced. Drinkers should have a particular appreciation for the higher end of the Scoville scale before trying these.)

Tickets can be pricey, but if you go to a single Chicago-area festival each year and you love weird, crazy, creative beers, put FoBAB on your calendar. The price of the festival also helps support the efforts of the Illinois Craft Brewers Guild. Tickets sell quick, so plan ahead accordingly. Your planning shouldn't stop once you get your tickets in hand, though—the 2-ounce pours may not look like much, but man, do they add up quickly when you're sampling a dozen 10 percent+ ABV monsters. (I skip the barleywine table each year, and though surely there are many great beers in there, they can simply be too much. Your beer style mileage may vary.) As beer festivals go, there are two that should be considered national beer holidays. Denver's Great American Beer Fest is one, and FoBAB is right along side it.

Your other festival must-attend is the annual **Beer Under Glass** event at the Garfield Park Conservatory, also hosted by the Brewers Guild. This fest kicks off the annual craft beer appreciation marathon known as Chicago Craft Beer Week (CCBW), a ten-day-plus celebration of the many brewers in and around the city and suburbs (and slightly beyond as well).

Beer Under Glass (or BUG for short) brings hundreds of beer fans to the nature-filled grounds of one of the Chicago

Park District's underappreciated gems, with acres of plants, trees, ponds, and fountains and many, many places for people to pour beer. If you've ever dreamed of drinking a beer poured for you from an elaborate jockey box by someone camped out beneath huge plant fronds in a greenhouse pouring some amazing beers, BUG is for you.

Since this festival is typically scheduled for mid-May, the weather tends to dictate that not all the beers are as high-intensity as FoBAB. Many more lighter options are available and many breweries take the opportunity to pour different versions of some old favorites. Beers can get infused with fruits, spices, and tons of different hops. In addition to being the CCBW kickoff event, it's also one of the very first beer festivals of the summer season, so the audience for this festival is less hardcore and a little more widely varied. For every guest hunting down the crazy downstate brewery that few have heard of, there are three others happy to try a pour of a light Half Acre pilsner or a pale ale from Revolution.

Both of these festivals are also notable for the participation of the brewery staff. At FoBAB, beers are poured by volunteers, but there's an extremely good chance that the person next to you sampling a beer or three is one of the participating brewers—FoBAB is as much a contest for breweries to win as it as a chance for brewery employees to get together and commiserate over a few strange brews. Since this festival is spread out over multiple sessions, those looking to occasionally run into the folks who make your favorite brews are probably going to want to get tickets for the Saturday evening session where awards are announced. Find someone wearing a medal and give him a high five.

At the single-session BUG, the booths are more often than not manned by the brewers themselves, getting beer fans right up close and personal with the folks slaving away over hot brew kettles for much of the year.

Not all the best festivals have a Brewers Guild imprint on them. **Festiv-Ale,** an annual gathering held downtown each fall since 2006 to benefit cystic fibrosis research, reliably has a great lineup of breweries and local chefs creating food pairings, and it benefits a good cause.

There's no shortage of street fairs in Chicago each summer, but the weekend of **Square Roots** in Lincoln Square has a great mix of local breweries, and you can even find homebrewers from the Square Kegs club making and pouring a few of their beers onsite.

Goose Island hosts their annual **312 Block Party** in mid-September, bookending BUG as the end of the festival season. The brewery brings in touring musicians for a concert in the West Loop where they pour tons of different Goose beers, including a reliable amount of rare and sought-after Bourbon County options.

Throughout the rest of the year, you can find a festival for every taste—there are events in every other neighborhoods and towns, there are events on boats and on rooftops, there are events where you can barely hear yourself think at Union Station, taste samples near the menagerie of Lincoln Park Zoo, and sip brews on the grounds of Soldier Field. There are even outdoor events in the dead of winter. We're not wanting for fests. Barring a flight to Denver in autumn for the annual Great American Beer Fest, FoBAB and Beer Under Glass are your two best bets in town.

Recipes from Beer-Friendly Restaurants and Brewpubs

It's one thing to read about all the beer and food at the many places that dot the Chicago landscape, it's another to create some yourself. I thought it'd be fun to let folks try their hand at them. The following are a collection of recipes from Chicagoland restaurants and brewpubs that either feature beer or go well with a freshly poured pint.

All recipes courtesy of Chef de Cuisine Cosmo Goss of The Publican (see page 175)

THE PUBLICAN'S MUSSELS
Serves 2

> 3 tablespoons butter, divided
> 1 tablespoon sliced celery
> 1 tablespoon sliced garlic
> 1 tablespoon sliced shallot
> 1 bay leaf
> 1 teaspoon thyme
> $1/2$ teaspoon chili flakes
> 2 pounds mussels
> 2 ounces Gueuze beer
> 1 tablespoon lemon juice
> 2 tablespoons chopped celery leaves
> Salt to taste

Over high heat, melt 1 tablespoon butter in a 3-quart sauce pot. Add celery, garlic, shallots, bay leaf, thyme, and chili flakes and sweat for 1 minute.

Add mussels to pot and stir to incorporate the ingredients. Add the Gueuze and cover pot until all the mussels open, 4 to 5 minutes. Uncover pot and stir in remaining 2 tablespoons butter.

Finish the mussels with a pinch of salt, drizzle of lemon juice and top with celery leaves. Serve with a fresh baguette.

THE PUBLICAN'S BARBECUE CARROTS
Serves 4

> 1 cup, plus 1 tablespoon The Publican's BBQ Rub (see recipe below)
> $1/4$ cup salt, plus more to taste
> 1 pound small farm carrots, cleaned and halved
> 1 tablespoon extra virgin olive oil
> $1/2$ tablespoon lemon juice
> $1/4$ cup toasted pecans, crushed
> 2 tablespoon Dill Yogurt Sauce (see recipe below)

Preheat grill to medium-high.

Meanwhile, in a large pot, add 2 gallons water, 1 cup Pelican's BBQ rub, ¼ cup salt, and bring to a boil. Add carrots and cook until almost done, about 5 minutes, then drain.

In a bowl, toss the blanched carrots with remaining 1 tablespoon Publican BBQ Rub and olive oil. Arrange carrots on a grill screen, and grill over direct heat until finished. Adjust seasoning as necessary.

Arrange grilled carrots on a plate, drizzle with lemon juice, garnish with crushed pecans and dill yogurt sauce

THE PUBLICAN'S BBQ RUB
Makes 1½ cups

  ½ cup dark brown sugar
  ½ cup kosher salt
  4 tablespoons hot smoked paprika
  1 tablespoon ground black pepper
  1 tablespoon granulated garlic
  1 tablespoon onion granules or onion powder
  ½ tablespoon celery salt
  1 tablespoon cayenne pepper
  1 tablespoon ground cumin

Combine all in bowl, mix well, and store in an airtight container.

THE PUBLICAN'S DILL YOGURT SAUCE
Makes 1 cup

  1 cup plain Greek yogurt
  2 tablespoon chopped fresh dill
  1 tablespoon lemon juice
  ¼ cup buttermilk
  Salt to taste

In a medium bowl, combine all ingredients and mix well. Reserve for use.

COFFEE/STOUT SEARED STEAK APPETIZER
Courtesy of Horse Thief Hollow (see page 128)

Serves 2 to 4

> $^1\!/_2$ *cup Coffee Stout*
> $^1\!/_4$ *cup maple syrup*
> *1 tablespoon plus 2 teaspoons butter, divided*
> *1 tablespoon cornstarch slurry*
> *1 butternut squash, peeled and seeded*
> *Salt and pepper*
> *3 shishito peppers*
> *1 (5-ounce) flat-iron steak*
> *2 tablespoons ground coffee*

Combine stout, syrup, and 2 teaspoons butter in a sauce pan over medium heat and reduce by a third. Whisk in slurry and set aside.

Preheat oven to 400°F.

Season squash with salt and pepper and roast for 25 to 30 minutes or until al dente.

In saute pan over medium heat, saute the peppers and slices of butternut squash in remaining 1 tablespoon butter.

Coat steak in coffee, salt, and pepper. Grill or sear to desired temperature.

Place peppers and squash on a plate, slice steak and fan slices over the vegetables. Glaze with Coffee Stout pan sauce and serve.

BACON FAT POPCORN
Courtesy of Revolution Brewpub (see page 135)

Serves 2

> *2 cups raw bacon lardons (bacon cut into $^1\!/_2$-inch pieces)*
> *2 to 3 sage stems with leaves*
> *1 cup popcorn*
> *1 teaspoon salt*
> *1 small block Parmesan cheese, grated*

Add bacon lardons to a cold saucepot and heat over medium heat. Cook bacon, stirring occasionally, until crisp. Remove and reserve for topping popcorn.

Heat remaining bacon fat over medium high heat until barely smoking. Turn heat down to medium, add sage (whole), and fry until leaves are crisp. Remove sage with slotted spoon and reserve for garnish.

Add popcorn kernels to bacon fat while moving saucepot back and forth continuously over heat. (Note: Popcorn kernels should always be moving in the pot or they will burn.) When first kernel pops, place lid on saucepot and continue moving vigorously back and forth over heat. Most kernels will pop within milliseconds of each other.

When popping slows to ½ to 1 second apart, remove saucepot from heat. Pour popcorn into large mixing bowl and season with salt to taste. Grate half the Parmesan over the popcorn and toss until evenly distributed. Sprinkle bacon over top of popcorn and cover with another layer of grated Parmesan. Garnish with sage leaves and enjoy with a Fist City Chicago Pale Ale.

SPENT GRAIN PASTA
Courtesy of Revolution Brewpub (see page 135)

Serves 4

For the pasta
7 ounces all-purpose flour
2 ounces spent grain "flour"
6 egg yolks
1 large egg
1 tablespoon milk
1 tablespoon extra virgin olive oil
1 tablespoon water

For the sauce
1 tablespoon extra virgin olive oil
½ cup cremini mushrooms, quartered
½ cup lamb braising liquid
4 ounces pulled lamb
2 tablespoons cold unsalted butter
1 cup fresh spinach, chiffonade
6 cherry tomatoes, halved
¼ cup shredded manchego cheese

To make the pasta

On a clean counter top, mix flours together and create a small crater in center large enough to hold liquids.

Add eggs, milk, and olive oil to crater. Mix liquids with your fingers in a circular motion (or a fork if you don't want to get your hands dirty), slowly pulling in flour from the sides of the crater. (Note: Be careful not to let the flour wall collapse or you'll have eggs all over your counter.) Keep mixing until most of the flour is incorporated and you're no longer in danger of liquids flowing out like a river.

Knead dough with your hands for 5 to 10 minutes or until it forms a smooth and elastic ball. Dough should spring back a little when you press it with your finger. Roll dough into a disc and refrigerate for 30 minutes to let gluten relax.

Roll pasta in sheets to #4 on any pasta roller and cut in 1-inch strips with a pizza cutter.

Blanch for 1 minute in heavily salted boiling water (½ cup kosher salt to 1 gallon water).

For the sauce

Heat olive oil to medium heat in a medium sauce pan. Add mushrooms and saute until golden brown (3 to 4 minutes), stirring occasionally.

Turn heat to medium-low and add lamb jus and pulled lamb. When lamb is heated through add spent-grain pasta, and season with salt and pepper to taste.

Turn off heat, add butter and fresh spinach, and toss.

Plate pasta and top with cherry tomatoes and manchego cheese. Enjoy with a Eugene Porter.

Per the folks at Revolution, spent grain "flour" is made from the spent grains left over from the beer-making process. Revolution Brewing dehydrates, grinds, and sifts these grains and adds them to their recipes for added depth of flavor. You can use spent grains from your own homebrew process or, if you do not have access to any spent grains, you can simply omit the spent "flour" and the extra tablespoon of water from this recipe and you have a basic pasta dough recipe.

PORTER BRAISED LAMB SHANK

Courtesy of Revolution Brewpub (see page 135)

Serves 4

> *2 (16-ounce) lamb shanks*
> *Salt and pepper for seasoning*
> *6 whole shallots*
> *6 whole garlic cloves, smashed*
> *2 sprigs fresh rosemary*
> *6 sprigs fresh thyme*
> *4 bay leaves (fresh or dried)*
> *¹/₂ cups beef tallow (or vegetable oil if not available)*
> *1 (12-ounce) can Eugene Porter*
> *¹/₂ cup port wine*
> *1 quart beef stock*
> *Dutch oven or cast iron skillet with lid*

Season lamb shanks with salt and black pepper.

Heat cast iron skillet or dutch oven on medium heat. Sear shanks on one side until golden brown. Flip lamb shanks, add shallots, garlic cloves, rosemary, thyme, and bay leaves. When shanks are brown, remove from pan, strain excess beef tallow and discard.

Deglaze hot pan with Eugene and reduce by 25 percent. Add port wine and beef stock and bring to a simmer. Pour wine/stock combination over shanks, cover, and cook at 325°F for 2 to 3 hours or until fork tender.

Remove shanks, separate meat from bone. Strain braising liquid and reduce by half or until it coats the back of a spoon.

HAYMARKET BREWPUB'S RANCH CHIPS
Courtesy of Chef Christopher McCoy of Haymarket Brewpub (see page 126)

Serves 4

According to Chef Christopher McCoy, this bar snack is, "f—ing delicious with a pint of Mathias. Kennebec potatoes are key, having to only cook them once yet achieving a perfectly crunchy chip."

> 2 tablespoons ground Indian Dill Seed
> 2 tablespoons ground whole black peppercorns
> 1½ tablespoons garlic powder
> 1 tablespoons onion powder
> 3 tablespoons diamond crystal kosher salt
> 7 tablespoons dehydrated buttermilk powder
> Oil for deep frying
> 5 Kennebec potatoes, sliced thin with a mandolin

Mix all ingredients except potato slices and oil together in a large bowl. Set aside.

In a deep pan, heat oil to 275°F. Add potato slices and cook, continuously moving chips around, until golden brown. Shake excess oil off, then immediately toss in seasoning until completely covered.

Homebrew Clone Recipes

For as many breweries around Chicago started as homebrew hobbies, I thought it'd be fun to see if brewers would be willing to share any of their recipes for current homebrewers to try in their kitchens and garages. Lo and behold, people were happy to open their files and allow us to take a look at what makes their beers what they are.

I requested some of the city's well-known brewers to dial down their recipes for a 5-gallon batch of brew. Sorry extract brewers, these are entirely all-grain (more reason to make the jump into the style). Aside from some minor formatting and streamlining, the following recipes are just how the brewer delivered them and we all thank them for being kind enough to supply them.

METROPOLITAN'S KRANKSHAFT KOLSCH & HELIOSTAT ZWICKEL

Brewer Doug Hurst's German style lagers are classics in Chicago. If you can regularly nail one of these recipes at home, I look forward to drinking some of your beer once you open your own brewery.

Krankshaft Kolsch
Makes 5 gallons, all-grain

> 8½ pounds German pilsner malt
> 10 ounces wheat malt
> 0.5 ounce nugget (12.5 percent) 60 minutes
> 2 ounces Santiam (7.5 percent) 0 minutes
> Wyeast 2565 Kolsch yeast
> Stats:
> OG 1.048
> FG 1.006
> IBU 24
> SRM 3.2

Mash-in with 3 gallons of water at 163°F to hit mash temperature of 152°F. Hold for 30 minutes before starting vorlauf. Sparge to collect 5 gallons in kettle. Boil for 60 minutes, adding hops at the appropriate times. Cool wort to 60°F and pitch yeast in fermenter. Ferment at 60°F for about 6 days until gravity drops to terminal. Rack to secondary fermenter and cold condition at 31°F to 35°F for an additional 12 to 22 days. This yeast strain is not flocculant and will require filtering or extended cold conditioning to be appropriately bright.

Heliostat Zwickel Lager
Makes 5 gallons, all-grain

> 9 pounds German pilsner malt
> 1 pound Vienna malt
> ¾ ounce Horizon (12 percent) 60 minutes
> ½ ounce Liberty (4.8 percent) 25 minutes
> 2¼ ounces Mt. Hood (5.8 percent) 0 minutes
> 1¾ ounces Sterling (7.5 percent) 0 minutes
> Wyeast 2042 Danish Lager
> Stats:
> OG 1.054
> FG 1.010
> IBU 38
> SRM 3.5

Mash-in with 3¼ gallons water at 160°F to hit mash temperature of 148°F. Hold for 30 minutes until conversion is complete. If the mash tun is large enough (at least 8 gallons), add 1¼ more gallons of water at 200°F to bring mash temperature to 161°F. Alternatively, use direct heat and vigorous stirring or a HERMS/RIMS system to raise temperature. Hold for 15 minutes before starting vorlauf. Boil for 60 minutes, adding hops at appropriate times. Cool wort to 52°F. Pitch a starter or two packs of yeast and aerate well.

Ferment at 52°F for 4 days, raise temperature to 60°F for 24 hours for diacetyl rest. Rack to secondary then drop temperature 5 degrees per day to 45°F. Hold at 45°F for an additional 15 days. Drop temperature to 31°F for 5 more days or until beer is somewhat bright. This Zwickel-style beer should not be filtered and should have a slight yeast haze in the bottle or keg. It should not, however, be turbid. A shorter lagering time is good, as this beer should be served fresh and raw.

SPITEFUL BREWERY'S ALLEY TIME

This pale ale from the tiny Ravenswood brewery sees release in six-packs of cans, the perfect beer for crushing in an alley after a bike delivery or two. It's nearly a SMASH beer—single malt and single hop—save for the inclusion of a bit of extra grain and dextrose. As pale ales goes, it's simple but immensely satisfying.

8½ pounds pilsen malt
2 ounces TF&S amber malt
10 ounces dextrose
4 ounces Simcoe at 0 minutes (whirlpool or let stand for 15 minutes)
6 ounces Simcoe dry hop
American Ale yeast
Stats:
ABV: 6 percent
OG: 1.051
FG: 1.005
SRM 2.75
Mash temp: 149°F

Owner Jason Klein says, "Fly sparge until you hit your volume, but batch sparge will work, too. Dry hop on day 10, bottle on day 22."

DRYHOP AND CORRIDOR BREWPUBS

The DryHop and Corridor brewpubs give head brewer Brant Dubovick lots of ways to play with different types of beers. The DryHop space pushes out a wide variety of hopped up ales, while the Corridor side is skewing saison and European. They've kindly given us examples of both to try at home.

Blame John Cusack

18-B Belgian Dubbel

Size: 5 gallons

Efficiency: 80 percent

Attenuation: 80 percent

Original Gravity: 1.068 (1.062 - 1.075)

Terminal Gravity: 1.014 (1.008 - 1.018)

Color: 17.5 (10.0 - 17.0)

Alcohol: 7.16 percent (6.0 percent - 7.6 percent)

Bitterness: 24 (15.0 - 25.0)

9.5 pounds (81.9 percent) Pilsen Malt - added during mash

13 ounces (7.0 percent) Special B Malt - added during mash

13 ounces (7.0 percent) Caramel Munich 60 Malt - added during mash

7.5 ounces (4.0 percent) Candi Sugar Amber - added during boil

1.5 g (5.3 percent) Polaris (17.0 percent) - added during boil, boiled 90 minutes

7 g (24.6 percent) Polaris (17.0 percent) - added during boil, boiled 60 minutes

10 g (35.1 percent) Tettnanger (4.5 percent) - added during boil, boiled 10 minutes

10 g (35.1 percent) Tettnanger (4.5 percent) - added during boil

Yeast - Omega Yeast Labs Abbey

Primary Fermentation - 74°F for 10 days

Secondary Fermentation - 70°F for 30 days

Mash Temp - 148°F

Shark Meets Hipster

14-B American"Wheat" IPA

Makes 5 gallons

Efficiency: 80 percent

Attenuation: 83 percent

Original Gravity: 1.059 (1.056 - 1.075)

Terminal Gravity: 1.010 (1.010 - 1.018)

Color: 8.56 (6.0 - 15.0)

Alcohol: 6.48 percent (5.5 percent - 7.5 percent)

Bitterness: 59.6 (40.0 - 70.0)

6.25 pounds (58.1 percent) 2-Row Brewers Malt - added during mash

2.5 pounds (23.3 percent) Red Wheat Malt - added during mash

1 pound (9.3 percent) Ashburne® Mild Malt - added during mash

1 pound (9.3 percent) Caramel Malt 20L - added during mash

3 grams (4.6 percent) Warrior® (16.0 percent) - added during boil, boiled 90 minutes

6 grams (9.1 percent) Warrior® (16.0 percent) - added during boil, boiled 60 minutes

0.5 ounces (21.6 percent) Chinook (13.0 percent) - added during boil, boiled 10 minutes

1.5 ounces (64.7 percent) Citra™ (12.0 percent) - added during boil, boiled 0 minutes

Dry Hop - 2 ounces Galaxy and 2 ounces Citra @ cold crash

Yeast - Omega Yeast Labs DIPA

Mash Temp - 152°F

Salts - 1gram CaSO4 to mash

Primary Fermentation - 7 days at 68°F

Secondary Fermentation - 7 days at 68°F

IMPERIAL OAK: BILLY DEE'S COCONUT PECAN PORTER

This is one of the many recipes that head brewer Brett Semenske plays with at their Willow Springs facility. They didn't specify, but I have a feeling this would be great with a few months of age in a rum barrel.

Efficiency: 75 percent
IBU: 35
9 pounds pale malt
1¼ pounds brown malt
1¼ pounds Cara Munich 40
4 ounces Black Patent Malt
8 ounces chocolate malt
60 minutes - 0.4 ounces Warrior (16 percent AA)
15 minutes -0.4 ounces Cascade (6.2 percent AA)
15 minutes -0.4 ounces Northern Brewer (8.6 percent AA)
0 minutes - same as 15-minute addition
In Secondary- 10 to 14 days
⅔ pound toasted pecans
⅔ pound toasted coconut flakes

HAYMARKET PUB & BREWERY'S ANGRY BIRDS AMERICAN BELGO RYE PALE

This recipe comes with some extra metal infused into it—it took gold at the 2011 GABF for American Belgo–style ale.

Grains:
Pilsner - 12.3 pounds
Rye - 4 pounds
Flaked Rye - 0.7 pounds
C60 - 0.2 pounds
570 Duvel Belgian yeast
Hops:
Bravo - 0.25 ounces @ boil
Citra - 1 ounce @ 60 minutes into boil
Amarillo - 2 ounces @ 85 into boil (90 minutes boil)
Amarillo - 4 ounces dry-hopped
Mash at 150, sparge at 170°F and ferment at 74°F

PENROSE BREWING COMPANY'S DEMINIMUS MANDARINA

Brewer Tom Korder says, "Our Deminimus series of beers were designed to highlight some of the new German aroma hop varieties and showcase the intersection of flavors between hops and tartness in beer. The Mandarina recipe highlights the Bavaria Mandarina hop layered on a kettle-soured medium golden ale. We decided to use hops that were processed by Hop Head Farms in Michigan, which makes a huge difference in the flavor profile."

Malts:	percent	5-gallon batch
Old World Pils	47 percent	3.5 pounds
Vienna	17 percent	1.5 pounds
Caramel 20	6 percent	0.5 pounds
Carapils	5 percent	7 ounces
Acidulated	10 percent	0.75 pounds
Spelt	15 percent	1.25 pounds
Hops	Time	Amount
Columbus	Beginning of boil	2 grams
Bavaria Mandarina	20 minutes left in boil	0.5 ounces
Bavaria Mandarina	5 minutes left in boil	1 ounce
Bavaria Mandarina	Dry hop	1.5 ounces

OG 9.0 Plato
FG 1.9 Plato
IBU   12 Platp
ABV 3.7 percent ABV
Yeast Type
Lactobacillus Delbrueckii
Saison

Tom's Process Notes

The tricky part of this process is the kettle souring. For ours, we use the following process:

1) Run off the wort into the kettle like normal.

2) Ramp to boil, and boil for 20 minutes.

3) Run through the heat exchanger to get the wort temp in the kettle down to 115°F.

4) Purge the cooled wort with a CO_2 source (we use dry ice).

5) Pitch your lacto and seal up the kettle with plastic wrap to keep out oxygen.

6) Wrap the kettle in a blanket or sleeping bag.

7) Pull samples daily (hopefully without opening the plastic wrap) until pH gets down to 3.3 to 3.4. If it hasn't reached the pH, bump the temperature to 110 to 115°F (remove the blanket!).

8) Once the pH is low enough (should be about 2 days), remove the plastic wrap and ramp temperature to boil.

9) Boil for 90 minutes to remove DMS and kill any remaining lacto, add hops during this stage.

10) From here on out, treat the beer like normal.

iecing together this book has been a long journey of beer research, conversations, interviews, storytelling and information hunting at all hours. I'd be remiss if I didn't thank (at least in a broad sense) the many journalists and writers who have helped cover the ever-growing array of breweries, brewers, bars, restaurants and other beer-centric spots around Chicago over the past decade or so. I owe you all (at least) a round of your preferred beverage of choice.

Karl Klockars has been writing about food, beer, and travel since 2008. His work has been featured in *Chicago Magazine*, *Draft Magazine*, the *Chicago Sun-Times*, *Thrillist*, *Time Out Chicago*, and on his own site, GuysDrinkingBeer.com, which has been thrice nominated as one of the nation's best beer blogs by *Saveur* magazine. When not writing about beer, you can find Karl hanging out with his wife, Nora, and their cat, Aoife. If you're buying, he'll have a porter or a pale ale.